The ASSERTIVE OPTION

Your Rights & Responsibilities

Patricia Jakubowski
Arthur J. Lange

RESEARCH PRESS
2612 North Mattis Avenue
Champaign, Illinois 61822

Contents

Figures

Exercises

Preface

A number of books have appeared over the past several years which focus on increasing assertiveness. Some offer suggestions for clarifying personal rights and explain the difference between nonassertive, assertive, and aggressive behaviors. Others provide descriptions of assertive attitudes and assertive behaviors which can be used in specific situations. In our opinion, no book yet has adequately provided specific techniques that readers can put into practice *to change* their thoughts, feelings, *and* behaviors. We have written this book because we believe that people have the ability to help themselves to become more assertive. And we are convinced that to become more assertive we need to learn how to identify the thoughts, feelings, and behaviors that support our nonassertiveness and aggressiveness; and how to substitute thoughts, feelings, and behaviors which are more assertive. We are convinced that people have the *capacity* to control, direct, and change their thoughts, feelings, and behaviors. The purpose of this book is to show how. The process is not difficult to understand but doing it requires systematic practice to achieve improvement.

The procedures in this book are for the person who wants to become more assertive. The fact is that almost no one is assertive, nonassertive, or aggressive all the time. Typically, each of us is able to handle some situations assertively and not others. Assertiveness is not a pervasive personality trait; rather, it is situationally specific. Almost everyone could become more effective in handling *some* situations they regularly encounter.

A major emphasis in this book is on providing a *process* or a collection of new skills which you can use in situations you do not handle as effectively as you would like. These tools are designed to help you reduce or prevent excessive anxiety, extreme anger, depression, guilt, worrying, or catastrophizing. Moreover, these tools can help you actually *behave* more assertively. We believe it is not enough to just provide you with a large number of new assertive behaviors. If you become extremely upset, angry, or depressed, the chances are you will be unable to use these behaviors. Therefore, we want to provide you with some ways to change the thoughts, feelings, *and* behaviors that are nonassertive or aggressive and also show you how to replace them with more assertive alternatives.

We describe a four-stage process to help you become more assertive: (1) identifying your personal rights and the rights of others in specific situations; (2) discriminating between nonassertive, assertive, and aggressive responses; (3) identifying and changing the thoughts which are barriers to assertive behavior; and (4) practicing specific, new, more assertive behaviors. We also strongly believe that assertiveness includes being *responsible* for your own behavior. That is, if you have rights, others have them too; if we are going to be responsibly assertive, we will maintain a high regard for the rights of others as well as our own rights in any given situation. We explain how to do this throughout the book. The point is that asserting yourself does *not* mean you can do or say anything to anybody under the guise of being "open" and "honest" or "just speaking your piece."

Following the chapters on the four stages of assertiveness, we have also included several chapters focusing on types of assertive behavior and specific situational contexts (making and refusing requests, handling anger, carrying on conversations, etc.). Although these by no means cover all situations, they are representative of the major assertion issues reported by people attending our workshops and group sessions.

We have provided exercises in each chapter because we believe that significant change requires step-by-step action. Understanding yourself is only half of the process; taking small, systematic steps toward a specific desired change is also necessary. Completing these exercises will help you to break the change process into manageable segments. Change seldom occurs in one sudden moment. Rather, it takes time—and energy. Changes which are accomplished systematically can be fun. And when attempted on a step-by-step basis, even those behaviors thought to be very serious or impossible to alter can become an enjoyable challenge.

We invite you to participate fully and actively in this book and its suggested activities. We have used the principles and procedures described in this book many times with significant success. Although we recognize the importance of additional research evidence, we believe that the successful changes that we and so many of our clients have made are a powerful valida- tion of this approach to becoming more assertive.

A NOTE FOR PROSPECTIVE MEMBERS OF ASSERTIVENESS TRAINING GROUPS

Many leaders of assertiveness training groups conduct interview sessions with prospective members. These sessions en- able the leader to describe the training group and to determine whether a prospective member's goals can be reasonably met in the group that is being organized. The interview also gives the prospective member an opportunity to ask questions. We sug- gest that you ask the leader these questions:

- What do you do in your group?
- What do you reasonably expect to accomplish? (Beware of people who seem to promise total personality change.)
- What are your qualifications for leading this group?
- Why do you think it's important to be assertive? (Beware of people who only view assertiveness as a method to get what they want or who seem to have little regard for the people with whom they are assertive.)
- Is role playing stressed? (Beware of people who provide little role playing experience.)
- How much is the expression of anger stressed? (Beware of people who see this as the main purpose of assertiveness training.)

In general a responsible professional leader can be expected to:

- clearly distinguish assertive from aggressive behavior.
- distinguish assertive training from psychotherapy.
- answer questions and respond to criticisms in a respecting way.
- conduct role playing exercises to help members acquire assertiveness skills.
- help members find assertive ways of communicating which *uniquely* fit them.
- conduct the group in an assertive way.
- indicate professional background and training.
- respect members' choice not to assert themselves.
- encourage a group climate where the emphasis is on positive suggestions and support.
- intercede if another person imposes suggestions.

As a member of an assertiveness group you can be reasonably expected to:

- make a commitment to attend group sessions.
- participate in assertiveness skills role playing practice sessions.
- identify specific issues that you'd like to work on.
- not force your viewpoints or suggestions on other members.
- focus on the positive aspects of other people's work.

As you go through the training experience, your self-confidence and personal awareness should increase. As you become more self-confident and motivated to change, you may have to *fight the temptation* to immediately rush off to "be assertive" with the most important person in your life or in an area where it's most difficult for you to be assertive. It's more important to start gradually with people you feel less anxious with; you have less to lose if things do not go as well as you'd like them to. At first there are likely to be a few rough edges on your assertions. But as you become more relaxed and self-assured and develop the skill of being empathically assertive, the rough edges will decrease. In general, you are likely to find that other people will respond favorably to your new communication efforts which show respect for their rights and feelings. A few people will be taken aback and will not respond the way you'd like them to. This is not a failure on your part; it just means that you need to learn how to deal with and adjust to some negative reactions without berating yourself or others in the process. You can feel good about yourself even if others do not respond in ways you'd ideally like them to.

Acknowledgments

We would like to thank Anne Johnson and Dr. Janet Clark Loxley for their creative suggestions and invaluable contributions to our efforts. We would also like to thank Dr. Rita Whiteley and Dr. Marion Jacobs for their thoughtful conceptualizations of assertiveness. Lastly, we greatly appreciate Richard Hagle's excellent editing work and Ann Wendel at Research Press for her patience and understanding. A special thanks to Joseph M. Strayhorn, Jr., for allowing us to use his definitions of I Feel, I Want and Mixed Feelings statements.

1
How *Do* People Communicate?

Have you ever had difficulty expressing your opinion in a group of friends or fellow workers? Was it difficult for you to be direct and clear in what you wanted to say?

Have you ever needed to give suggestions to or correct someone who was doing a poor job of typing, public relations, organizing an activity, or doing household repairs? Did you ignore the situation, hoping it would take care of itself? Did you come on too strong when you finally gave the correction?

Do you self-consciously deny a sincerely made compliment? Do you respond with humorous remarks that make the other person look foolish?

Have you ever worked with someone on a project—a business report, a class project, a shower—only to find that the other person wasn't doing her share? Did you quietly seethe? Did you blow up and afterwards feel uneasy about how you handled the situation?

Have you ever been verbally abused? Did you passively accept the abuse and feel hurt and resentful? Did you respond in kind and put the other person down?

Are you intimidated by the high-pressure tactics of people selling magazine subscriptions, business equipment, religious items? Do you agree to buy things you don't really want? Do you refuse in a very cold, curt manner?

Have you ever avoided asking for a favor? Did you feel that you might be intrusive or pushy? Were you concerned about being rude or demanding?

Have you ever avoided asking someone to change his behavior, especially when it affected you? Did you talk yourself out of saying anything about it?

1

You probably have had to deal with at least one of these situations. Most people have. And like most people, you probably felt trapped, unhappy with how you handled the situation, but thought that you had no other choice. When you felt this way, chances are that you saw only two options.

What *can* you do? You can say nothing about the unpleasant situation and simply try to ignore your feelings and desires. This is nonassertive behavior and, while it may prevent conflicts with others, you probably will wind up feeling helpless, exploited, angry, and disappointed with yourself. Also, you may lose the respect of others and, most importantly, lose respect for yourself.

The second option is to be aggressive. You can use sarcasm and intimidation to get what you want. Or can you? When you blow up at someone who isn't doing her work, do you then get the cooperation you want, or do you just get a sullen withdrawal? When you belligerently complain about a neighbor's loud party, you may get the quiet you want, but what happens to the relationship afterwards? And don't you usually feel uncomfortable with the way you acted?

There is a third option, one you may never have considered, yet it often helps people reach their goals without sacrificing important relationships. This is the assertive behavior option (see Figure 1). *Acting assertively* means *standing up for your assertive rights and expressing what you believe, feel, and want in direct, honest, appropriate ways that respect the rights of the other person.*

Figure 1   The Assertive Behavior Option

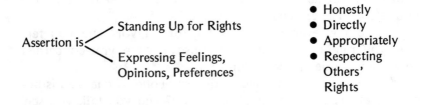

2

THE NONASSERTIVE OPTION

A common dating situation illustrates the differences among the three behavior options.

Situation: Fran met Joe at a party, where they had a short, pleasant talk. Although Fran enjoyed the conversation, she decided that she wasn't interested in getting to know Joe better. Joe, on the other hand, decided that he wanted to date Fran and gave her a phone call.

Joe: I enjoyed talking with you at the party and would like to get to know you better. How about dinner and a movie this Saturday?

Fran: (lying) I'm having my parents over for dinner that night; I'm sorry.

Joe: Well, then, how about Sunday?

Fran: Sunday's kind of bad for me with work starting on Monday and all.

Joe: Then how about if we make it just for dinner? That wouldn't take all that long. You'd still have more than enough time for your beauty rest.

Fran: Don't you think that would be hard on you? I live pretty far away, and there aren't any good restaurants around here. You'd be spending half the time in the car driving out here and back just for a couple of hours of dinner. Are you sure that's what you really want to do?

Joe: You're worth it. And if that's the only time we can get together, I'm sure willing to do it. Let's say seven o'clock.

Fran: Well, OK.

Outcome: By being nonassertive and letting herself get talked into a date, Fran exchanged momentary escape from a confrontation for a week of feeling upset. On their Sunday dinner date, Fran was very cool and distant, all in an attempt to get Joe to decide that *he* didn't want to go out with her. When he commented on how distant she was, Fran got defensive. The result was that Joe felt confused, hurt, and angry, and Fran felt guilty and embarrassed.

When you react like Fran did, you usually get trapped into acting nonassertively because you become overly concerned about hurting someone else's feelings. In the process your feelings and wants get left by the wayside. It's as though you have taken all the responsibility for the other person's feelings. You react as though you have signed a contract that says you must have the same feelings and wants as someone else and that it's all your fault if you don't. You are likely to feel this way when you mistakenly reason that there is a perfect way to handle all situations so that nobody feels bad and that it's all your fault for failing to find this mythical perfect solution.

When you become overly concerned about hurting another's feelings, it is easy to get trapped in the Nonassertive Circle (see Figure 2). The circle starts with a sincere desire to avoid hurting someone's feelings or your relationship with them. Then you decide not to say what you really feel, which leads you to act in ways that hurt the other person or your relationship even more than if you had been assertive in the first place. In the Fran-Joe example, Fran didn't want to hurt Joe's feelings, so she didn't tell him that she didn't want to date. As a result she eventually hurt Joe even more than if she had politely but firmly refused the date in the first place.

You can recognize a potential Nonassertive Circle by asking yourself these questions:

- What will be the long-term effects on this relationship, on the other person, and on myself if I don't say what I want, feel, or believe?
- Will these long-term effects be worse than any short-term discomfort I or the other person may feel if I am assertive in the first place?

A second way you can trap yourself into nonassertion is by fooling yourself into believing that your feelings aren't real (e.g., I'm probably just nervous about dating); that you shouldn't have

4

Figure 2   The Nonassertive Circle

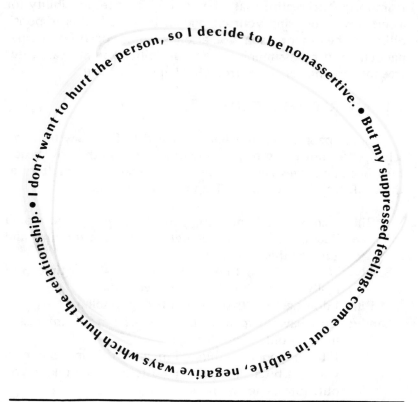

the feelings you have (e.g., He's a nice guy and I *should* be happy he asked me out); that your feelings don't matter when compared to someone else's (e.g., I'll be uncomfortable at dinner; what's that compared to how bad he'll feel if I say no); that if you are assertive, an unbearable scene will definitely occur; or that you have no choice other than to comply with what the other person wants.

A third trap is manipulative. You try to get the other person to withdraw his request so that you don't have to take the responsibility of saying what you believe, feel, or want. In the Fran-Joe example this occurred at two points. First, Fran tried to persuade Joe that the date would be too hard on *him*. Second, she acted cool and unfriendly at the Sunday dinner date in an effort to make him decide that *he* didn't want to date her. It is important to realize that when you give up responsibility for assertively expressing yourself and instead push this responsibility on the other person, you also lose some control over what happens. But by assuming this responsibility you have a greater freedom and power to control what happens to you.

THE AGGRESSIVE OPTION

Some people, seeing what happened to Fran, say to themselves, "I'm not going to put up with that." So they overreact; they become aggressive, but this doesn't really help matters, as the confrontation between Bill and Sandy illustrates.

Bill: I enjoyed talking with you at the party and would like to get to know you better. How about dinner and a movie this Saturday?

Sandy: Well, I'm going to be tied up for a real long time. So I really don't think that would work out.

Bill: I don't get it. What are you trying to tell me?

Sandy: Do I have to spell it out for you? I'm not interested in going out, so don't bug me!

Bill: I'll tell you one thing. I'm glad I found out now you're a bitch. I wouldn't waste my time taking you out! (Slams down phone.)

Outcome: Though Bill and Sandy may have felt self-righteously proud that they didn't put up with each other's "mistreatment," they both ended feeling more agitated than they would have if either person had handled the situation assertively. Meeting fire with fire, their mutually cutting remarks escalated into an unnecessarily upsetting experience.

Instead of overreacting to Bill's irritated comment ("What are you trying to tell me?") Sandy might have nondefensively accepted the fact that she had been vague and politely but firmly said, "I can see where I sounded pretty vague. What I mean to say is thank you for asking me out, but I want to be

6

straight with you. I'm really not interested in starting a dating relationship."

To Sandy's cutting comment about "spelling it out for him," Bill could have assertively expressed his irritation and firmly stated his limits: "I was asking for clarification; I didn't mean to bug you. If you don't want to go out with me, that's OK. I don't object to your decision, but I do strongly object to the way you put me down in the process." Perhaps Sandy would have started thinking about the aggressive way she reacted; perhaps she would have regretted her behavior. Perhaps not, but Bill's assertive goal wouldn't be to make her regret what she had said or to make her feel bad but rather to simply let her know what reactions he had. He wouldn't have been trying to make himself feel better at her expense by personally putting her down. By assertively stating his limits, Bill could have felt good knowing that he hadn't just passively accepted what Sandy did and yet hadn't stooped to her tactics.

In this example, Sandy initially responded nonassertively, only hinting that she didn't want to go out, but upon meeting resistance to her nonassertive refusal, she aggressively overreacted. When we meet with less-than-immediate compliance, we often feel that we are being attacked and our goals threatened. We may not even be aware that at some level we have suddenly become afraid that we are about to lose control of the situation and will be overwhelmed by the other person. Deep down inside we often are afraid that we will be unable to get what we want or will be forced to do something we don't want to do. Feeling vulnerable can set off an automatic stream of exaggerated thoughts that propel us into aggressive action. Though these thoughts vary according to our unique backgrounds, some typical ones are:

- I'm going to have to show him who's boss around here!
- She's not going to get away with making a fool out of me!
- I've put up with this treatment long enough, and I've got every right to get nasty now!
- Apparently he doesn't understand anything except someone coming down hard on him, and if that's what it takes, I'm just the person who can deliver it!

7

These three options—nonassertion, assertion, and aggression—may at first seem to be on a continuum, with assertion being the "golden mean," but this view really isn't accurate. Aggression is the flip side of nonassertion. Both nonassertion and aggression typically stem from feeling threatened and helpless, feelings that ultimately control us. With assertion we manage our fears, not letting them dominate us or force us into submission or an overreactive attack.

Aggression is the opposite of nonassertion in yet another way. Both tactics put someone in the inferior position. When we use nonassertive behavior, we make ourselves less than the other person; aggression, on the other hand, makes the other person less than us. It is as if we are used to thinking that the only way a person can get his beliefs, feelings, and wants acknowledged is by forcing someone else into an inferior position.

THE ASSERTIVE OPTION

Assertive behavior avoids both of the extremes that aggression and nonassertion lead to. Kate's responses to Mark show how a person can protect her own interests without abusing someone else in the process.

Mark: I enjoyed talking with you at the party and would like to get to know you better. How about dinner and a movie this Saturday?

Kate: Thanks for the compliment in asking me out, Mark. I enjoyed talking with you at the party, but I'd prefer not to go out.

Mark: What do you mean? Why don't you want to go out with me? What's wrong with me?

Kate: I did enjoy our talk, and I don't think there's anything wrong with you. I don't want to go out on a date.

Mark: Stop giving me the run-around. You haven't even given me a chance—you're not even giving yourself a chance.

Kate: It may very well be that I'm not giving you a chance. I don't want to offend you, but I also don't want to go out.

Mark: Why?

8

Kate: Mark, I'm starting to get real uncomfortable with this. I've already said I don't want to go out a couple of times. I guess you'd like me to have a specific reason, and I don't have one to give you. I simply don't want to go out. Pursuing this is not getting either of us anywhere, and I'd like to drop it.

Mark: Isn't there any way I can persuade you?

Kate: (friendly but firm) No.

Mark: OK, good-bye. You don't know what a good time you're missing.

Kate: Good-bye, Mark.

Outcome: Afterwards Kate felt good. She didn't feel guilty because she was able to accept her right to refuse. She knew she hadn't done anything wrong. Her small irritation with Mark's persistence easily passed. Mark was disappointed but not really hurt or angry because Kate did nothing to put him down.

In simple situations, being assertive may simply involve one sentence or a short statement. However, in complex situations like this one, listening skills and persistence are needed. Although many callers would have stopped after the first polite refusal, this extended dialogue illustrates how it is possible to use assertion to deal with manipulation without having to resort to the same kinds of manipulative tactics the other person is using.

Kate didn't get pulled into the "why-because" trap where each answer is systematically knocked down by the other person. In Kate's situation, it was appropriate not to say why she didn't want to date. She had the right to not *have to* defend her feelings and keep providing explanations until she finally hit on one that was acceptable to Mark. In this case, acting on her right did not violate any rights of the other person.

Kate avoided getting hooked into anger or guilt by Mark's use of red-flag phrases. These red flags were "Stop giving me the run-around" and "You haven't even given me a chance." She followed the general assertive principle of recognizing that these statements reflected Mark's perception and that her behavior could reasonably be interpreted that way even though it was incorrect. Simply acknowledging that his perceptions could be accurate rather than arguing about them and, instead, using her energy to simply restate her refusal enabled her to maintain her assertive presence of mind.

Kate handled her growing irritation with Mark's persistence by concentrating on her goal of refusing to date and focusing her mind on such thoughts as "I can get through to him without getting nasty. Take a deep breath and relax. I don't like his pushing, but I don't have to hit him with a sledge-hammer—all I have to say is no." Thus she avoided getting hooked into aggression that would have occurred had she focused her mind on such thoughts as "He's got no right to persist! He has his nerve thinking that I must give him a reason for not going out!"

Being assertive sometimes takes more time than being aggressive, but the extra four or five minutes can make the difference between walking away feeling strong and good or walking away feeling self-righteous and upset.

ADVANTAGES OF ASSERTION, NONASSERTION, AND AGGRESSION

Assertive Behavior
Assertive behavior helps us feel good about ourselves and other people. It increases our self-esteem, leads to the development of mutual respect with others, and helps us achieve our goals. Though some people fear that they will become hurtful by becoming more assertive, assertive behavior actually minimizes hurting and alienating other people. Expressing ourselves assertively does not mean that we must become obnoxious, crude, and insensitive people. Just the opposite is true: One of the ultimate goals of assertion is developing caring, honest, and accepting relationships with others.

Nonassertive Behavior
Nonassertion hurts us directly by causing us to lose respect

for ourselves. Continued nonassertion erodes our sense of self-esteem and in some cases leads to a general sense of worthlessness and depression. We see ourselves as a doormat the world walks on and we usually don't reach our goals or get our preferences respected. Instead, nonassertive behavior invites others to infringe upon us and teaches them to take advantage of us. Though some people may like our nonassertiveness, in many cases they like us simply because we are not inconveniencing them, not because of *who* and *what we are*—full human beings who have unique feelings, needs, preferences, and opinions—all of which at times will inconvenience others because they sometimes run counter to what other people feel, want, believe.

Nonassertion can also hurt other people, too. Parents who raise their children nonassertively, allowing them to do whatever they want without regard to the consequences of their actions or to their parents' feelings, unintentionally teach their children to expect the world to give them everything they want and to be insensitive to the needs of others—an attitude that surely will hurt their relationships with others on the playground, at school, and later in life. The mother who allows herself to be victimized by others may cause her daughter to feel ambivalent about being a woman, especially when her daughter begins thinking that being a woman means being abused and hurt. The supervisor who bends with every pressure, whether it comes from her boss or her subordinates, eventually hurts the job morale of her subordinates, who sense that they can't depend on their supervisor. The worker who cannot ask for a raise eventually hurts his family's financial security. The friend who rarely says what he genuinely wants or feels denies other people a real person to form a relationship with. The person who gives everything to anybody under any circumstances eventually fails everybody (including himself) as he becomes drained and resentful.

This does not mean that we *must always* be assertive and that nonassertion is never appropriate. There are times when we may choose to act nonassertively, for example, with an employer or teacher who, when disagreed with, is known to retaliate with a job dismissal or lowered grade.

Though nonassertion can be costly, it also has certain advantages. We can experience momentary relief when we are nonassertive and avoid potential conflicts with others. Nonassertion can help perpetuate a self-image of always being available to help others and never needing help ourselves. Also, many of us have learned how to use nonassertive tactics to manipulate others so that we can get what we want without having to be direct and honest. But there is a price for achieving our goals this way. Other people eventually catch on to the manipulation and become suspicious and guarded, and engaging in such manipulative behavior erodes our self-esteem as we come to realize that people are doing things for us not out of a sense of respect or affection but merely because they've been fooled. We then cheat ourselves out of genuine encounters with other people, encounters that may be anxiety producing and not always get us what we want but are still part of the essence of life and help us become more fully human.

Aggressive Behavior

When we react aggressively, we usually are making our best effort to handle a threatening situation. It enables us to let off steam without regarding the feelings and rights of others, and it can scare others into giving us what we want; but it is an inefficient method of protection. What may happen is that other people become less likely to give us what we want: They may not really hear what we are saying because of the way we are saying it. When people are attacked, often they automatically set up a mental barrier and become actively or passively resistant to our message. Where they might have cooperated if they'd been approached assertively with some common courtesy, they oppose us just to show that they can't be pushed around. Thus aggression can defeat our goals.

Continued aggression in ongoing relationships at home or work typically leads others to become guarded and to withdraw from us. Unfortunately, others usually do not directly confront us with our aggressive behavior; thus often we do not fully realize to what extent we are aggressive and how much our behavior disturbs others until it is too late and the love or work relationship is damaged badly. Continued aggression can cheat us out of one of life's major joys: having others trust and value us enough to reveal themselves genuinely to us.

Finally, there is the unnecessary stress we put ourselves through, the extra weight of the needless irritation and quarrels we make ourselves carry by getting overly upset when other people don't behave the way we think they *should*. Making ourselves upset over small events like cars moving too slowly in traffic, secretarial errors, waiting in lines, or tactless remarks of strangers simply adds to the stress in our lives and leads us to feel a little out of control. Some of these things are not worth getting upset over.

Acting aggressively does not make us bad human beings, but assertion *is* a better way to handle conflicts with other people. By holding ourselves and others in high esteem, there is more to be gained from life.

The Risks of Acting Assertively

Although assertion has its benefits, there are some risks as well. One of the biggest risks is that others may not approve of the assertive behavior. For example, if you refuse a friend's request, you take a risk—he may or may not understand your feelings. He may be pleased that you respected him and yourself enough to be honest with him. He may feel good because your refusal gives him the freedom to occasionally refuse you, and he may simply accept your refusal without any further thought. But he may be surprised because he didn't expect you to refuse, and he may feel disappointed because he is inconvenienced. He may feel angry and hurt because he thinks you have no right to refuse and that you no longer value him as a friend.

This example points out two things: One, since all people are unique to some extent, they will react uniquely to your behavior, and their reactions in large part will be based on their own psychology and the frame of reference they use to evaluate your behavior. For example, if, in their frame of reference, friends exist to be of service, they will strongly disapprove of your refusal. On the other hand, if they feel that every friend, regardless of how close he is, has limits, they won't necessarily resent being turned down. Even if they are disappointed, they may simply accept the refusal. Two, a negative reaction to your

13

assertive behavior does not automatically mean that you have done something wrong, and it certainly does not mean that you are a bad person. It is very important to remember that you cannot make other people change their frame of reference—and thus approve of your assertion and make life easier for you—any more than they can make you change your frame of reference to fit theirs.

A second risk is that, when you regard others' rights as well as your own, there will be times when you won't get what you want. For example, when you assertively ask if you may smoke and make it clear that you respect the other person's right to say no, the risk is greater that the other person will refuse than if you use nonassertive tactics when you make your request.

There is a third risk with assertion: You may find out that you are wrong. For example, if you assertively ask a teacher why you got a C instead of a B, you may discover that you haven't been doing as well as you thought. By acting aggressively and never giving the teacher a chance to respond, you could walk away still convinced that you were right. Likewise, when you assertively ask your supervisor to evaluate your performance, you may find out that you need to improve your work habits or that there are good reasons why you did not get a raise. This is painful information. You probably would never have found out the truth if you had walked in with an aggressive chip on your shoulder and discounted your supervisor's comments—you could then still have the comforting, though incorrect, belief that you are a great worker and that the supervisor simply doesn't like you.

The major disadvantage of assertion is that it involves risk. However, our fears about risk taking are often unfounded. Much of the time other people accept, understand, and in some cases appreciate our assertiveness, especially when they are approached in a way that shows we have as high a regard for their rights, feelings, and preferences as our own.

CHANGE: WHAT IT TAKES

Regardless of how nonassertive and/or aggressive we have

learned to act, we can change. The available research strongly favors the idea that assertion is not a personality trait that some lucky people are born with.[1] Instead it is a kind of behavior that occurs in specific situations. In other words, in some situations we react assertively, in others nonassertively, and yet others aggressively. Even if we think we are nonassertive or aggressive in every area of our life, chances are that we are not and that somewhere we do respond assertively. All of us can expand our assertive skills even though now they may be quite limited. To become more assertive we need:

- some desire to change our behavior.
- a willingness to take some risks, initially in low-threat situations and then, as our confidence and skills increase, in more scary situations.
- a willingness to value ourselves as well as other people.
- a willingness to live with the fact that sometimes we will not get our way.
- a willingness to accept the fact that there is no such thing as a perfect response that will handle every situation.
- a willingness not to demand magic, gimmicks, or pat answers to complex situations.
- a willingness to examine ourselves and be open to new ways of thinking and handling situations.
- a willingness to accept the fact that we will not dramatically change overnight.
- a willingness to set small, reasonable goals.
- a willingness to want to be liked by other people but to work on not being terribly upset when it doesn't happen.
- a willingness to want fairness and to do everything we can to be treated fairly but to work on not allowing ourselves to be excessively upset when it doesn't occur.
- a willingness to accept the fact that acquiring skills requires effort and practice.
- a willingness to put forth some effort and to practice.

Change: How To Do It
The problem isn't so much a matter of should we change; the question is how. That is where this book comes into the

picture. It is designed to help people acquire information and skills in four basic areas.

The first area involves learning to distinguish assertion from aggression and nonassertion from politeness. These are important distinctions, for without this knowledge you may suppress spontaneous assertive reactions because you mistakenly think they are aggressive. With this knowledge you can more quickly recognize when you have gone too far and have become aggressive rather than assertive. By becoming skilled in making these distinctions you can be in a better position to correct other people's misunderstandings about assertion. People who don't understand the idea of assertion sometimes become afraid of your behavior. This may include people who are important to you, such as your boss, your teacher, or a close friend. If you can make these distinctions, you can give both them and yourself an important gift. Making these distinctions also becomes important when people tease about reading this book or about joining an assertive communications group.

The second area involves learning about basic assertive rights and the limits on these rights. This is important so that you can maintain a high regard for your own rights as well as for the rights of others. If you fail to consider the rights of others, you can easily become aggressive or inappropriately assertive. Recognizing these assertive rights helps you avoid feeling guilty when you exercise them, and recognizing that others have rights helps you avoid aggressive behavior.

The third area involves understanding the causes of aggressive and nonassertive behavior and developing skills that will enable you to assess how beliefs cause people to feel excessive anxiety, inappropriate guilt, self-righteous anger, or depression. And, most important, you will learn how to constructively cope with these feelings so that they do not interfere with your ability to be assertive in given situations.

The fourth area involves learning how to listen effectively, negotiate workable agreements, express wants and feelings, deal with others' aggression, and initiate, maintain, and terminate conversations. This section involves integrating all the skills acquired in the previous three areas and practicing specific behavior skills.

16

Although this book will give you much information, there is no substitute for practice. This book is about communication *skills,* and you will need practice in order to translate your insights into action. Each chapter includes exercises. You can complete the exercises as you read the chapters; you can read the book first and then make a schedule to complete the exercises; or you can complete particular exercises as you encounter specific assertion problems in your day-to-day life.

If you are in an assertive training group, you may be assigned readings by your group leader. A large part of your group experience will involve practicing assertive skills in the group, where you will get a lot of support, encouragement, and concrete suggestions for developing assertive skills.

NOTES

1.   Most current research supports a situation-specific view of assertive behavior. See: Bates H., & Zimmerman, S. Toward the development of a screening scale for assertive training. *Psychological Reports*, 1971, *28*, 99-107. Gambrill, E., & Richey, C. An assertion inventory for use in assessment and research. *Behavior Therapy*, 1975, *6*, 550-561. Lawrence, P. The assessment and modification of assertive behavior. (Doctoral dissertation, Arizona State University, 1970); *Dissertation Abstracts International*, 1970, *31*, 396B-397B. Eisler, R., Hersen, M., Miller, P., & Blanchard, E. Situational determinants of assertive behaviors. *Journal of Consulting and Clinical Psychology*, 1975, *43*, 330-340.

2
Responsible Assertion

Knowing what to do and knowing how to do it are two very different things. It is easy to realize that assertive behavior is better than nonassertive or aggressive behavior, but how can you recognize which is which? Assertive behavior can be recognized by several qualities and certain kinds of actions. This chapter will describe them.

RESPECT FOR OTHERS AND SELF

Respect—Not Deference

Treating others with respect simply means honoring their basic human rights, but it does not mean deference, the unquestioning approval of what others think or do. Sometimes someone knows more about or has had more experience with a certain kind of situation, and it makes sense to go along with her. But too often we act as though others are right or are better than we are *simply because* they are older, or more powerful, or richer. We incorrectly tell ourselves that:

- As a wife, I'm supposed to defer to the wishes of my husband.
- As an employee, I'm not supposed to question the opinions or policies of my boss but act as though I agree with everything she says.
- As a child I'm not supposed to question my parents' rules or disagree with their views.
- As a student, I'm not supposed to question the relevance of certain school assignments.

Anyone who expects that his views, preferences, or feelings will automatically take top priority simply because he has greater power is confusing deference with respect. But many people do equate respect with agreement and disrespect with lack of agreement, as the following example illustrates:

> Frank was extremely angry with Mr. Orzo, his boss. Mr. Orzo heard from Lucille, one of Frank's co-workers, that Frank had offended a company client. He took Lucille's word for it, didn't ask Frank for his side of the story, and bawled Frank out in the office reception area for how he handled the client. Frank was mainly angry about Mr. Orzo's lack of respect. As Frank put it, "He showed he had no respect for me or my professional judgment by taking Lucille's side of the story and thinking I was wrong in the way I handled the client. If he had respect for me, he would never have believed her, and he would have checked with me first and agreed with the way I handled the whole thing."

Mr. Orzo had a right to form his own opinion and to disagree with Frank. Disagreeing with him did not in itself constitute showing lack of respect. On the other hand, Mr. Orzo did violate (didn't respect) some of Frank's rights: He didn't give Frank a chance to have his say before being criticized (Mr. Orzo jumped to conclusions without checking out all the facts), and he criticized Frank in a way that unnecessarily humiliated him.

> As Frank finally said, "I guess the fact that he didn't automatically back me up doesn't necessarily mean that he has no respect for me; he doesn't have to agree with me to show respect. Not giving me a chance to express my side of the story and jumping on my back in public was pretty poor judgment; he sure didn't respect my rights there. What I can do is assertively tell him that I'm concerned with the way the situation was handled and the way it lowered me in the eyes of the other clients and my co-workers; I'd simply like to tell my side of the story and ask that in the future he call me into his office when he has a complaint about me."

Exercise 1 can help you to better sort out the respect, deference, and rights issues when you get very upset with another person's disrespect.

Exercise 1 Sorting Out Respect, Deference, and Rights

1. Describe a specific situation in which you believe the other person showed disrespect for you. Don't interpret the other person's motives for acting this way.

   Was condescended by Jeremy for not taking a girl's info when she rear-ended me.

2. How would you have liked the other person to have acted? How reasonable is this?

   Reasonably, I would have preferred to be taught what to do in the situation.

3. Are there any other explanations for the person's behavior other than he had no respect for you?

   Jer had been going thru a very stressful situation.

4. List the rights the other person has in this situation.*

   Express being angry @ someone you love.

5. List the rights you have in this situation.*

   treated w/ dignity & respect

6. State in positive terms what you would like the other person to do in the future.

7. Write out your assertive statement.

---

*For information on basic human rights, read Chapter 4.

Self-Respect and Self-Caring

Responsible assertion also means having respect—valuing—for yourself. This means taking care of yourself, treating yourself with as much kindness, intelligence, and good will as any human being deserves. It means, in short, being your own best friend. Specifically having self-respect means:

- putting limits on what you are willing to do for other people.
- being able to evaluate situations; in other words, distinguishing imaginary fears from the genuine possible consequences of an act and figuring out ways to deal realistically with these alternatives instead of letting yourself be overwhelmed by a situation.
- being realistic about what you can accomplish and not putting unrealistic demands on yourself.
- not letting yourself get so outraged that you hurt others and consequently cause yourself to feel disgusted and disappointed with yourself.
- allowing yourself to feel good about small gains in assertive skills.
- not making yourself miserable when someone treats you unfairly.
- forgiving yourself for making so-called mistakes and reverting to your more familiar nonassertive or aggressive behavior.

The Balancing Act: Respecting Self and Others

The following examples show the two aspects of responsible assertive behavior—self-respect and respect for others—that a person must balance when confronted by a potentially troublesome situation.

A woman was desperately trying to get a flight to Kansas City to see her mother who was sick in the hospital. Weather conditions were bad and the lines were long. Having been rejected for three standby flights, she again found herself in the middle of a long line for the fourth and last flight to Kansas City. This time she approached the person who was at the head of the line and said, pointing to her place, "Would you mind exchanging places with me? I ordinarily wouldn't ask, but it's extremely important that I get to Kansas City tonight." The man nodded yes and, as it turned out, both of them were able to get on the flight.

When asked what her reaction would have been if the man had refused, she replied, "It would have been OK. I hoped he would say yes, but after all he was there first."[1]

This woman showed self-respect for her own needs by asking whether or not the man would be willing to help her instead of automatically assuming that everyone else's needs were far more important than her own. At the same time, however, she respected the man's right to refuse her request and not fulfill her need.

Making apologies also involves both aspects of respect. Dave arrived about twenty minutes late for a casual dinner party; his friend waited until Dave arrived before serving the dinner. By simply saying, "I'm sorry I'm late; I hope I haven't messed things up for you," he acknowledged his lateness and also showed concern for the host without demeaning himself. If Dave had been nonassertive, he would have groveled about his late arrival, making a self-deprecating apology, saying, "I'm a real louse. Now I've messed up your whole dinner. I wouldn't blame you for never inviting me again"; or he would have apologized ad nauseam, saying, "I'm surprised you kept dinner waiting for me. I would have thought any host would have started without me. Now everybody's going to have a rewarmed dinner," which actually would be a subtly aggressive way of absolving himself of any wrong-doing and putting the blame on the host for ruining everyone's meal.

How can giving criticism show both aspects of respect? If you are dissatisfied with the way a painter is working on your garage, saying, "There are some parts of the garage door that are still rough—I'd like those sanded down some more before you put the primer on," shows that you have respect for yourself as well as respect for the painter's right to be given corrective information in a way that doesn't involve putdowns. Saying, "You've done a sloppy job of sanding that door. Now I'm paying you good wages, and I expect good work. Now do it right for a change," implies that the painter is lazy and dumb. (Perhaps the painter is incompetent by your standards, but that's not really relevant; what is relevant is that you are dissatisfied with the work and want it redone.) Aggressive criticism shows no respect for the other person (in this case, the painter) as a human being. Nonassertive behavior shows that you lack regard for yourself, either by keeping silent about your dissatisfaction or by registering your complaint in a self-deprecating way ("I know you know your trade a lot better than I do. But these spots over here—aren't they kind of rough?").

DIRECTNESS

Assertive behavior communicates feelings, beliefs, and needs directly and clearly, while nonassertion and aggression are indirect forms of communication.

Hinting

One of the best examples of indirectness is hinting, for example, yawning when friends stay longer than you want them to. If, on a long car drive, you say, "Are you planning to stop?" you are being indirect; you really mean, "I'd like to have a rest break soon." A man whose marriage had just broken up phoned a close friend and in a wavering, sad voice said, "I was wondering if tonight was a good night for you to have a little company," when he really meant, "I'm very upset and really want to see you tonight."

When people don't take our hints, we usually get angry. Instead of getting angry, we would have more personal power if we were direct and freed ourselves from having to depend on others' willingness and ability to mind-read what we want. Being direct can be very difficult, however, when we resent having to tell others what we want and why we want it: "Why should I have to tell him to take out the garbage; he should know!" or, "Why should I have to tell her what I want; if she really cared about me she'd know and do it without my asking!" This reasoning is self-defeating because it gives the other person all the decision-making power. Realistically, it's irrelevant whether another person *should know* something; what is relevant is what *we* know. Focusing on what others *should* know does not help us deal with situations. It merely makes us frustrated. And besides, often others aren't denying us something we want; they simply don't know what we want because we haven't asked for it.

Aggressive Indirectness

Aggression also can be indirect because it often does not clearly communicate what someone is upset about or wants. However, many people mistakenly believe that aggressive messages are direct since the other person "gets the message"; however, the message the receiver usually gets is that he is stupid or not OK in some other way. The receiver often gets stuck on this message and then never figures out what the aggressor wants. Compare these two communications:

Aggressive Message Sent	First Messages Received
Can't you see I'm too busy to do that now?	He thinks I'm inconsiderate. He thinks I can't see. He thinks he can shove me around. He thinks I haven't got important things to do, too.

Assertive Message Sent	First Messages Received
I'm willing to do that as soon as I finish this rush project.	He'll do it for me. He's too busy to do it now.

In order for people to decipher aggressive comments and respond assertively, they have to use extra energy to deal with the first rush of negative thoughts and hurt feelings that these remarks elicit—energy they may not have or be willing to use. Thus aggressive comments make us dependent on other people.

HONESTY

Assertive honesty means expressing yourself in ways that accurately represent your feelings, opinions, or preferences without putting down yourself or others in the process. It does not mean saying everything that crosses your mind or giving all the information you are privy to. Assertive honesty is always balanced by appropriateness.

Nonassertive Honesty and Dishonesty

Someone who cuts himself down while expressing his honest feelings is acting nonassertively. For example, the job applicant who, when asked why she applied for a job, responds with, "This is the only job I heard about; that's why I applied," is being nonassertively honest. Similarly the fledgling teacher is nonassertively honest when he begins the term with an apology like, "I feel very inadequate to teach this subject; I've never taught it before." Nonassertive dishonesty involves lying, for example, saying that you don't mind chatting on the phone when really you are tired and want to go to sleep.

Aggressive Honesty and Dishonesty

Being aggressively honest means saying what we honestly think without regard for the appropriateness of what we say or how it will affect the person we are speaking to. Sometimes we use aggressive honesty as a cover for our hostility or as an excuse for injuring others. Telling a good friend whose loved dog is arthritic, "If I had a dog in as bad shape as yours, I'd just put it out of its misery," or telling your grandson who recently has put on a lot of weight, "I'm really disgusted by how fat you've become," is pursuing honesty with a vengeance. These statements imply a total lack of concern for the listener's feelings.

Some kinds of aggression are actually dishonest. They involve a subtle kind of emotional dishonesty that, consciously or unconsciously, enables you to use your anger to cover up less personally acceptable feelings, such as hurt, worry, affection. This can happen when you are only aware of your immediate anger and aren't aware of how it may be a secondary reaction to other feelings. The Smith family's situation is probably more common than many people realize.

> Constant quarreling was common in the Smith family. In one particularly bitter incident, Steve attacked his teenage son Ian saying, "You're a bum and you're going to be that way the rest of your life unless you straighten up and stop goofing off at school. You're

26

a disgrace to the entire family!" Only much later did Steve realize that, besides feeling angry and frustrated with his son, he also deeply loved Ian, was very much worried about his future, and felt help-less to prevent Ian from making mistakes with his life.

After several hours thinking about it, Steve was finally able to say to Ian what all his feelings were, not only his angry ones. Ex-pressing these in terms of "I feel" instead of "you are" statements, Steve haltingly said, "Ian, I think you have a lot of ability and I'm real worried about what's going to happen to you in the future. I see your grades going down and I feel helpless to do anything that would help you. Then I get angry. I love you and I don't know what to do." Though this did not immediately change their relation-ship, it started them on the path toward relating to each other in more constructive ways.

Whenever Steve found himself becoming really angry with his son, he stopped and checked what other feelings he was also having and expressed these in nonattacking "I feel" statements. As Ian saw his father's concern and effort to communicate more constructively, he gradually started to care more about his studies.

Figure 3 (page 28) can help you distinguish emotionally honest assertion from emotionally dishonest nonassertion and emo-tionally dishonest aggression.

APPROPRIATENESS

All communication, by definition, involves at least two people and occurs in a particular context. The context of com-munication, assertive or otherwise, includes such things as the location, timing, degree of firmness, frequency, and the nature of the relationship. When a statement is inappropriate in its context, the entire communication may, depending on the situation, become aggressive, border on aggression, or it may simply lower the effectiveness of the communication. Respon-sible communication fits the demands of a particular context.

Location
Location is *where* the communication takes place. Usually an appropriate location is a private rather than a public place. On the next page are some examples of inappropriate locations.

Figure 3 Distinguishing Responses

Emotionally Honest Assertion	When we go to a party and you get sexy with other men, I think I'm not attractive to you. That hurts and scares me. What's happening to us?	I'm worried that with our different tastes in furniture, we'll never be able to find anything we both agree on.
Emotionally Dishonest Nonassertion	I don't mind your flirting with other men. But I'm just worried about what other people will think.	I guess that couch is nice, but I don't think that you really like it. So let's not get it.
Emotionally Dishonest Aggression	You're disgusting. You're always leering at men. Won't you ever grow up?	How could you possibly like that couch? You've got absolutely no taste in furniture. You'd better leave all the furniture decisions to me.

- The supervisor of a bank teller, who has made an error, loudly criticizes the teller at his window as other tellers, customers, and supervisors witness the scene. This shames the person.
- An employee who is dissatisfied with his salary complains to his boss during the office Christmas party.
- A workshop participant objects, in front of the group, to the leader's starting late after the lunchbreak. The matter could have been handled just as effectively and with less discomfort by speaking privately to the leader.

The following is an example of a situation in which it would be more appropriate to respond in public:

In a committee meeting where highly confidential matters were discussed, Tom announced that there had been leakage of confidential material to students, after which he paused with a significant look at Denise, who was the only one who had direct access to the information. Though she was innocent of his implied accusation, she said nothing, intending to speak privately to Tom. The rest of the committee interpreted her silence as guilt. Since Tom's indirect accusation was made in public, it would have been reasonable for her to respond publicly.

Timing

The person who uses appropriate timing considers the desires and feelings of others in deciding *when* to be assertive. People usually like to finish saying what they think. When you interrupt others they often feel that you haven't really been listening to them. In some cases your interruption may be interpreted as a power play, as the following example shows.

> Two members of a small committee were disagreeing with each other. Instead of waiting until they had finished speaking, the chairperson interrupted them with her idea on how to resolve the conflict, with the result that the members felt that they had not been heard and that she was pulling a power play on them. Waiting a minute or two before talking would have been more effective.

Sometimes interrupting is inappropriately used to dominate others:

> Byron, a job interviewer, asked applicants lots of questions—too many, in fact. He interrupted so frequently that he was actually badgering and being aggressive.

Under some circumstances it is appropriate to interrupt, for example, when someone is monopolizing a discussion or when you want to ask a short question that will clarify what the other person is saying. But timing—when you interrupt—can be as important as why you interrupt. Appropriate timing means being aware of the other person's emotional state, as in the following example.

> Robert came home, very happy that his job promotion had just been confirmed. As he was expressing his great joy, his wife Mary's only comment was how bad she felt about having to move out of the city. Robert felt hurt and angry and interpreted her reaction to mean that she didn't care about him. It was OK for Mary to have

29

different feelings than Robert, but expressing them at that particular moment was not good timing.

Certain kinds of situations are not good times to raise important issues or problems. For instance, when the other person is absorbed in another activity (e.g., watching a football game) or has just walked in the door and is already tense from an unrelated bad experience (e.g., a bad day at work), it is not a good time to bring up another problem or demanding issue to consider. Good timing means taking into consideration just how much information a person can handle at one sitting and timing it so that you don't overload her with all your complaints.

When raising emotion-laden issues with others, it's important to consider whether or not there is sufficient time to deal with them adequately. This means not starting serious discussions as you are on your way out the door, headed for a meeting or a party. An employer who has a good sense of timing may schedule performance evaluations on Friday afternoon. This gives employees who get poor evaluations time to think about the evaluation and work through their feelings about it. Instead of having to come in to work the next morning, maybe emotionally overwrought, they have the weekend to think things over and get an objective, rational perspective on the situation.

When criticizing others' behavior, you generally should do it as soon after the occurrence of the disturbing behavior as possible. In work situations this means not waiting until the biyearly work performance review or yearly salary review to tell an employee that you are dissatisfied with his work. If you haven't immediately said that you were irritated with someone's behavior or were confused by a remark she made, it doesn't mean that you have forfeited your chance of ever saying anything about it; it simply means that bringing up the issue at a later time will be more difficult and somewhat less effective than if you had done it sooner.

You can increase the effectiveness of assertive communications by making them when it is easiest for the other person to respond to them. For example, it generally is more effective to discuss salary with an employer when you are interviewing for the job rather than waiting to raise the money issue until after you have been offered the job. It's more effective and considerate to immediately tell a waiter that you are in a hurry to be served than to wait until half way through the meal. In general it is more effective as well as considerate to ask for favors as soon as you realize that you need one instead of waiting to the last minute to ask and possibly creating an unnecessary emergency.

Good timing also considers *your* emotional state. When you are very upset, it is better to give yourself time to sort out your reactions before dealing with important issues or problems.

This doesn't mean that you must wait for the "perfect moment." In some cases waiting for the perfect time when all conditions are right might mean waiting a very long time—maybe too long.

Intensity

The firmness of your statement can also affect the impact it makes. In general it is appropriate to become increasingly firm when another person persistently ignores your assertions and consequently violates your rights. The confrontation between Karen and Vince shows the importance of the right degree of intensity.

Situation: Karen has just met Vince at a friend's party.

Vince: So you're a real estate saleswoman. That sounds like a really interesting job. Just how much money do you make on it?

Karen: I can appreciate your being curious about that, Vince, but for me that's something I consider private, and I'd prefer not to say.

Vince: What! Make so little money you're ashamed of it?

Karen: (pleasantly) No, that's not it. It's just something I don't discuss with people.

Vince: Well you're becoming a real challenge to me now. Do you make ten, fifteen, or twenty thousand?

Karen: (firmly) I don't want to be your challenge, Vince. I've said a couple of times that I don't want to discuss my income, and I think I've been polite in saying it. Now I'd like to change the subject . . . . Have you seen the new art exhibit at the museum? I saw it last week and I was very impressed.

Each of Karen's assertions was appropriate in its particular context. It was appropriate to start with a minimal assertion that was least likely to cause the other person to react negatively and still enable her to state her limits.[2] As Vince kept pushing the issue, it was appropriate for her to become increasingly firm until she took charge and changed the conversation, after first stating her intention to do this. If she had responded to his first inquiry about her income by coldly refusing to discuss it and abruptly changing the subject, she would have been overreacting and would have at least been bordering on aggressive behavior.

Many people appear to be aggressive because their *initial* response is highly escalated. When a salesperson comes to the door some people coldly say no and slam the door in his face just as he starts his sales pitch. This highly escalated, aggressive overreaction is inappropriate because it puts the other person down.

Our Relationship with the Other Person
Being assertive does not mean making the same pat statements to everyone. You deal with many different people every day: your boss, your parents, your lover, a young child, or a stranger on the street. It is appropriate to firmly but pleasantly say "no thanks," offering no explanations to a telephone solicitor who wants to sell you magazines. Giving that same response without explanation would not be appropriate if someone in your office asks you to cover her desk while she takes a break, or if a friend says he would like you to come over and visit, or if your mate asks you to go with her to a basketball game. Responsible assertive communication takes into consideration our relationship with the other person. If Walter, a close friend of Karen's, had asked her about her income, she probably wouldn't have reacted the way she reacted to Vince:

32

Walter: You really sound excited about your new real estate job! How much are they paying you for that?

Karen: Yes, I really do like the work, and as far as salary goes I'm making out OK. I don't want to go into the specifics of how much I'm getting, though.

Walter: Hey come on now. I'm not just anybody. I'm your friend, and I'd like to know how much money you're making.

Karen: Walter, I do value you as a friend, and you're not just anybody to me. It's just that my salary is something that feels real private to me.

Walter: Well just tell me this. Do you make ten, fifteen, or twenty thousand?

Karen: Walter, I'm really feeling pushed. I said a couple of times that I don't want to talk about it, and yet you're still asking me . . . . What's the matter? Have you had a bad day, or have I offended you in some way?

Because Walter was a close friend, Karen wanted to do more than simply refuse to discuss her salary; she also wanted to keep the relationship. By asking what was wrong, she discovered that Walter was feeling hurt and angry because she hadn't called him since she had gotten the real estate job; he was feeling left out and unimportant in her life.

Appropriate Frequency

Enthusiasm is a valuable quality; so is repetition. You can use them to emphasize a point you want to make, but it is easy to go overboard. Bob's attempt to become more assertive shows the importance of appropriate frequency.

Bob, a part-time student and a full-time telephone installer, usually didn't express his opinions in classes, at home, or at work. Getting tired of being so nonassertive, he started expressing his opinions at every opportunity regardless of how unimportant the situation was. Though his opinions often made sense, he stated them so often that others thought he was on an ego trip; they didn't really listen to him and didn't take him seriously. Bob needed to identify his

33

priorities and decide which issues were important enough to merit assertive comments. Going overboard was self-defeating, and it unnecessarily alienated others.

By the same token, the indiscriminate use of "I want" statements can give the impression that you are only interested in what you want and are insensitive to others. Overuse of "I feel angry" or "I feel put down" statements gives others the impression that you are constantly angry and defensive, thus reducing the effectiveness of your communications. Going overboard with any type of assertive communication alienates others, who often see such statements as manipulative ploys rather than authentic communication.

BODY LANGUAGE

Body language also is important in communicating messages to other people. It not only is what we say but how we say it that affects how we come across to other people and how they react to what we say. In fact, body language may account for as much as 80 percent of what we communicate to people.[3] Consider how simply saying, "I don't agree with you," could communicate different messages depending on our body language.

Body Language	Body Language Message
Face flushed with anger, shaking head disgustedly from side-to-side, contemptuous tone of voice. (Aggressive)	"I don't agree with you, dummy. Push me and you're in big trouble."
Even tone of voice, straight eye contact, speech pattern is expressive. (Assertive)	"I mean what I say. I don't agree with you."
Ingratiating tone of voice, hand covering the mouth, averted eyes. (Nonassertive)	"I don't have any right to say this. Disagree with me and I'll feel stupid and crumble."

34

Body language can easily get in the way of effective communication, especially when much of a person's body language has these two components:

1. Unfriendly component: generally looking stern, frequently frowning, rarely smiling.
2. Constantly angry component: generally speaking in a clipped or professional tone of voice, being overly firm, appearing tight-lipped, and repeatedly expressing opinions in a flat, final way that leaves no room for others' viewpoints.

Many people will interpret this kind of body language to mean that you have a chip on your shoulder and are apt to fly off the handle, or that you think you are better than they are. With this body language even simple assertive communications come across as aggressive overreactions.

Becoming Aware of Body Language

An important step in developing assertive body language is becoming aware of your body language. Figure 4 (page 36) lists behaviors that are commonly believed to be associated with assertive, aggressive, and nonassertive behavior. Since the list is not all-inclusive, you may want to add any behaviors that are particularly characteristic of your body language. Checking this list can help increase your awareness of the kind of body language behavior that decreases the effectiveness of your verbal messages. It is often helpful to ask a friend or co-worker to also rate your body language behavior. This is particularly helpful if you tend to be aggressive. Aggressive people often are unaware of how their body language affects others.

Changing Your Body Language

You can change your body language in at least two important ways. One way is to become aware of and change negative thoughts you have about yourself. These thoughts cause people to assume less effective body language. (Chapter 5 discusses such thoughts in depth.) The example on page 39 shows how important evaluating and changing your body language can be.

Figure 4 Assessing Your Body Language

Assertive body language is congruent with what is being said verbally, adds strength and emphasis to what is being said, and is generally self-assured.

Aggressive body language conveys an exaggerated sense of self-importance, overbearing, strength, and/or an air of superiority.

Nonassertive body language conveys weakness, anxiety, and lack of self-confidence. It softens the impact of what is being said verbally to the point that the verbal message loses most of its power. This is particularly true when the person's verbal message and body language are in conflict with each other, for example, laughing when saying, "I'm really angry with you." In general when there is such a discrepancy between a verbal message and a body language message, other people seem to take the body language message more seriously. Use the following system to check your body language:

OK = Satisfactory level
S = Some improvement needed
L = Lots of improvement needed

Eye Contact

Assertive	Aggressive	Nonassertive
____comfortably direct	____looking down nose ____staring off into distance with ____bored expression	____looking away or down ____blinking rapidly

Figure 4 Assessing Your Body Language (Continued)

Facial Expression

Assertive

_____open, frank, relaxed

Aggressive

_____clenching teeth
_____flaring nostrils
_____jutting jaws
_____pursed, tight-lipped mouth

Nonassertive

_____constant smiling
_____smiling, laughing, or winking when express-ing irritation
_____biting or wetting lips
_____swallowing or clearing throat
_____tensing and wrinkling forehead

Voice and Speech Expression

Assertive

_____appropriately firm
_____appropriately warm
_____expressive, emphasizing key words
_____clear

Aggressive

_____overly rapid
_____deadly quiet
_____overly loud or strident
_____sarcastic or condescending

Nonassertive

_____overly soft
_____mumbled
_____whiney
_____monotone
_____overly slow

37

Figure 4 Assessing Your Body Language (Continued)

Gestures

Assertive	Aggressive	Nonassertive
_____ well-balanced	_____ pounding fists	_____ covering mouth or
_____ erect	_____ stiff and rigid	lower face with hand
_____ relaxed	_____ finger waving or pointing	_____ excessive head nodding
_____ hand gestures, emphasizing	_____ shaking head as if other person	_____ tinkering with clothing or
key words	isn't to be believed	jewelry
	_____ hands on hips	_____ constant shifting of weight
		_____ scratching or rubbing head
		or other parts of body
		_____ wringing or rubbing hands
		_____ wooden body posture

Note: Research has yet to clearly establish which of these body language behaviors is critical in communicating assertion, aggression, and nonassertion. These lists of behaviors were taken from A. Lange, and P. Jakubowski, *Responsible Assertive Behavior: Cognitive-Behavioral Procedures for Trainers* (Champaign, Ill.: Research Press, 1976); S.A. Bower, and G.H. Bower, *Asserting Yourself* (Reading, Mass.: Addison-Wesley, 1976); and L. Bloom, K. Coburn, and J. Pearlman, *The New Assertive Woman* (New York: Delacorte Press, 1975).

A young working woman found that she went through her day with this mental set: "I am thoroughly competent in all respects regardless of what *you* may think, and I'm going to prove it to you. You'd better not mess with me because you're going to be in for a big surprise!" She felt better about herself and improved her body language and subsequent work relationships when she changed her mental set to "I basically like these people, and I don't think most of them are out to get me. They'll probably give me at least half a chance."

Adopting this attitude helped put her into a more relaxed, self-confident frame of mind in which she could view other people as well as herself as basically OK people. She came across less defensively and acted less defensively with other people. Some people find Exercise 2 (page 40) useful in identifying more constructive thoughts they can give themselves to improve their body language.

A second way to improve body language is to give yourself simple instructions, such as, "Look at the other person," "Stop staring, glance around," "Relax and stop frowning." If this is not effective, you can practice better eye contact by looking at yourself in a mirror and making eye contact with yourself as you practice delivering assertive communications that are particularly hard for you to say, such as, "Thank you; however, I'm not available to serve on that committee," or, "When I get a lot of complaints the first thing I walk in the door, I get irritated and I'd appreciate your giving me an hour to relax and collect my thoughts before you tell me everything that's gone wrong during the day."

One type of nervous body language that often takes more elaborate practice to change is that of swallowing repeatedly or excessive throat clearing, both of which tend to communicate fear and lower self-confidence to others. The following exercise can help to correct this habit. "Take a sip of water before speaking. Stop speaking each time you swallow, relax and take a deep breath. Swallow while concentrating on the wave of relaxation that follows the wave of throat tension. Exaggerate and memorize the feeling of an open, relaxed throat. Practice relaxing your throat by recalling that feeling in your throat several times a day."[4]

Exercise 2   Changing Your Body Language Through Changing Your Thoughts

In completing this exercise, it is often helpful to ask close friends about the message or impression that comes across to them in your body language. The following are two sample exercises that have been completed.

Specific Body Language	Message Given to Others	Message You're Trying to Get Across	Thoughts You Give Yourself	More Constructive Self-Thoughts
Soft voice	I'm not confident.	Don't take offense.	I'm not trying to offend you.	It's OK for me to say things that you might not like to hear. Having a different opinion doesn't make me offensive.
Overly loud, strident voice	I'm better than you are.	You'd better listen to me.	If I don't come on strong, I won't be listened to.	Relax. Take a deep breath. I don't have to win in order to be OK. I can make myself heard without shouting.

Now complete the exercise for your own body language.

1.

2.

For people who find themselves freezing like a statue when they assertively communicate, the "silent movie exercise" can be helpful. Stand in front of a mirror and practice delivering an assertive communication that you find difficult. Exaggerate your gestures and simply mouth your words as though you were in a silent movie. Though in real life you would not use such exaggerated gestures, practicing this exercise once a day can help free up your body and help you find a way of constructively channeling the body tension you experience in the process of acting assertively.[5]

Another exercise can be particularly helpful for people whose inappropriately strong, clipped tone of voice and excessive speech rate cause their communications to come across as aggressive. Tape record yourself reading several newspaper paragraphs aloud at your normal speaking rate. Then read at two other rates. Replay the tape, asking a friend to help you determine your best speaking rate and check the degree to which you speak clearly at the various rates. Read aloud until this optimal rate feels natural for you. Then write out an assertive communication that is difficult for you to say; read it at the optimal rate. Then practice delivering this communication from memory at the optimal rate and intonation, emphasizing key words. Finally, monitor your speech rate in social conversation and reward yourself for changing your speech pattern.[6]

SUMMARY

Responsible assertive communication involves expressing ourselves in ways that are respectful of self and others, direct, honest, and appropriate in the context of the particular situation. Body language should be congruent with what is being said verbally, adding strength and emphasis. Figure 5 (page 42) compares assertive, nonassertive and aggressive behaviors.

Aggressive communication dominates, humiliates, or puts others down, showing no respect for the other person. These communications are typically indirect attacks on others, emotionally dishonest, and inappropriate in their location, timing, intensity, or frequency. Aggressive body language is so powerful that it can turn assertive communications into aggressive ones.

Figure 5 A Comparison of Nonassertive, Assertive, and Aggressive Behavior

	Nonassertive	Assertive	Aggressive
Characteristics of the Behavior:	Does not express wants, ideas, feelings, or expresses them in self-depreciating way. Intent: to please	Expresses wants, ideas, and feelings in direct and appropriate ways. Intent: to communicate	Expresses wants, ideas, and feelings at the expense of others. Intent: to dominate or humiliate
Your Feelings When You Act This Way:	Anxious, disappointed with yourself. Often angry and resentful later.	Confident, feel good about yourself at the time and later.	Self-righteous, superior. Sometimes embarrassed later.
Other People's Feelings About Themselves When You Act This Way:	Guilty or superior	Respected, valued	Humiliated, hurt
Other People's Feelings About You When You Act This Way:	Irritation, pity, disgust	Usually respect	Angry, vengeful

Figure 5   A Comparison of Nonassertive, Assertive, and Aggressive Behavior (Continued)

	Nonassertive	Assertive	Aggressive
Outcome:	Don't get what you want; anger builds up.	Often get what you want.	Often get what you want at the expense of others. Others feel justified at "getting even."
Payoff:	Avoids unpleasant situation, avoids conflict, tension, confrontation.	Feels good; respected by others. Improved self-confidence. Relationships are improved.	Vents anger, feels superior.

Source: This chart is a modification of the charts of Cheri May, Karen Coburn, and Joan Pearlman, unpublished chart, from Robert E. Alberti and Michael L. Emmins, *Your Perfect Right: A Guide to Assertive Behavior* (San Luis Obispo, Ca.: Impact, 1970), and from Patricia Jakubowski-Spector, "Facilitating the Growth of Women through Assertive Training," *The Counseling Psychologist* 4 (1973): 75-86.

There are two types of nonassertive behavior. The first type is letting ourselves down by not doing anything when our rights or feelings are infringed upon or by lying about how we feel or what we want. The second type of nonassertion is speaking in such a self-deprecating, anxious way that lack of self-respect is shown. Nonassertive body language can make such an impact that it can turn an otherwise assertive statement into a nonassertive one.

Although these concepts may seem clear, it is often more difficult to accurately discriminate between assertive, aggressive, and nonassertive communication in specific situations. The Jakubowski Discrimination Test in Exercise 3 can be used to help you assess the degree to which these differences are clear to you.

Exercise 3   Discrimination Test on Assertive, Aggressive, and Nonassertive Behavior

Carefully read each situation and then rate the response as either assertive (+), aggressive (−), or nonassertive (N). The correct scorings appear on page 49.

Situation	Response
1. Plans to vacation together are abruptly changed by a friend and reported to you on the phone. You respond,	Wow, this has really taken me by surprise. I'd like to call you back after I've had some time to digest what's happened. _____
2. Parent is reprimanding the children when they haven't cleaned up their room and says,	You've got to be the worst kids in the whole city! If I had known parenthood was going to be like this, I would never have had any kids at all! _____
3. Your roommate habitually leaves the room a mess. You say,	You're a mess and our room is a mess. _____

*Adapted from P. Jakubowski, "Discrimination Test on Assertive, Aggressive, and Nonassertive Behavior." In A. Lange and P. Jakubowski, *Responsible Assertive Behavior: Cognitive-Behavioral Procedures for Trainers* (Champaign, IL: Research Press Co., 1976).

Exercise 3   Discrimination Test on Assertive, Aggressive, and Nonassertive Behavior (continued)

Situation	Response
4. Your husband wants to watch a football game on TV. There is something else that you'd like to watch. You say,	Well, ah, honey, go ahead and watch the game. I guess I could do some ironing. _____
5. Parent is annoyed that school counselor has not done anything about son's conflict with a teacher. Parent says,	I have asked the school to investigate the situation in my son's classroom and it concerns me that nothing has been done. I must insist that this situation be looked into. _____
6. Supervisor has just berated you for your work. You respond,	I think some of your criticisms are true, but I would have liked your being less personal about telling me about my shortcomings. _____
7. Your ten-year-old child has interrupted you three times with something that is not urgent. You've assertively asked her not to interrupt you. The child has now again interrupted you. You say,	I can't listen to you and talk on the phone at the same time. I'll be on the phone a few more minutes and then we'll talk. _____
8. It is your turn to clean the apartment, which you have neglected to do several times in the last month. In a very calm tone of voice your room-mate asks you to clean up the apartment. You say,	Would you get off my back! _____
9. You're the only woman in a group of men and you're asked to be the secretary of the meetings. You respond,	I'm willing to do my share and take the notes this time. In future meetings, I'd like us to share the load. _____

Exercise 3 Discrimination Test on Assertive, Aggressive, and Nonassertive Behavior (continued)

Situation	Response
10. A fellow teacher always tries to get out of doing his turn of team teaching and asks you again to take his turn. You say,	Well . . . I guess that'd be OK even if I do have a splitting headache. ____
11. An acquaintance has asked to borrow your car for the evening. You say,	Are you crazy! I don't lend my car to anyone. ____
12. Loud stereo upstairs is disturbing you. You telephone and say,	Hello, I live downstairs. Your stereo is loud and is bothering me. Would you please turn it down. ____
13. A good friend calls and tells you she desperately needs you to canvass the street for a charity. You don't want to do it and say,	Oh gee, Fran, I just know that Jerry will be mad at me if I say yes. He says I'm always getting involved in too many things. You know how Jerry is about things like this. ____
14. You are at a meeting of seven men and one woman. At the beginning of the meeting, the chairman asks you to be the secretary. You respond,	No, I'm sick and tired of being the secretary just because I'm the only woman in the group. ____
15. You are team teaching, but you're doing all the planning, teaching, interacting, and evaluating of students. You say,	We're supposed to be team teaching, yet I see that I am doing all the work. I'd like to talk about changing this. ____
16. The bus is crowded with high school students who are talking to their friends. You want to get off but no one pays attention when you say, "Out please." Finally, you say,	What is the matter with you kids? I'm supposed to get off at the next corner! ____

46

Exercise 3 Discrimination Test on Assertive, Aggressive, and Nonassertive Behavior (continued)

Situation	Response
17. Student comes late to class for the third time. Teacher responds,	When you're not here at the beginning of my lecture, I have to repeat parts of my lecture and that takes extra class time. I'm getting bothered by your tardiness. _____
18. The local library calls and asks you to return a book you never checked out. You respond,	What are you talking about? You people better get your records straight—I never had that book and don't you try to make me pay for it. _____
19. You are in a line at the store. Someone behind you has one item and asks to get in front of you. You say,	I realize that you don't want to wait in line, but I was here first and I really would like to get out of here. _____
20. Parent is talking with a married child on the telephone and would like the child to come for a visit. When the child politely refuses, the parent says,	You're never available when I need you. All you ever think about is yourself. _____
21. Employer sends a memorandum stating that there should be no more toll business calls made without first getting prior permission. One employee responds,	You're taking away my professional judgment. It's insulting to me. _____
22. Your mate expects dinner on the table upon arriving home from work and gets angry when it is not there immediately. You respond,	I feel awful about dinner. I know you're tired and hungry . . . it's all my fault. I'm just terrible. _____

Exercise 3 Discrimination Test on Assertive, Aggressive, and Nonassertive Behavior (continued)

Situation	Response
23. You have set aside 4:00 to 5:00 for things you want or need to do. Someone asks to see you at that time. You say,	Well . . . I can see you at that time. It's 4:00 Monday, then. Are you sure that's a good time for you? _____
24. Mate gets silent instead of saying what's on his mind. You say,	Here it comes. The big silent treatment. Would it kill you to spit it out just once? _____
25. Mate has criticized your appearance in front of your friends. You say,	I really feel hurt when you criticize my appearance in front of other people. If you have something to say, please bring it up at home before we leave. _____
26. A friend often borrows small amounts of money and does not return it unless asked. He again asks for a small loan which you'd rather not give. You say,	I only have enough money to pay for my own lunch today. _____
27. A neighbor has been constantly borrowing your vacuum sweeper. The last time, she broke it. When she asks for it again, you reply,	I'm sorry, but I don't want to loan my sweeper anymore. The last time I loaned it to you, it was returned broken. _____
28. A woman is being interviewed for a job, in the process of which the interviewer looks at her leeringly and says, "You certainly look like you have all the qualifications for the job." She responds,	I'm sure I am quite capable of doing the work here. _____

Exercise 3 Discrimination Test on Assertive, Aggressive, and Nonassertive Behavior (continued)

Situation	Response
29. You're walking to the copy machine when a fellow employee, who always asks you to do his copying, asks you where you're going. You respond,	I'm going to the Celtics ball game . . . Where does it look like I'm going? ⎯⎯⎯
30. Parent is talking with a married child on the telephone and would like child to come for a visit. The parent says,	I had a funny dream last night. I dreamed that the grandchildren came to visit me. ⎯⎯⎯

Scoring Key to Discrimination Test

1. +	11. −	21. −
2. −	12. +	22. N
3. −	13. N	23. N
4. N	14. −	24. −
5. +	15. +	25. +
6. +	16. −	26. N
7. +	17. +	27. +
8. −	18. −	28. +
9. +	19. +	29. −
10. N	20. −	30. N

NOTES

1.   Jakubowski, P. Assertive behavior and clinical problems of women. In E. Rawlings & D. Carter (Eds.), *Psychotherapy for women: Treatment towards equality.* Springfield, IL: Charles C. Thomas, 1977.

2.   This type of assertion is called the escalating assertion and was developed by: Rimm, D. C., & Masters, J. C. *Behavior therapy: Techniques and empirical findings.* New York: Academic Press, 1974.

3.   Mehrabian, A. *Nonverbal communication.* Chicago: Aldine/Atherton, 1972.

4.   Bower, S. A., & Bower, G. H. *Asserting yourself.* Reading, MA: Addison-Wesley, 1976.

5.   Serber, M. *Assertive training.* Paper presented at the Association for the Advancement of Behavior Therapy, New York, 1972.

6.   Bower, S. A., & Bower, G. H., 1976.

3
Causes of Nonassertive and Aggressive Behavior

Many people simply attribute their nonassertive or aggressive behavior to a lack of self-confidence, low self-concept, or quick temper, and although there may be some truth to these observations, they do little to help deal with communication problems. Generalizations about behavior tend to lead to generalized remedies (e.g., "I simply need to develop more confidence"). The purpose of this chapter is to develop a broadened understanding of nonassertive and aggressive behavior so that you will start thinking more precisely about your behavior. The following two chapters provide more specific information about how to change nonassertive and aggressive behavior.

COMMON CAUSES OF NONASSERTION

Fear of Displeasing Others
One reason that many people don't act assertively is their fear of displeasing others. Experiencing others' disapproval is usually disappointing and uncomfortable. However, when people are nonassertive, they seem to carry their disappointment one step further.

There are several ways to do this. We tell ourselves that we *must* have others' approval and *can't stand* their disapproval. And when we get disapproval from other people, we incorrectly interpret this to mean that it is all our fault and that we are bad, worthless human beings. Many people believe in a kind of magic: If they are good enough (try hard enough, care enough, sacrifice enough, overlook enough, assert enough), they will get others' approval, and they incorrectly interpret disapproval to mean that they are not good enough people.

This line of reasoning fails to account for the fact that a person's negative *thoughts* about you do not *make* you bad: You are a good and worthwhile person even when a very significant person is angry or displeased with you. Your own opinion of yourself and your behavior is worth at least as much as someone else's opinion. Another person's opinion is just an opinion and not an indisputable, irrevocable fact.

It is important to remember that your behavior is more likely to get disapproval when it is unexpected and doesn't conform to others' expectations, especially societal expectations. For example, an employer who feels that any woman is lucky to have a job will be surprised by a female employee's request for a raise; and he probably won't approve, regardless of her personal worth as a human being. Thus others' disapproval of your actions often has little to do with your personal worth. The following is a case in point.

> During an assertiveness seminar one of the authors (Pat) used the phrase "feeling shitty" several times while describing the effects of nonassertive behavior. One woman was so angered by this that she turned her back, muttering comments to her neighbor about Pat's upbringing. Later in the seminar, Pat helped another woman practice assertively asking men whether they were married before she decided to accept a date; and Pat defended the woman's right to do this when a male criticized the practice session because he felt that the woman was cutting herself off from potentially enjoyable relationships and that "just because a man was married didn't mean that he couldn't just take her out and be a friend." After the seminar Pat received praise and positive comments about her moral character from the same woman who earlier had disapproved of her as a bad, immoral human being!

When other people leap from disliking something we do to negatively evaluating our entire personhood, it is not necessary or good to make the same illogical leap. There is no reason to conclude that we are unlikable, unworthy human beings.

Reasoning that causes us to feel depressed and unworthy when other people disapprove of us fails to take into consideration that even if we have done something that is, objectively speaking, a wrong or thoughtless *act*, we are not bad and worthless *people*. When we agree with others' disapproval of our behavior, instead of berating ourselves because we are imperfect, fallible human beings, we can choose to change what we and others don't like—not because we're bad or *must* have others' approval but because we can see there is a valid point to the criticism. Sometimes we may decide to change our ways even though we don't really agree with another's criticism, for example, when we value the other person and the relationship and are willing to make some accommodations to improve the quality of the relationship. Such behavior is assertive (rather than nonassertive) when it involves no loss of personal integrity.

You can be assertive in spite of your fear of displeasing others when you are able to accurately evaluate whether you are doing something that is wrong—objectively speaking—or whether the other person's negative reaction to your assertion is due to the fact that you simply haven't met her personal expectations, haven't conformed to what she wanted, or have done something which in her *opinion* you shouldn't have done.

Rejection and Retaliation
Often what we really fear about displeasing others is that the other person will withdraw his affection or end the relationship or use his power over us to get back at us.

The likelihood that other people will withdraw or retaliate after you have been responsibly assertive depends a great deal on the nature of the relationship. More specifically, it depends on such things as individual definitions of what is acceptable behavior in a relationship, the kinds of expectations people have, the give-and-take pattern that has been established in a relationship, and the degree to which a person can accept or tolerate differences or disagreements. Other important factors are the moods and the degree of fairmindedness of the individuals involved, the value they place on the relationship, the importance of the issue, and their assessment of power in the situation.

The questions listed in Exercise 4 (page 56) can be used to help assess how likely it is that the other person will retaliate. In personal relationships it is also helpful to complete and discuss these incomplete sentences with the other person:

- If I really cared about this relationship (or the other person) I would . . . .
  (Example) " . . . show interest and concern when my friend is in need, and I would do the best I can, within limits, to be of help."
- If he really cared about the relationship (or me), he would . . . .
  (Example) " . . . generally understand and accept me, and when he disapproved, he'd be up front with his disapproval and would be willing to discuss it rather than just immediately demand I change."

Discussing these sentences can help individuals become more aware of their hidden expectations. This knowledge can help you to better predict others' reactions when you act assertively and help you to decide whether or not you want to continue the relationship.

The discussion itself can help clarify expectations and potentially lead to the discovery that one or both parties' expectations are unrealistic and need to be changed. If both parties refuse to change or modify their conflicting expectations, then they will need to be prepared to handle the disappointments and hurt feelings that will inevitably arise. In some cases people may discover that what is expected in the relationship is so rigid and narrow that responsible assertive behavior does indeed threaten the very foundations of the relationship. In such cases it's a matter of weighing the benefits and costs to acting assertively. Francine made such a decision.

> Francine's husband expected her to always agree with him and to be available when he wanted to relax. When she disagreed with the way he disciplined the children or said that she didn't want to go to a movie on a particular evening, he became sulky and withdrew into a cold silence. Francine then apologized and did what he wanted. This pattern continued for fifteen years in their marriage until she got a divorce.
>
> Retrospectively, Francine now wishes that she had withstood his silent, moody period so that this might have forced the issues

to come out in their marriage, be discussed, and possibly resolved. Though she could never know for sure whether this course of action would have had any more beneficial results, at least her self-esteem would not have suffered in the years of keeping quiet about her own views and acquiesing to him.

What makes fear of rejection so difficult to deal with often is not the consequence of rejection itself but rather the way we react to it. When faced with the prospect of being rejected, we often see ourselves as helpless victims with no recourse other than to passively accept the treatment we have been given. We scare ourselves so much that we forget to stop and think how we could protect ourselves from the retaliation or how we could make the other person's withdrawal or ending the relationship an easier experience to bear.

The following are some examples of catastrophizing thoughts that many people unknowingly give themselves. The catastrophizing elements are italicized.

- Fear of a Lover's Moodiness: "It's *all* my fault. He'll *never* feel good about me again. I *can't stand* his moodiness. I'll *never* be loved again. My assertiveness will *totally destroy* our relationship *forever*. I *must* have hurt him *terribly* for him to get so moody."
- Fear of Losing a Job: "If I get fired as a result of my assertiveness, I'll be *totally* without resources. I'll *never* be able to get another job. I *absolutely couldn't stand* being temporarily out of work. *Everyone* would think I am a failure. I'll *never* be able to get any good references so I'll *never* get another job."
- Fear of Being Bad-Mouthed: "If I speak up, *all* my co-workers will *definitely* talk badly about me. I'll *never* get them to talk nicely about me again. This will *never* blow over. I'll *never* be able to hold up my head again. I'll be *totally* alone, and there's *absolutely nothing* I can do about it. *Everyone* will hate me, and there's *nothing* I can do to change *anyone's* mind about me."

Chapter 8 discusses how people can deal with negative thoughts.

Exercise 4   Assessing the Likelihood of Retaliation

1. Describe the specific situation in which you wish to be assertive but are concerned about retaliation.

2. What do you fear will happen?

3. What's the concrete evidence that this person will retaliate in the way you fear? (Has this person retaliated in the past, either with you or anyone else? What were the circumstances surrounding that retaliation? Are they the same or different than yours?)

4. Is there any evidence that the person will *not* retaliate in the way you fear?

5. What do you think will actually happen?

6. Is there any way you can protect yourself from the person's retaliation?

Mistaken Sense of Responsibility:
The Hurt Feeling Issue

A third cause of nonassertion is a mistaken sense of responsibility. We unduly hold ourselves responsible for others' hurt feelings, in effect saying to ourselves that if someone feels hurt, it *must* be *all* our fault because we failed to find a perfect way of being assertive which wouldn't have resulted in another's feeling hurt. We tend to overreact or overdramatize, saying to ourselves, "It would be *awful* if the other person's feelings got hurt when I asserted myself. I could *never* forgive myself. The person would *never* recover from the hurt. She'd be *permanently* damaged. Her life would be ruined *forever*, and I'd be *totally* responsible."

Also, we often make the error of assuming that it is the other person's positive or negative reactions that determine whether or not we have an assertive right in a situation. Unfortunately some people do feel upset, scared, or hurt *even when* our assertion is justified, sensitively expressed, and is not intended to hurt them. We cannot automatically assume that we don't have a right to be assertive *just* because the other person may feel bad or hurt.

The key issue is whether *you hurt* the other person or whether the other person *simply felt* hurt because he misinterpreted your assertiveness to mean that you didn't care for him and don't value the friendship; it is this interpretation that caused the person to feel hurt. If you made a snide remark, ridiculed the other person, or knowingly violated his rights, then you have hurt the person and can hold yourself accountable. If you have simply refused a date, expressed a contrary opinion, suggested that a relative's holiday visit last for four days instead of two weeks, then your assertive *action* was not in itself hurtful even though the person may have *felt* hurt. The following example may clarify this important point.

Don ate everything his hostess had provided at dinner except for the meat. When the hostess asked if there was something wrong with the meat, Don complimented her on the meal and said that the only reason he wasn't eating the meat was because of religious reasons. When Don described this incident to his assertiveness group, he was pleased with how he handled the situation, didn't eat the meat, and didn't make fun of his religious beliefs. The group was equally pleased with the way Don handled the situation—all except for Ruth who said that she would have felt very hurt if she had been the hostess.

When the group leader asked what thoughts would run through her mind if Don were to say that to her, Ruth replied that she'd think, "Oh! It's all my fault. I'm a terrible hostess. I should have known about his dietary restrictions. Now his meal is totally ruined, and everybody thinks I'm a terrible hostess!"

All these thoughts were exaggerations and distortions. Don's dinner was not ruined; in fact, he made it clear that he was enjoying himself. There was no particular reason why the hostess "should" have known about his dietary habits; one doesn't routinely ask guests about their religion. It's doubtful that anyone at the party thought she was a terrible hostess on the basis of this single incident.

This example illustrates an important point about assertive behavior: A person can feel hurt even though, *objectively speaking,* you have done nothing to hurt him. It is difficult enough to control your own negative thoughts without also holding yourself responsible for others' stream of self-condemning thoughts. This is not to say that you should go to the opposite extreme and become insensitive and indifferent to others' feelings. Responsible assertion involves trying to do the best you can to avoid hurting others, with full recognition that this will not always be possible. When your assertion involves friends and other people who are close to you, responsible assertion calls for trying to clear up the other person's misinterpretations of your assertion (e.g., thinking that suggesting that your parents come for four days instead of two weeks means that you don't love them), again with the full recognition that it takes two people to clear up a misunderstanding.

Mistaken Sense of Responsibility: The Guilt Issue

Justified guilt occurs when you do something that violates realistic moral standards and personal values, such as stealing, taking advantage of others, or allowing a mate to abuse a child.

Justified guilt, however, occurs far less often than the frequency of guilty feelings would suggest. People often feel guilty when there is no objective basis for feeling this way.

When you feel inappropriately guilty any or all of the following events may be involved:

1. You see yourself as the only one who can help and therefore *should* take responsibility.
2. The person in need often appears very helpless.
3. A message is communicated that "If you *really* care, you will do this for me," or you give yourself this message.
4. You do not define your own behavior.
5. You are confused about the legitimacy of your own wants when they conflict with or might lead to inconvenience or displeasure for others.

People often see themselves as the *only* resource available to someone in need simply because the other person has defined the situation that way. People often believe the message from others: "You are the only person I know who can do this for me, and I know you will do it if you really love me." Sometimes it is true; you really are the only person who can help in a specific situation, but the pressure of "if you really care" often can lead you to ignore other available options. Even more disruptive than the inaccurate message of being the "one and only source of help" is the suggestion that "If you really love me, you will do what I want." This message equates doing something like spending more time together with caring and love for that person. This is not unreasonable in itself, but the message, "You should spend such and such amount of time with me and do such and such for me; if you do not, you are a bad person, selfish and inconsiderate and uncaring," is an unreasonable tactic. The irrational quality of such a message is that the other person is defining *your* competence or goodness as a person in terms of *his* preferences and *his* definition of a caring person. Amelia's relationship with her grandfather illustrates the dilemma that this kind of reasoning can pose.

Amelia visited her grandfather regularly once a week. During her visits her grandfather continually asked her to do chores for him, like food shopping, taking clothes to the cleaners, and having his car serviced. Grandfather regularly complained of being alone and forgotten, especially by Amelia. He would make indirect and sometimes direct demands that Amelia should come over more often than once a week if she really cared.

Grandfather acted as though Amelia was the only person who could do these things for him. Although Amelia had initially accepted this as true, she realized that several of her brothers and sisters who lived nearby were willing to help out, but Grandfather simply preferred Amelia's help. Initially Amelia felt guilty because she believed that if she really loved her grandfather, she should do all these things and see him more frequently. Actually Amelia preferred to spend her visiting time doing something enjoyable with him. She enjoyed seeing him once a week; more than that would have resulted in her feeling burdened and resentful.

In rethinking how she was allowing her behavior to be redefined by her grandfather, Amelia decided that she would continue to visit him once a week and that she would spend most of that time doing something enjoyable with him. As Grandfather attempted to define Amelia's commitment as "not enough" and Amelia as "bad and selfish," Amelia defined her own self by reaffirming her love for him and stating her limits: "I do love you and care about you very much. I look forward to visiting you once a week, especially now that we are spending more of that time together. I know you would like to see me more often, but I'm not willing to increase my visits." The conversation continued with Grandfather initially, but briefly, expressing hurt and rejection. Amelia continued to express her caring and clearly yet firmly stated the limits of her commitment. Amelia refused to allow herself to be defined as a "bad" person.

In other cases we get hooked into feeling inappropriately guilty when we mistakenly believe that the other person will be helped if we put aside our own feelings and desires and take responsibility for solving their problems, as the following examples illustrate.

A teacher constantly found himself spending hours helping his students. He wanted to set more realistic limits on his time, yet he felt guilty because he saw the students as helpless and unable to get along without all the help he provided. He saw himself as indispensable. He would do such things as spend hours of extra time with students and essentially end up writing half of their themes.

A brother, over a period of years, kept borrowing money from his sister to the tune of $8,000. She wanted to refuse his requests for money, but each time his pleas were dramatic: Because of his gambling debts, he was in danger of being beaten up unless she would loan him the money. On other occasions, he wanted the money to have his bad checks covered so that he wouldn't go to jail.

Were these individuals really helping with their nonasser-tive behavior? The teacher found that his hours of work with students left him with little time to devote to his personal life. The teacher felt victimized. The students, on the other hand, weren't being taught how to think on their own but rather learned how to be passive and let the teacher do their thinking for them. In fact, their limited self-confidence in writing in-creased even more because they couldn't see how they could possibly write their themes as well as the teacher. As the teacher felt increasingly taken advantage of by his students, he became highly critical and attacked them for not doing more on their own. Some of the students simply counterattacked by accusing the teacher of not really caring, while others felt guilty.

What happened was that the teacher's nonassertion was not really helping but rather was rescuing. When someone is genuinely helped, her behavior changes in positive ways, and at some point she no longer needs the assistance. When someone is rescued, the *rescuer eventually ends up as the victim and often in the persecutor-aggressor position. The so-called victim con-tinues the same unhealthy behavior and eventually assumes the persecutor-aggressor position.*[1]

The sister who loaned money to her brother was being taken advantage of. Her brother had an excellent job, took expensive vacations, and in general just frittered away his money. The brother actually lived off his own income plus half of his sister's. Classically, the sister then became the victim and felt abused, powerless, and had no money to take care of her own desires for relaxation, clothes, savings, etc. Occasionally she became persecutor-aggressor and attacked her brother for his failure to repay the loans, yet every time he came begging for help, she again rescued him, and the cycle started again (see Figure 6). As long as she was hooked into rescuing her brother, she could not assertively refuse his demands for money.[2]

Figure 6   The Drama Triangle

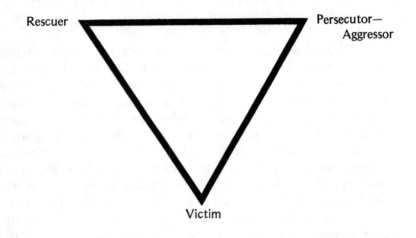

Rescuer

Persecutor—
Aggressor

Victim

Source: Stephan Karpman, "Fairy Tales and Script Drama Analysis," *Transactional Analysis Bulletin* 7, 26 (April 1968): 40.

One way you can assess whether you are really being help-ful or are nonassertively rescuing is to ask yourself the following questions.

1. How much of my urge to help is caused by feeling guilty?
2. Do I see the other person as a helpless victim? Does the other person have options, resources, or abilities to solve the problem that I am failing to recognize?
3. What kind of assistance would really help the other person?

4. What can I reasonably expect the other person to do to help herself?
5. What price will the receiver pay when I feel obligated and resentful?
6. How much assistance can I give without feeling resentful?

The last question can be particularly difficult to answer for those of us who often fool ourselves about the importance of our desires or the costs we will pay if we are not assertive. If you tend to underestimate the strength and importance of your own desires, the following guidelines are useful.

When you decide to do what others want instead of what you want to do, it is helpful to pay particular attention to how you feel afterwards. If you discover that you feel resentful, hurt, or depressed, you probably have miscalculated the importance of your preferences. On the other hand, you probably will also find times when you feel satisfied afterwards. It is true that you can feel happy and fulfilled when doing things for other people, even if they entail making sacrifices. The key is to know when choosing to give up your preferences will bring peace and when it will bring resentment. Analyzing the differences between those times when we feel glad and when we feel resentful can help you assess when it is appropriate to give to other people and when you are letting yourself down by ignoring important preferences and limitations.

Noticing how your body feels when you agree to do something someone else wants is also helpful. Sensations like sinking heart, quickening breath, tightened stomach, or rigid facial muscles give you important information about your feelings and the real importance of your preferences.

When you are not sure how you will feel afterwards, it is important to take time to think before you give your answer. It often is helpful to picture yourself doing the activity, then not doing it (doing what you want to do instead), and notice what differences there are in your feelings. When your sense of what is right (conscience) and your desires are at odds, there are several things you can do. You can ask yourself what compromise you can strike with *yourself.* You can analyze which of your desires are most important and make plans to fulfill them.

As in Ted's case you can determine whether or not the dictates of your conscience are realistic.

Ted's mother, who had been widowed for several years, wanted to spend two weeks visiting Ted during the summer. Ted dreaded the whole idea, fearing that his mother, who had limited interests, would only talk about her deceased husband, her loneliness, and her financial worries. Ted's conscience dictated that he should have his mother stay for several weeks and devote himself to entertaining her, taking care of her every need. Picturing himself doing this, Ted felt tense, depressed, and angry. Picturing himself living his usual life without his mother being there, he felt relieved but also guilty.

After some thought Ted realized that he believed he had some responsibility to be available to his mother and that he wanted to help her to be a little more happy—and that two weeks would result in his feeling bitter, a bitterness that would undoubtedly show in subtle ways to his mother, who really didn't want to take advantage of him or be a burden upon him.

Ted struck a compromise with himself by asking his mother to stay for an extended weekend. When he pictured himself having this visit, Ted realized that he still felt more bitter than was good for him. Analyzing it further, Ted discovered that he pictured himself waiting "hand and foot" on his mother and that this is what was creating his feelings of resentment. Realizing that he needed to reduce his feelings of resentment, he planned to include some activities that he enjoyed, not only those that his mother might like. He decided not to wait on her hand and foot and to plan some time when his mother would be alone or could do a few things for him, realizing that his mother probably would enjoy doing a few simple things for him.

The end result was that Ted felt a lot better about his sacrifice. The visit was quite a bit more pleasant than he had expected. By taking care of his most important needs, Ted was able to welcome his mother without hidden resentment.

Whether guilt is justified or not, feeling guilty does not mean that you are a bad, worthless person. Guilt simply gives you information: Whatever you have done—or are thinking of doing—violates your conscience; you need to act rather than simply sit back and feel bad or automatically give in to other people in order to appease your conscience. If you decide that

64

your guilt is unwarranted, you can work toward changing the unrealistic demands you put on yourself. If you conclude that your guilt is warranted, you can take the kind of action that will change your behavior, or decide to remain as you are and take the consequences.

Misinformation about Basic Human Rights

A fourth common cause of nonassertive behavior is the mistaken belief that you don't have the right to act assertively. It is very difficult to be assertive when you believe that you are stepping beyond your prerogatives. This is particularly true when you have come to believe that you have rights only under special circumstances (e.g., not having the right to express irritation unless you have become so angry that you are about to explode; not having the right to refuse a date unless there is absolutely no doubt that you can't stand the other person). It also is difficult to be assertive when you deny yourself certain rights simply on the basis of your sex or position (e.g., incorrectly concluding that you, as a parent, don't have the right to take some time out for yourself because your children didn't ask to be born; that you, as a child, don't have the right to disagree with your parents because they know best; that you, as a boss, don't have the right to make mistakes because you "should know better").

Chapter 4 discusses the rights that people do have. It also provides an exercise you can use to help yourself feel more comfortable about accepting and acting on these rights while still respecting the rights of others.

Reluctance to Give Up
the Hidden Benefits of Nonassertion

There are disadvantages to acting nonassertively, such as loss of self-respect, increased anxiety, and resentment, but there are also advantages. By presenting yourself as helpless and unable to act in your behalf, other people may act for you. Nonassertive behavior can help you to perpetuate certain public images. For example, by not asking for information you need, you can appear all-knowing; by not expressing irritation, you can appear to be very understanding and accepting of other people; by not expressing controversial opinions, you can appear to be in agreement with other people. By finding out what the hidden payoff of your nonassertive behavior is, you may become more aware of why you continue such behavior and what you will need to give up in order to change (see Exercise 5).

**Exercise 5 Assessing the Hidden Payoffs
of Nonassertive Behavior**

Step One: Describe a specific situation in which you are nonassertive.

Step Two: Complete this sentence two or three times:
                 The neat thing about being nonassertive in this situation is:

Step Three: What would you have to give up or change in order to be assertive in this situation?

Step Four: What are some other more direct ways you can get or replace what you would give up?

Step Five: What small steps could you take today to incorporate this change into your life? (Remind yourself of the costs of your nonassertive behavior; give yourself permission to be less than the image you are trying to protect; remind yourself that you are generally what your image is, but not 100 percent of the time.)

The idea for Exercise 5 came from B. E. Thomas, who is a practicing psychologist in Conway, Arkansas. This exercise can also be used for assessing the payoffs which come from aggressive behavior.

Lack of Skills or Information
Many times people act nonassertively simply because they have not yet developed the skills of assertive communication and need practice and information. For example, people who have never negotiated for a salary increase, headed a committee, or supervised workers may lack the information on how this is done.

COMMON CAUSES OF AGGRESSIVE BEHAVIOR

Underlying Cause
The underlying cause of aggressive behavior seems to be the feeling of being vulnerable or unsafe *and* powerless in a threatening situation. In such circumstances, people often over-react in an attempt to protect themselves from a threat. For example, some people, anticipating that a car salesperson is out to take advantage of them, feel threatened and attempt to protect themselves by approaching the salesperson with a chip on their shoulder and an attitude that broadcasts, "I know you're out to take advantage of me, but I'm going to get you first."

The following model of anger is useful for understanding the dynamics of our own and others' aggressive behavior.* According to this model, people quickly go through these stages:

Threat Stage: The cycle starts with seeing a person or object as threatening to our physical or psychological well-being. Unmet expectations or demands are frustrating and can also be felt as a threat.

---

*The idea for this model comes from the Anger Cycle, J. E. Jones & A. G. Banet, "Dealing with another's anger." *The 1976 Annual Handbook for Group Facilitators.*

Assessment of Danger Stage: The next step is making automatic assumptions about the possible danger of the threat, for example, by assuming that the threat is a major one.

Assessment of Power Stage: This is quickly followed by determining the other person's power in the situation and our own perceived power for dealing with the threat. If we decide that we are powerful enough to handle the threat successfully or conclude that the threat is not very great or important, we can calmly deal with the situation. But if we decide that we are powerless to handle the threat, then anger occurs to destroy or reduce the threat and protect ourselves.

Anger Stage: Anger is more likely to emerge as aggression if we do not have the verbal skills to handle the situation assertively; if we have allowed the anger to build to high levels before expressing it or dealing with it; if we have a belief system which supports the view that aggression is the only way to get through to people; if we exaggerate the seriousness of the "misdeed" of the other person or the unfairness of the situation; if the other person frustrates our attempts to deal with the situation. On the other hand, when the emotion of anger is itself very threatening or the consequences of expressing anger are perceived to be very dangerous, the anger can be turned inward and result in depression or nonassertive behavior.[3]

The cycle occurs so rapidly that you can become aggressive almost instantaneously. In dealing with this cycle and your aggressive behavior, it is very important to recognize when you feel threatened so that you can interrupt the cycle and handle situations more constructively. You may be unaware of the fact that you feel threatened or deny this feeling because you think that you shouldn't feel threatened or that you are bad for feeling this way. One major way you can become more aware of your feelings is to pay attention to your body's reactions and watch for those things that indicate increased tension (e.g., increased breathing, tightening facial muscles, tensed shoulders or chest). Recognizing and accepting the fact that you feel threatened can help you to get in touch and more objectively evaluate the stream of automatic assumptions you are making about the threat and your power in the situation.

Second, you can determine what you are frightened about.

You may often discover that the threat was simply that the other person's values, opinions, or behaviors are different than yours. You can come to realize the extent to which you are exaggerating the threat—you may even discover that there is no threat (see Chapter 5).

Third, you can more accurately assess your own and others' power in the situation. When you do this, you should remember that just because the other person has more power, you probably still have some power. Not having all the power or even more power does not make you totally helpless.

Fourth, you can learn how to cope with increased body tension, develop assertive ways of protecting yourself, and dispute erroneous and emotionally charged beliefs that support aggressive behavior, all of which are dealt with in Chapter 5. It is possible to acknowledge and "own" your anger by using I statements ("I disagree") instead of You statements ("Your opinion is stupid"). Owning your anger helps avoid putting unwarranted blame on others and locates the anger where it is—inside of you. You also can learn to differentiate the various levels of anger you experience, which can help you more accurately determine your capacity for dealing with your anger and learn to measure your response from mild reactions like "I'm disturbed" through medium responses such as "I'm angry" to intense reactions like "I'm furious."[4]

The underlying cause of aggression—feeling vulnerable and powerless in a threatening situation—is related to six other factors, namely, the presence of beliefs that increase the level of threat, the rubber band effect, self-denial of basic human rights, underlying nonassertion, lack of desire to give up the benefits of aggression, and lack of skills or information.

Beliefs That Increase the Level of Threat
There is a mind-set, or group of beliefs, which promotes aggressive behavior:

- I *must* win in order to be OK.
- If I don't come on strong, I won't be listened to.
- The world is hostile, and I *must* be aggressive in order to make it.

69

- To compromise is to lose.
- I *must* make an impact.
- I *must* get my way.
- Aggression is the *only* way to get through to some people.
- I *must* prove I'm right and they're wrong.
- The world *must* be fair; it's *intolerable* when people mistreat me.

These beliefs make us feel unsafe since they increase our level of threat. Believing that you must win in order to be OK turns a simple difference of opinion into an immediate threat and if someone disagrees, this imminent danger becomes mortal combat.

These beliefs tend to set a self-fulfilling prophecy in motion. If you believe that you won't be listened to if you don't come on extremely strong, you deny yourself an opportunity to find out whether assertive behavior would work just as effectively without arousing negative reactions in others. Besides, aggression can set in motion exactly what you fear will happen: The other person may become uncooperative and antagonistic because she feels that she is being pushed against a wall. As one new car dealer said, "The guy who comes in here ranting and raving about the trouble he's having with his new car, I figure, 'OK buddy you can just wait. I don't have to take that treatment. You can just cool your heels.' Now the guy who comes in and just says what the problem is and comes across like he's got a little consideration for me, too, I'll go out of my way to help and see that he gets the service he needs." The dealer's comment illustrates that people will often go out of their way to accommodate us when they are approached in a way that shows respect for them.

Such beliefs as "The world is hostile," or "The only way to get through to some people is to get aggressive," lead you to anticipate the worst of people, jump to conclusions and create threats where in reality there are none. It can be difficult to change these beliefs because they are self-fulfilling and often have some element of truth though it is exaggerated and distorted. Figure 7 gives examples of some of these distinctions. It is easier to be assertive when you defuse or eliminate as much

Figure 7 Exaggerated Beliefs

Belief	Element of Truth	Exaggeration
The world is hostile, and you must be aggressive in order to survive. You've got to fight tooth and nail to get anywhere.	People sometimes are hostile, uncooperative, or unpleasant to deal with. Sometimes you need to become physically aggressive to protect your life or belongings.	The whole world is hostile. Most people are uncooperative or out to get you. Aggression is the only way you can protect yourself.
If you don't come on extremely strong, no one will listen to you.	At times *it is* necessary to be very firm and blunt.	You must come on strong most of the time. Coming on strong guarantees that others will listen to you.
To compromise is to lose.	You do lose something.	You lose everything. You lose getting your most important needs recognized. Losing something makes you a loser.

71

threat as possible. Changing those beliefs that unjustifiably increase your threat level necessitates first recognizing how distorted and exaggerated they are and then replacing them with more realistic thoughts, for example: "I would like to make an impact; if I don't, it doesn't mean I'm worthless or weak" or "I would very much like to get my way; if I don't, I can stand it; it doesn't mean I'm a loser." Chapter 5 presents a model of how we can identify and counteract exaggerated beliefs.

The Rubber Band Effect

When a rubber band is held loosely, it has little tension, but when it is drawn back and then snapped, it has much more impact. Similarly a mildly threatening situation has considerably more impact when it reminds a person of a previous negative experience. The new situation is like a rubber band, snapping the individual's consciousness back to that unpleasant event.[5] For example, a child who was frequently told that his accomplishments were "not enough" may overreact strongly when, as an adult, his boss tells him that he didn't do enough to deserve a pay increase. His reaction to this current experience is colored by his past; this current "threat" is partially an unresolved threat from the past. Kathy's conflict with her husband is a good illustration of the rubber band effect.

> Sitting with her husband and a woman friend, Kathy was trying to explain the need for refuge centers for women who are abused by their husbands. Her husband casually asked why it was needed. Kathy overreacted and started to berate him for his ridiculous question.
>
> After the outburst, her woman friend calmly asked the husband whether Kathy always reacted so strongly. Her husband responded, "Yes, when we start talking about issues like this, Kathy gets pretty uptight." The calm way in which both her friend and husband reacted caused Kathy to realize that she had acted as though she had been personally attacked when in reality her husband had only asked for additional information. In thinking about her overreaction, she realized that the feelings she had while discussing the need for women's centers were familiar ones to her. She asked herself this question: "When have I had these feelings before?" These feelings of powerlessness and personal attack she felt with her husband

on this issue were similar to feelings she had experienced as an adolescent, arguing to no avail with her unyielding father about religion and other issues. Discussing this emotionally charged issue was similar to discussing religion in the past with her father and triggered the same feelings of powerlessness and aggression, even though her husband did not respond like her father.

In later disagreements with other people, Kathy made a conscious effort to remind herself that the other person was not her father, that she was no longer a child, and that she was OK even if the other person did not accept her opinions. This self-talk helped her to maintain her perspective, composure, and assertion when presenting her opinions to potentially rejecting individuals.

The rubber band effect helps explain why some people react very strongly to seemingly minor situations. You can become more aware of this effect by asking yourself these questions:

- What am I experiencing now?
- Does my reaction fit the situation or is it an overreaction?
- Are these feelings familiar ones? If so, what was happening in my life when I experienced them in the past?

You can help control the rubber band effect by reminding yourself how you are different now as a person and/or how the other person or situation is different than it was in the past.

Self-Denial of Basic Human Rights

It is clear that aggressive behavior denies other people's rights. It's less obvious that our aggression may be partially the result of denying ourselves particular rights. For example, when we deny ourselves the right to make mistakes, we may blame others for causing us to make an error.

Andy agreed to drive with a co-worker to a conference in Milwaukee, but later he changed his mind and felt guilty. Instead of acknowledging that he had made an error and apologizing for the inconvenience he was causing, he blamed his co-worker for not giving him sufficient time to think through his decision.

Vicky felt very threatened and aggressive when friends asked why she wasn't planning on having children. After some self-examination it became clear that she was not fully comfortable with her right to decide that she didn't want to have children. Only when she could accept her decision and her right to make that decision was she able to be confident and nondefensive when people questioned her.

When someone doesn't feel that he has the right to ask for affection or support, he may try to get it by manipulating others, for example, by allowing misunderstandings to grow and then aggressively attacking the other person over the misunderstandings and expecting that the person will feel guilty for the mistake and make up for it by becoming more affectionate and thoughtful. Chapter 4 provides an in-depth discussion of basic human rights.

Underlying Nonassertion

As discussed in Chapter 1, aggression and nonassertion appear to be flip sides of each other. People who change nonassertive behavior often go through an aggressive period before they become assertive, especially when they decide to "express themselves" but don't think about *how* or when to do it. People who change their aggressive behavior sometimes make a similar kind of overcorrection: They go through a nonassertive period before becoming assertive, especially when they give themselves a lot of "stop" messages (e.g., "Stop being aggressive") and not enough "go" messages that provide constructive alternatives (e.g., "Before you disagree, take a deep breath, relax, and tell yourself that you don't have to win in order to be OK").

People sometimes act aggressively to prevent themselves from becoming nonassertive. For example, when you have been assertive in repeatedly refusing someone's request, you may become threatened by your own nonassertive impulses, feeling that you will give in if you are asked one more time. To prevent yourself from becoming nonassertive, you may feel self-righteously angry and blame the other person: "Who does she think she is anyway? I've already said no three times!" These thoughts and feelings may then erupt into aggression.

People sometimes have a nonassertive-aggressive cycle going as in the following example.

74

Gerald was very much in love with Cynthia, yet she had a habit of criticizing him for what seemed like the smallest things. Gerald didn't want to criticize her. Above all he wanted to keep peace, but underneath his seemingly quiet exterior, he was really starting to seethe until he finally blew up. Afterwards he thought he was a destructive person and vowed to keep his anger under better control, in other words, to suppress it. The next time Cynthia did something that he didn't like he said nothing—and started the nonassertive-aggressive cycle all over again.

In other cases, people deliberately allow their rights and feelings to be violated so that they can feel justified in expressing their feelings and aggressively standing up for themselves. This is like collecting resentment in a gunny sack until the sack is full so that you can "cash it in" for a justified aggression. ("After all the years I silently took his abuse, well he just had it coming; I should have told him off years ago!")

Aggression and nonassertion are related in yet another subtle way. People who have reacted nonassertively in one situation sometimes express their suppressed anger in a different situation. For example, you may feel that you cannot afford to risk expressing your true thoughts or feelings at work or school and discharge this tension at home, where you feel your family will understand and accept you for what you are.

Lack of Desire to Give Up
the Benefits of Aggression

Aggression has its price: It alienates others, it creates a lot of personal stress and agitation, and it makes close, trusting relationships more difficult; but aggression also has its benefits. It does scare some people into giving you what you want; it can give you a sense of power; it enables you to let off steam without regard for others; it helps you see yourself as all-knowing, and it leads others to regard you as all-powerful.

It is easier to give up the benefits of aggression when you value yourself enough to avoid getting agitated over minor issues and when you can accept yourself even when you are imperfect and incorrect. If you can recognize and value the costs of aggression and accept the fact that you cannot always get what you want, you will achieve a reasonable degree of self-confidence that will enable you to find more constructive ways of meeting your needs (e.g., to let off steam, to be heard, to be powerful, to be taken seriously) and handling threatening situations.

Lack of Information or Skills

In a great many cases people are aggressive because they haven't learned any other way of expressing themselves. Many people genuinely do not know how to express tenderness except indirectly, by acting rough; or how to express affection for another person except through sarcasm; or how to ask for a favor except by commanding. Another skill that many people simply don't have is the ability to be aware of their own increasing levels of tension and how to cope with it.

SUMMARY

What is so difficult about acting assertively? All of us are creatures of habit. It is "more comfortable" in the short term to act as we have always acted, never thinking about what it does to us or to those around us. Changing our behavior means, first of all, analyzing it. This chapter described the basic causes of nonassertion and aggression. The four common causes of non-assertion—fear of displeasing others, fear of rejection, fear of hurting others' feelings, and an unwarranted sense of guilt—hurt others as well as us. Nonassertive reasoning leads us to under-value our own worth, engage in self-pity, and sometimes causes us to be the greatest obstacle to improvement because we feel that we must "shoulder the burden" all by ourselves. Other common causes of nonassertion, including the belief that we don't have the right to act assertively, the reluctance to give up the hidden benefits of nonassertion, and our perceived lack of skills or information to act assertively, can lead to the kind of inaction that produces precisely the kind of outcome we were trying to avoid.

Although aggressive behavior is manifested in different ways than nonassertive behavior, it can be just as unproductive. The sense of vulnerability and powerlessness in the face of a per-ceived threat that leads us to overreact, like nonassertiveness, often produces the consequences we sought to avoid. The four stages of the cycle of aggression—the feeling of threat, assessment of the danger, assessment of our power and the others' power, and anger—describe how beliefs, such as, "I must win in order to be OK," set in motion a self-fulfilling prophecy that causes the other person to become uncooperative and antagonistic, behaviors that our aggression was supposed to prevent. With this knowledge hopefully you will soon develop the power to avoid the excesses of both the nonassertive and aggressive approaches to problems and begin to act assertively.

NOTES

1. Karpman, S. B. Fairy tales and script drama analysis. *T A Bulletin*, 1968, 7 (2), 39-43.

2. This is similar to what Margaret Adams calls the "compassion trap" in which we feel we *must* be compassionate at all times and serve others and suppress our feelings in order to take care of other people's feelings. See: Adams, M. The compassion trap. In V. Gornick & B. Moran (Eds.), *Women in sexist society: Studies in power and powerlessness.* New York: Basic Books, 1971.

3. Jones, J. E., & Banet, A. G. Jr. Dealing with anger. In J. W. Pfeiffer & J. E. Jones (Eds.), *Annual handbook for group facilitators.* La Jolla, CA: University Associates, 1976. This model is probably most useful for understanding spontaneous aggression. It doesn't fit as well for people who consciously choose to use aggression as a power tactic or who enjoy the verbal repartee of aggression.

4. Jones, J. E., & Banet, A. G. Jr., 1976.

5. Haimowitz, M. L. Therapeutic interventions: Rubberbands NOW (or when the past is NOW). Unpublished, n.d.

4
Personal Rights and Responsibilities

An important key to becoming more assertive is developing the ability to accept your assertive rights. When you deny yourself these rights, you deny an important part of your humanity, and you can work harm on yourself and on those close to you. When you fail to accept these rights, you in effect tell yourself that you must prove your worth by doing all you can to please others, forgetting about yourself and never inconveniencing or upsetting others. What happens when you do this? You suppress your assertive impulses and avoid saying what you want, think, or feel so that you won't feel guilty. Instead, you feel hurt, resentful, or disgusted with yourself.

Accepting rights and acting on them in a responsibly assertive manner does not mean demanding more than you deserve. It only means asking for a share of consideration and courteous treatment. It does not mean thinking only about yourself and becoming insensitive to other people: Assertive rights can be expressed in humane, considerate ways. Accepting rights means acting in ways that tend to equalize power rather than overpower others. When you are responsibly assertive, you express who you are without infringing on others.

BOUNDARIES, RESPONSIBILITIES AND BALANCE

Before describing some basic assertive rights, keep three points in mind.

First, having assertive rights is not like having a license to act any way you want with total disregard for other people. There are ethical boundaries on all rights. In general, you have the right to refuse to explain your behavior but this right does not apply in situations where such refusals would violate another's rights. A student has the right to know why she was given a C instead of a B or an A; similarly an employee who has been given a bad work performance review has the right to a civil explanation.

Second, accepting rights brings personal power, which brings responsibility. For example, everyone has the right to make mistakes, but we also have the responsibility to accept our mistakes rather than blame "the system" or other people and to sincerely attempt to avoid making the same mistake over and over again.

Third, our assertive rights do not negate the other person's rights in a situation. You have the right to make a mistake, but the other person has the right to dislike the fact that you have made one, to feel disappointed about it, to ask you to rectify it. (She does not have the right to malign or ridicule you because you have made a human error—that's going beyond the boundary of her rights.) This balance of rights provides protection for both parties, neither of which has to become a powerless victim whenever one person is acting on her rights in any given situation.

Basic Assertive Rights

Participants in assertion training groups have identified more than 100 rights from which these 11 most basic ones were derived:

1. The right to act in ways that promote your dignity and self-respect as long as others' rights are not violated in the process
2. The right to be treated with respect
3. The right to say no and not feel guilty
4. The right to experience and express your feelings
5. The right to take time to slow down and think
6. The right to change your mind
7. The right to ask for what you want
8. The right to do less than you are humanly capable of doing
9. The right to ask for information

80

10. The right to make mistakes
11. The right to feel good about yourself.[1]

Your Dignity and the Rights of Others. You have the right to decide your values and lifestyle so long as you don't violate the rights of others. This basic right means that you have a right to be yourself and that you have a right to feel good (not guilty) about yourself so long as you do not damage others in the process. It is not healthy to feel guilty about being yourself.[2]

Since everyone is unique, assertions that will promote one person's sense of self-respect will differ a bit from those that others find important. Some people may want to assertively respond to someone cutting in line, while others may choose to overlook it. There is a danger in going overboard and interpreting virtually every situation as a threat to your personhood, for example, thinking that you cannot have self-respect unless you express your opinion at every possible point in conversations. Such behavior quickly becomes obnoxious assertion and is ultimately a self-defeating way of promoting self-respect.

The Right to Respect. You have the right to be treated courteously by salespeople, teachers, parents, employers, doctors and, more generally, you have the right to be treated as a capable human being and not to be patronized. As discussed in Chapter 2, respect does not mean deference, the unquestioning approval of your actions or automatic compliance with your wants. Since all people are equal as persons, everyone deserves to be treated in a way that recognizes his human dignity.

The Right to Say No and Not Feel Guilty. Like all people, you have a limited amount of time and energy, and deciding how to use them partially determines the quality of your life. Consistently placing what you want below the wants of other people is self-defeating. You are a person, too, and sometimes you must say yes to yourself and no to others. If you don't set reasonable priorities and draw the line somewhere, you will be so exhausted that when something really important happens, you won't have the energy necessary to respond. On the other hand, consistently placing your wants first and refusing to do anything for others unless you directly benefit is equally self-defeating. Living this way can deprive you of the joys of sharing and unnecessarily alienate you from others; and it denies the fact that you live in an interdependent world where some give and take is necessary to have a reasonably satisfying life.

Many people have trouble saying no because they tell themselves that they should be unselfish. This is a worthy objective, but too often "unselfish" really means "Unless I think of others first and give until I hurt, I'm being selfish." This is a self-destructive message. Being selfish means placing your desires before practically everyone else's, but saying no and not giving until you hurt doesn't automatically mean that you are selfish. It simply makes you a healthy, reasonable person who realizes that:

- It is not healthy to hurt yourself.
- Caring for others does not require caring less for yourself.
- You have a personal responsibility to yourself to value yourself as much as you value others.
- Your wants do not have less value than other people's simply because of who you are (a parent, student, employee, or a woman) or what you have (less power or experience or are younger).
- You are not an open energy system with limitless energy and capacity to fulfill other people's desires.

The Right to Experience and Express Your Feelings. Instead of accepting the right to have feelings, we often tell ourselves that we shouldn't feel the way we do: "I shouldn't be depressed, I shouldn't be so sensitive, I shouldn't feel like having sex." These feelings accomplish nothing except to make us feel guilty about having the feelings we already have. Since we are human and our feelings are a natural part of being human, it is more logical to accept the human right to experience our true feelings than to feel guilty about them.

We also tell ourselves that we should be understanding of other people—another worthy objective that is often misinterpreted to mean that *we* should not feel. This misinterpretation occurs when we incorrectly reason that if we understand other people we will not—*should not*—feel irritated or disappointed with them. This ignores the reality that we can think and feel at the same time. We can understand that an important relationship needs to end but still feel bad about its ending; and we may realize that when an intimate makes sarcastic digs, he is feeling insecure, but we can still be irritated by his behavior. However, understanding and accepting other people doesn't mean passively accepting their abusive behavior, especially when their behavior has concrete and tangible negative effects on us. Our resulting irritation can be a healthy emotion that tells us that we need to take action in our behalf, and denying these feelings can leave us unable to protect ourselves when we are being taken advantage of. Believing that we should not have certain feelings can cause us to neglect our feelings until they build to the point that they come out in abrasive explosions, which can lead us to view our genuine feelings as a dangerous part of our humanity.

Experiencing and expressing our feelings are two separate issues, however. After accepting the fact that we have certain feelings, we often realize that our feelings are way out of proportion, as the following examples illustrate:

- Alicia couldn't stand it when waitresses didn't immediately bring her a menu, regardless of how busy they were.
- Jack felt depressed and hurt whenever anyone, including newly introduced strangers, forgot his name.
- Marc got extremely angry when his secretary made the slightest error.

In these situations it often is more appropriate to deal with our feelings than to continually express them to others. (A detailed guide for coping with feelings that are blown out of proportion is discussed in Chapter 5.)

Should you act this way all the time? No, sometimes you may decide that it is not in your own—or others—best interest to express your feelings. For example, you probably would not tell your boss that you are bored by her jokes. Not expressing your feelings in such a situation affirms your assertive right to choose when and with whom you will share your feelings. Of course, there are limitations on this right; you have the right to withhold your feelings from others, but you don't have the right to use your silence to hurt other people.

When you decide to express your feelings, it is important to accept responsibility for them. Saying "You make me feel inadequate when you criticize my disorganized way of doing things" is blaming the other person and putting him on the defensive, but saying "I get upset when you criticize my disorganization, so I'd like you to stop it" is taking responsibility for expressing your feelings and doesn't involve attacking the other person. Assertively expressed irritation does not destroy people. On the contrary, it can lead to greater understanding of each other's limits and greater closeness, and it can help other people become aware of how their behavior affects you. In contrast, the cold, unresolved anger that you hold in while trying to appear understanding can eventually decrease your ability to express genuine warmth and caring to others.

The Right to Slow Down and Think Before You Act. People who deny themselves the right to pause for a moment and think about how they will respond to a situation and instead tell themselves "I'll never get what I want unless I hurry up" often fall into such self-defeating, aggressive behaviors as jumping to conclusions; interrupting others; being so much in a rush to get a conflict settled quickly that they impose premature solutions to difficult interpersonal conflicts; and attacking others who seem to be doing things too slowly.

Hurrying a decision doesn't automatically lead to getting things accomplished any more effectively. Just the reverse is likely to happen; you are more likely to make more mistakes when rushing. Instead of telling yourself to hurry, it is better to tell yourself "Stop . . . think . . . take enough time."

The Right to Change Your Mind. Decisions like volunteering to help in a charity drive, making a luncheon date a week in advance, disagreeing with someone's opinion, refusing to give a worker a day off are all based on the facts that you have at the time. At a later time you may become suddenly aware of new information, including information about your feelings, that legitimately calls for changing your mind. Katherine's change of heart is a good example.

> Only after Katherine told her son that she would loan him money for a new car did she realize just how much that decision upset her, how much she worried about having sufficient savings for her own peace of mind, how resentful she felt that her son didn't want to take out a bank loan and make the interest payments himself, and yet he apparently didn't mind that she would lose her savings interest. At the time Katherine made her initial decision, she didn't realize that she would have these feelings.

Changing your mind on the basis of new information shows flexibility, and refusing to change your mind when it is realistic to do so shows rigidity and stubbornness rather than true strength.

When you discover that you must change your mind, it may be because you hurried when making your original decision—that you haven't accepted your right to deliberate—and therefore forced yourself into making an immediate decision before you really thought the question through. Of course you may try to handle the problem of appearing wishy-washy by rigidly sticking to hasty stands that don't make sense, but it won't take long to realize that this won't work. Instead, act on your right to take your time to think, get information, and sort out your reactions. You can assert this right by making such statements as, "That's an important question, and it deserves some thought; I'll get back to you later on it," or "I'd like some time to think about it before I make up my mind." These kinds of statements will give you the time you need to make an intelligent decision. Of course, you also have the responsibility to give your answer within a reasonable amount of time. You have other responsibilities as well, such as the responsibility to let the other person know you have changed your mind and to accept the consequences, which may include experiencing the other person's irritation.

It should be noted that acting on the right to change your mind sometimes is not appropriate, for example, agreeing to do house painting for a specified sum and then, after completing the job and finding that it took more time than expected, presenting a bill that is higher than the price you originally quoted.

The Right to Ask for What You Want. A natural part of our humanity is having wants. When we don't assertively ask for what we want, we may consciously or unconsciously resort to trying to get what we want in devious ways that are likely to cause bad feelings and damage relationships. For example, you may deny that you want to go out for the evening, but insist that the other person "needs" to have a relaxing night out, even if she really doesn't want to go anywhere. It takes a lot of energy to keep yourself from asking for what you want—perhaps even more energy than if you simply ask for what you want in the first place.

Asking for what you want gives the other person a kind of permission to clearly and directly ask for what she wants too. There is an advantage to this: Neither person has to second guess what the other wants, which will probably increase the total amount of satisfaction in the relationship.

Though there is no guarantee that you will get what you want by simply asking for it, it is more likely that you won't get what you want if you say nothing and don't make your desires known. The fact that others have the right to refuse your requests helps protect you from accidentally taking advantage of them. In close relationships these occasional refusals are kinds of gifts that give us permission also to refuse. A friend's refusals let you know that when he says yes he really means it, and you can trust him not to feel secretly resentful because he would have preferred to say no but couldn't bring himself to do it.

The Right to Do Less Than You Are Humanly Capable of Doing. You have the right to give less than 100 percent all the time. You have a perfect right to waste your own time, to know what you want, and to ask for help even if you don't need it but just for the fun of having other people help you with unpleasant tasks. You have the right to organize your work so that you can maximize your enjoyment, and you have the right to do less than your best. (Lots of things aren't really worth doing our best at, and you are probably better off—and not less of a person—for having recognized this.)

When we deny ourselves these rights, it is as though we are telling ourselves that we must be strong, which we frequently misinterpret to mean that really strong people can handle virtually everything by themselves, that we do not need help, and that we should ignore our need for rest and fun. We incorrectly reason that we can have needs only when we have exhausted every other personal resource. Believing this can lead people to take on more work than they can reasonably accomplish, to work to the breaking point, and to have difficulty asking for directions until they are hopelessly lost.

It is more humane and realistic to do what you can reasonably do. You have a basic human right to not have to continually push yourself to the physical, mental, and emotional limit. Continually pushing yourself this way is treating yourself like a work robot instead of a human being. If you set some time aside for yourself and your so-called lazy pursuits and let other people know when you would like some support, some company, or a kind word, you can improve the quality of your life, get more enjoyment out of living, give yourself a chance to get emotionally and physically recharged and thus be better able to do those things that are important to you. Notice the difference between how Iola and Paula dealt with unpleasant situations.

Iola badly injured her back; the first day she had a friend stay with her. She thought this was OK to do because she literally couldn't get out of bed. Iola's internal rule was that she had the right to ask for help if she was totally incapable of taking care of herself and had suffered enough. On the succeeding days, since she was capable of taking care of herself with some difficulty, Iola not only didn't ask friends to help her, she refused any offers unless they forced their help upon her. Then she felt lonely, depressed, unloved, and as her only comfort had the thought that she was really "strong."

In contrast, though Paula realized that she could handle having the experience of dental surgery for several impacted wisdom teeth by herself, she decided to take better care of herself and told herself that it was OK to make the experience as pleasant as she possibly could. Though she initially thought that none of her friends would arrange to get off work to take her to the surgeon's office, when she asked one of her friends, she found much to her surprise that he was more than willing to do so. She arranged to have him drive her to the office and made an agreement that she could whine about the pain all she wanted to afterwards and that her friend didn't have to do anything about her whining except listen. Paula's friend stayed with her during the day, taking care of her by changing the dental packing and bringing pain medication. Paula arranged in advance to have several friends keep her company in the evening and through the next two days until she decided that she wanted to be alone. The end result of this experience was that Paula felt very cared for and proud of herself for the way that she took care of herself. What she remembered most about her dental surgery was the kindness of her friends and how much fun she had allowing herself to complain about her pain and letting other people take care of her. The way that she handled the surgery added richness and enjoyment to her life.

When someone tries to be a pillar of strength, that often is exactly what she ends up looking like: a rock, a piece of stone that others don't realize is actually a human being. People tend to take her at her word (or appearance), thinking that she really can absorb everything and take anything, accidentally tending to abuse her by taking her for granted. If you allow yourself to think this way, you can work yourself into a corner: You try to be a pillar of strength—that is, ignore your needs until they become overwhelming and frightening, thus appearing dangerous—and then resolve to be stronger and feel less. The fallacy that motivates this vicious cycle is that you do your best when you are pushing yourself and being a pillar of strength. Yet deep down inside you know that this isn't true because you don't feel good—and you don't feel good because you are missing out on a lot of life. In reality your "best" is your humanity and your ability to create a good life for yourself.

However, this right isn't justification for failing to live up to an agreement. If, for instance, you agree to do a piece of work, you have an obligation to do the quality of work you agreed to produce. If you become convinced that you agreed to do an unreasonably high quality of work, you can request a change of agreement with the other person.

The Right to Ask for Information. When you are making a decision, oftentimes you are unsure of your facts or feelings.

You have the right to get a second opinion, to ask that inadequate work be redone at no extra charge, to ask for references and bids, to get what you paid for, and to say "I don't understand." You have the right to know exactly what services professional and tradespeople will perform, how the work will be done, how long it will take, how much it will cost.[3] You have a right to ask pointed questions so that you can make an informed decision, and doing so is likely to save you lots of trouble later on.

If someone reacts defensively or condescendingly to your probing questions, it does not mean that you are ignorant or don't have the right to ask those questions. Rather it is another piece of information about that person's professional attitude, and it is reasonable to think that people who treat you poorly before you have hired them will be just as uncooperative when it comes to carrying out the work.

Getting answers to your questions is a reasonable way of building your own trust in a person whose services you may use. There is no logical reason to automatically trust professionals simply because they have good credentials, were recommended, or have more knowledge and expertise than you have. Trust is not their automatic due; they earn your trust by how they treat you, respond to your legitimate questions, and perform their services.

The Right to Make Mistakes. No one has made it through life mistake-free. It is impossible to avoid making at least a few mistakes since it is impossible to be perfect and to know everything. Moreover *if* you truly could have avoided making a particular mistake, you probably wouldn't have made it in the first place. For example, if you drive a car too fast and get into an accident, you made an error in assuming you could stop safely. It's true that the accident could have been avoided *if* you had been a different person *at that moment* and had not made an incorrect assumption, but telling yourself that you *shouldn't* have made the incorrect assumption is reasoning after the fact and fails to consider that at any moment in time you can only be who you are at that time and act according to the beliefs and assumptions you hold then. Instead of berating yourself for making mistakes, it is more humane and realistic to remember that a mistake is simply a life experience that you can learn from. And, of course, as with any right, it is your responsibility to accept the consequences of your mistakes and to rectify your errors. Also there is an important distinction between an honest mistake and reckless behavior. If, in the example given above, you are driving on wet pavement that is more slippery than you realize, you have made an honest, though maybe fatal, mistake. However, if you are driving sixty miles an hour in a hospital or school zone, you have little defense. If you have a driver's license, you have passed a driver's test and have probably studied *The Rules of the Road;* you know better than to drive so fast under such circumstances. Unless there was some life-or-death emergency or some other extenuating circumstances, you didn't just make an honest mistake; you were reckless and irresponsible.

The Right to Feel Good about Yourself. Many people have difficulty giving themselves this right because they have been taught to believe that they must be modest or humble. This is another worthy objective that is often misinterpreted to mean, "I must not feel good about myself; I must act as though I am nothing; otherwise I am conceited and getting too big for my britches."

Being humble or modest doesn't mean humiliating yourself. Being humble simply means recognizing that though some of your talents or accomplishments are better than those of other people, they do not make you a superior human being. Having the right to feel good about yourself does not mean expressing honest happiness about yourself in superior or condescending ways. It is the right to express your self-worth and human dignity—not conceit or lack of humility—to be able to accept compliments graciously and to share your good feelings of self-worth with others.

The Tenets of an Assertive Philosophy listed in Figure 8 express the spirit of the eleven basic assertive rights just discussed. When we abide by these tenets, we are able to live fuller, more honest lives, treating others and ourselves with dignity and respect.

Figure 8   Tenets of An Assertive Philosophy

1. By standing up for ourselves and letting ourselves be known to others, we gain self-respect and respect from other people.
2. By trying to live our lives in such a way that we *never* cause anyone to feel hurt under any circumstances, we end up hurting ourselves— and other people.
3. When we stand up for ourselves and express our honest feelings and thoughts in a direct and appropriate way, everyone usually benefits in the long run. Likewise, when we demean other people, we also demean ourselves and everyone involved usually loses in the process.
4. By sacrificing our integrity and denying our personal feelings, relationships are usually damaged or prevented from developing. Likewise, personal relationships are damaged when we try to control others through hostility, intimidation, or guilt.
5. Personal relationships become more authentic and satisfying when we share our true reactions with other people and do not block others' sharing their reactions with us.
6. Not letting others know what we think and feel is just as inconsiderate as not listening to other people's thoughts and feelings.
7. When we frequently sacrifice our rights, we teach other people to take advantage of us.
8. By acting assertively and telling other people how their behavior affects us, we are giving them an opportunity to change their behavior, and we are showing respect for their right to know where they stand with us.

Source: P. Jakubowski, "Self-Assertion Training Procedures for Women," in E. Rowlings and D. Carter, eds., *Psychotherapy for Women* (Springfield, Ill.: Charles C. Thomas, 1977).

HELPING YOURSELF ACCEPT ASSERTIVE RIGHTS

Though other people may deny our rights, many people find that often the greater problem is within themselves. For instance, they may have been raised to believe that others always come first and consequently may have come to the conclusion that they are not good enough to have rights. Having trouble accepting assertive rights is not a sign of their weakness;

more often it is because they have learned to give themselves internal messages that talk themselves out of rights and they do not have more accurate internal messages to give themselves. Or, they may be surrounded by people who consistently deny that they have any rights.

You can help yourself accept assertive rights by following these four steps:

Step One: Become aware of the internal messages you give yourself that cause you to believe that you aren't entitled to rights.

Step Two: Develop more realistic messages that you can use to counter your rights-denying messages.

Step Three: Repeatedly practice internally giving yourself the countermessage. Having others say that you have rights or reading books that confirm your rights is a helpful middle step. Ultimately you need to be able to give yourself these messages.

Step Four: In small, appropriate ways, *act* on the right while internally affirming your right to do so.

Steps One and Two: Awareness and Change

People can usually accept assertive rights in principle. However, when it comes down to specific situations, they often find it more difficult to put the principle into practice. For example, some people accept that they have a right to refuse requests, but they will not refuse a request from their father.

When you think about the rights-denying messages you give yourself in a specific situation, you may find that initially you are only aware of thinking, "I can't do that; I don't have the right." You can increase your awareness of these rights-denying messages by answering the first three numbered questions in Exercise 6. These questions are guidelines; you may find that it isn't necessary to answer all of them, or you may think of other questions that work better for you.

Most rights-denying messages contain an element of truth, but they are exaggerated and distorted, so changing them involves ferreting out these distortions from what is realistically true. The small-letter (a, b, etc.) questions may help this process. (Some people find that instead of completing this exercise, it's just as effective to simply ask a friend to give them a rationale as to why they have an assertive right.)

Exercise 6   Developing Self-Enhancing Messages About Assertive Rights

Describe a specific situation in which you have difficulty accepting an assertive right: *Always giving in current living situation/relationship, and feeling terrible with the neglected emotionally; not happy*

What would you ideally like to do in this situation?
Be given as much as I give.

What are the other person's rights in this situation?
To be committed.

What is the right(s) that you realistically think you have and want to feel more comfortable in accepting?
Feel good about self

1. What do you tell yourself will happen if you accept this assertive right?

    Life will be difficult

    a. What is the evidence that this is likely to happen? How realistic is this?

        Have tried in past, very realistic

    b. If you don't really know what's likely to happen, think of ways in which you might be able to find out.

        Take small steps

93

Exercise 6 Developing Self-Enhancing Messages
About Assertive Rights (continued)

2. What do you tell yourself you "should" do instead of accepting and acting on the assertive right?

live w/ it

a. Always? No exceptions? Where is it written that you "should"? Who says you should? Is this person's judgment trustworthy?

Always; parents say so; he's rich, not two.

b. What other options, strengths, or abilities does the other person have?

to change;

c. What will be the costs to you and the other person if you don't accept this right?

Unhappiness for me,

d. What's reasonable for you to do?

Take small steps

3. What negative conclusions would you draw about your whole character if you were to act assertively and not follow the "shoulds" you place on yourself? For example, if I tell my friend that I don't want her to move in with me, that makes me a selfish person who doesn't really care about people.

a. Does doing this one act of ___defiance___ automatically make you ___bitchy___ ? What evidence do you have

94

to the contrary that you are not what you tell yourself you are?

*I know I'm not, I just
don't want to confront.*

b. What does doing this one act of _____ more
realistically suggest about you instead? For example,
telling her that I don't want her to move in with me
more realistically means that I have limits and feelings
as a person, even though I do care about her.

*I recognize that I'm allowed
to be happy.*

4. Reread your answers to the above questions and put together a realistic, self-enhancing message about your assertive rights.

5. Write a possible assertive statement that you could make in
this situation. Experiment with phrasing your statement in
the positive (saying what you want) instead of in the negative (saying what you don't want). For example, "About
your moving in with me, I've given it a lot of thought and
realized that it's important for me to live alone."

Step Three: Practicing the Countermessage
After developing a meaningful internal countermessage, it
is important to practice saying it to yourself. There are several
ways to do this. One method is to write the message on cards
and put them where you will see them often during the day.

You can do the same thing with stars: Put the stars in various places around the house. The stars will serve as reminders of the countermessage: Each time you notice the cards (or stars) repeat the message silently or aloud to yourself.

A second approach is to associate the message with some activity you frequently engage in.[4] For example, if you often open the refrigerator door, put the card or star on the door and repeat the countermessage before you open the door. Putting it on the telephone would involve practicing the message just before you pick up the phone. Using this method, you will find that after awhile, the countermessage will be more likely to occur to you spontaneously during the course of the day.

A third method is to tape record the message; play it several times a day while you are relaxed. Make sure that the tone of the taped voice is reassuring and comforting, not nasty or pushy.

A fourth method uses your feelings as a cue to turn on your countermessage. If you find yourself feeling guilty or very anxious when you think of acting assertively, use these feelings as a cue or reminder to immediately turn on your countermessage instead of letting your mind continue to run off rights-denying messages.[5]

Step Four: Acting on Rights in Small, Appropriate Ways

If possible, devise small ways to practice using the right you are learning to accept. For example, Pedro practiced affirming his right to have needs as important as those of others by taking thirty minutes a day to do whatever he wanted to do for himself. Obviously not all rights lend themselves to practicing in small steps. For example, affirming your right to express irritation by expressing all the slightest irritations you feel during the day probably would unnecessarily alienate others and make you feel miserable by the end of the day because you focused too much on irritations.

If you devise small, appropriate ways of acting on your rights, yet find yourself never getting around to actually practicing them, you may need to reassess whether or not you are ready to give up the benefits of nonassertive or aggressive behavior. It is also possible that you're talking yourself out of acting

96

on the right. The following are some common ways people do this.

Thoughts	Countermessage
I'll do it later.	Exactly when is later?
It's not really that important.	You're important. If it's important enough to bother you, it's important enough to do something about it.
I couldn't stand the consequences.	How many times have you said, "I can't stand it," but did? The fact that you're living and breathing today means that you can stand it.
I'm not strong enough.	Maybe not now, but that doesn't mean you never will be. Practicing in small steps can make you stronger.
It's not my nature.	Your nature is what you do and believe and feel. You can change all of these and thus in a sense change your nature.

THE RIGHTS-DENYING PROBLEMS OF AGGRESSION

While individuals with nonassertion problems stand to gain by helping themselves accept rights, people who have aggressive problems often think that they will lose if they accept others' rights. Facing this prospect often evokes strong reactions like, "Why should I grant others rights?" There's at least one reason why.

By increasing your ability to accept others' legitimate rights, you can gain at least as much if not more than you lose. You can gain calmness, an increased ability to be objective, and an increased ability to think clearly because you will no longer be unnecessarily agitating yourself with distracting, nonproductive thoughts like, "He has no right to ask me that! He's got some nerve!" You will be more able to focus on what you want to communicate and on your objectives in the situation, which will help you feel more in control of yourself and less the victim of other people or of your self-righteous anger.

Even when it is clear that the other person has clearly gone beyond her rights, for example, by being nasty, it is more productive to focus on what rights you do have in the situation and on how the other person's behavior concretely affects us, rather than on what rights the other person doesn't have.

When someone acts aggressively she seems to be very sure of her rights, yet closer examination sometimes reveals her uncertainty and insecurity: She is simply reassuring herself of her right-ness by focusing on the wrong-ness of others. As discussed in Chapter 3, aggression may be partially the result of denying ourselves particular rights. Discovering which rights you may be denying yourself is not easy since the process can be quite subtle; however, the following questions can help:

- Is the right I am aggressively affirming one that I actually feel comfortable with?
- Is part of my aggression caused by my feeling guilty? If so, is there a particular right I deny myself that results in my feeling guilty?
- Is the right I deny for other people the same or similar right I deny myself?

The answers to these questions are the crux of Eric's inner conflict.

> Eric found himself getting sarcastic when students were disinterested in schoolwork. He reasoned that they should care and didn't have the right to not value schoolwork. Though he wanted to accept their right to have their own priorities, he couldn't develop any rationale he really believed. Finally, upon asking himself where he got the idea that his students shouldn't/mustn't feel disinterested, he discovered that instead of using his own judgment, he had accepted what other teachers told him: that it's the teacher's responsibility to force students to learn and to come down hard on students who

aren't interested and that any teacher who lets disinterest pass isn't worth a hill of beans. Eric realized that what he needed to do was to focus on accepting the right to make his own professional judgments and that he had the right to not have to *make* students conform. Interestingly, the right Eric realized he needed to accept for himself was very similar to the right he had been denying students, i.e., to set their own priorities.

COMMONLY ASKED
QUESTIONS ABOUT RIGHTS

What If My Rights Conflict
With the Rights of the Other Person?

The philosophy of responsible assertion is that of taking a flexible stance, not a rigid one. When conflicts of rights occur, it is appropriate as well as reasonable to try to work out a compromise where both parties can get some satisfaction. It is important, of course, that such compromises do not involve a loss of personal integrity. Chapter 7 describes how people can develop skill in constructively resolving conflicts.

If Both Parties Are Equally Assertive,
Won't This Lead to Dead-End Conflicts?

Dead-end conflicts are much less likely to occur when both parties are responsibly assertive because they will realize that it is necessary to try to understand the other person's position as well as their own; they will consider compromise without loss of integrity a logical and humane way of handling many conflicts and they will believe that people do not have to win in order to feel OK about themselves. For instance, if you are in a theater line and a couple obviously cuts in line in front of you, what could you say or do if you assertively point out that the line forms to the rear and one of the people responds, "Oh yeah! Make me go back!"? If you are responsibly assertive in this situation, you will stop to figure out what's really important to you. You do not have to win. You do not have to make the other person confess that she was trying to cut in line in order to feel good about yourself. The question is, in this situation how can you be assertive even if you are not going to get what you want? A reasonable goal would be to simply let the person know that you are irritated without saying it in such a way that you get hooked into a power struggle with her. You might say, "Obviously I'm not going to drag you to the end of the line, but I don't like what you're doing, and I'd just like you to think if this is really necessary for you to do." Then turn away, leaving the other person emotional space to deal with that question herself. Perhaps your assertion would cause the person to reconsider her action; perhaps it wouldn't. But you would know that you expressed yourself on the situation and could feel good that you took care of yourself. You would know that you didn't fail—you were assertive and the other person simply didn't act in the way you wanted. You *do not have* to make people act the way you want.

Must I Always Assert My Rights?
No. You are always free to choose not to assert yourself, assuming that you are also willing to take the responsibility for whatever consequences may then occur. It is important to decide for yourself when and how you will be assertive and that you do not allow yourself to become trapped by a new set of restricting rules to live by such as "Thou Shalt Be Perfectly Assertive at all Times or Else Thou Hast Failed and Should Feel Guilty."

Don't I Have to Develop
Greater Self-Confidence Before I Am Assertive?
People generally find it easier to act assertively if they have greater self-confidence. However, waiting until you develop more self-confidence may mean waiting a long time. What seems to be faster is first to take risks in small areas, where you are not likely to get punished by the other person and where you have little to lose. As you succeed with small assertions, your self-confidence and sense of self-worth are likely to increase.

How Can I Accept My Rights
When Others Deny That I Have Any?
Ultimately other people do not give us rights. We accept the rights (and their accompanying responsibilities) ourselves.

There is no doubt that it is a lot easier to act assertively when others support your behavior and acknowledge your right to do so. Unfortunately, this may not happen, so it is very important at least to understand why you have rights and to be able to defend them to yourself. Thus you can give yourself permission to act assertively even when others do not support you.

Are There Any Rights I Don't Have?

Yes. You do not have an inalienable right to have others act "correctly." Other examples of assertive rights no one has are the right to use our feelings as a bludgeon to control or bully other people, to use feelings manipulatively to make the other person responsible for them,[6] or to mistreat people just because we're in a bad mood.

SUMMARY

An important key to becoming more assertive is developing our ability to accept assertive rights. Although all rights have limitations and bring with them responsibilities, they are all part of a process that will expand your personal horizons. The most important thing to remember is that, regardless of what others might say, you do have rights. While listing them as we have done in this chapter may seem a bit artificial, hopefully you will now have a firmer grasp of the basis of responsible assertive behavior.

NOTES

1. Many of these rights are also found in other books dealing with assertiveness. See: Bloom, L. Z., Coburn, K., & Pearlman, J. *The new assertive woman*. New York: Delacorte Press, 1975. Smith, M. J. *When I say no I feel guilty*. New York: Dial Press, 1975.

2. Alberti, R. E., & Emmons, M. L. *Your perfect right* (2nd ed.). San Luis Obispo, CA: Impact Publishers, 1974.

3. Bloom, L. Z., Coburn, K., & Pearlman, J., 1975.

4. This principle is based on the Premack Principle of Reinforcement. See: Premack, D. Reinforcement theory. In D. Levin (Ed.), *Nebraska symposium on motivation, 1965*. Lincoln, NE: University of Nebraska Press, 1965.

5. Meichenbaum, D. H. Cognitive factors in behavior modification: Modifying what clients say to themselves. In C. Franks & T. Wilson (Eds.), *Annual review of behavior therapy: Theory and practice*. New York: Brunner/Mazel, 1973. Also see: Meichenbaum, D. H. The cognitive-behavioral management of anxiety, anger, and pain. In P. Davidson (Ed.), *Behavior management of anxiety, depression, and pain*. New York: Brunner/Mazel, 1976.

6. Waukasch, L. Personal communication, January 1978.

5
Changing Your Thinking

When dealing with certain people or situations, it is difficult to think about personal rights, setting goals for oneself, and
choosing certain assertive responses. Why? The answer people
usually give is, "I can't be assertive because I just get so upset
[angry, depressed, guilty, anxious] that I can't think. My emotions get in the way because the other person is so obnoxious
[mean, crude, awful, boring, stupid, domineering]." Obviously
a person's emotions and reactions to others' behavior play an
important role in the ability to think clearly and act assertively.
This chapter discusses two methods for more constructively
dealing with upsetting feelings that can interfere with your ability to act assertively. Before presenting these two methods, it is
first necessary to discuss how thoughts, feelings, and behavior
are related.

THINKING, FEELING,
AND BEHAVING

The A-B-C's
Many people think that thinking, feeling, and behaving are
three separate, unrelated entities, but an increasing amount of
evidence is pointing to how they are related and how they
influence each other.[1] In your efforts to become more assertive,
the relationships among thinking, feeling, and behaving become
crucial since often it is not enough to simply believe in personal
rights or learn specific assertive behaviors. The following section
presents one model—the A-B-C model—developed by Dr. Albert
Ellis for understanding the relationships among thinking, feeling, and behaving.[2]

Point A represents a particular activating event or situation,

103

such as going for an important job interview, responding to your boss when he criticizes your work performance, or asking for a date. Point *C* represents your feelings and behavior in the situation. For example, when you ask for a date and feel extremely anxious and upset, your behavior might be any of the following: fidgeting, looking helpless, hesitating or stuttering, not looking at the other person, and saying meekly, "I know I'm really probably out of place to say this but, . . . (pause) oh gosh, I've gone this far (laugh) . . . would you ever consider going out with me?" Or you might sound pushy or defensive, become sarcastic and critical, act like it really doesn't matter, and sarcastically say, "Hey, I know you probably think you're God's gift to women, but that's not my problem. I've got two tickets to the Stones concert, so I figured why not ask you."

The important point about the A-B-C's is that most people mistakenly believe that *A* (the situation or person) directly causes *C* (the feelings and behaviors), like in the following:

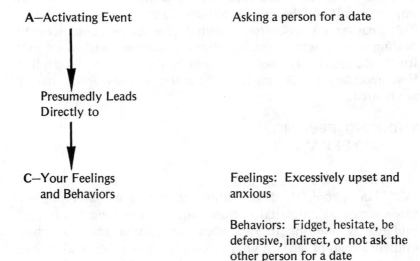

A—Activating Event   Asking a person for a date

Presumedly Leads
Directly to

C—Your Feelings   Feelings: Excessively upset and
   and Behaviors   anxious

                                       Behaviors: Fidget, hesitate, be
                                       defensive, indirect, or not ask the
                                       other person for a date

One common-sense explanation for this mistaken belief is that the situation (*A*) is highly visible and people are very much aware of their own feelings and behaviors (*C*). If *A* doesn't cause *C*, what does? Actually something very important happens *between A* and *C* that does influence your feelings and behavior significantly: You *think*. Though you think about all kinds of things, three of the most important are:

- what you think about yourself
- what you think about the other person
- what you think about the situation itself.

All people have little inner conversations with themselves as they think about these questions. These "inner dialogues" occur at point *B* of the A-B-C's. Sometimes you may be well aware of the important parts of these dialogues, but other times they occur so quickly and subtly that you are almost unaware of them. Yet you are very much aware of the resultant feelings and behaviors. The A-B-C model for understanding the relationships among thoughts, feelings, and behaviors can be shown this way:

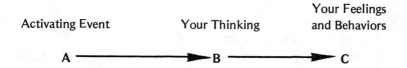

| | | Your Feelings |
| Activating Event | Your Thinking | and Behaviors |

A ➝ B ➝ C

Dating situations can demonstrate how thinking influences feelings and behaviors. If, when asking for a date at point *A*, Diane finds herself feeling extremely anxious and behaving non-assertively at point *C*, at point *B* she is likely to be having these kinds of thoughts about the other person: "He's so attractive. I've *got* to get him to say yes. But what if he says no or laughs at me? Or even worse, what if he acts nice, but it's really clear that he doesn't want to have anything to do with me? And what if he thinks I'm just a brazen, aggressive woman? Besides, what would he really want with me except sex?" Thoughts such as these about the situation are also likely to be present: "Damn! This dating stuff is such a hassle! Why can't it be easier?" Lastly, she'd likely have thoughts about herself: "What's wrong with me? I can't even ask someone for a date without getting all upset!"

Everyone has his own style of talking to himself. Diane's

statements are only one example of a dialogue that is likely to lead to greater anxiety and distress. The significant point is that the internal dialogue itself influences the resultant feelings and behaviors during that specific situation.

Rational Thinking vs. Irrational Thinking

The thinking you do at point *B* can be either rational or irrational. *Rational* means reasonable, self-enhancing, logical, accurate, and realistic. *Irrational* means catastrophic, absolutistic, illogical, inaccurate, self-defeating, and unrealistic.

The common components of irrational thinking are the tendency to:

1. Turn wants or preferences (including strong ones) into absolute, vital needs
2. Convince oneself that if the need isn't met, it will be awful, terrible, catastrophic, unbearable, and the end of the world
3. Draw incorrect conclusions
4. Not consider the evidence
5. Automatically attribute negative motives to other people
6. Focus exclusively on self-deprecating thoughts.

When Diane contemplates asking someone for a date and thinks to herself, "He's so attractive, I've *got* to get him to say yes," she is thinking *absolutistically*. She is telling herself that she *must* get this person to accept or else it will mean that she is a terrible failure. When she thinks, "But *what if* he laughs at me, or, even worse, *what if* he acts nice but it's really clear that he doesn't want to have anything to do with me? That would be *so* embarrassing!" she is using catastrophic, "what-if" questions that tend to increase anxiety. Instead of answering these by problem solving and figuring out what she could do (e.g., "If he laughs at me, I could treat the whole thing lightly, I could express my disappointment," etc.), she makes no plans and answers these questions with "It would be unbearable, awful, horrible, and I couldn't stand it!" After thinking these absolutistic ("I must, . . . he must . . .") and catastrophic thoughts ("What if . . ."), it's no wonder that she feels upset and acts nonassertively. Thus, the situation of asking for a date stimulated thinking that led to undesired, self-defeating feelings and nonassertive behaviors.

Few people think irrationally all the time, but most of us do think irrationally some of the time. And it is often a rather subtle process that ultimately leads either to nonassertive or to aggressive behaviors. Through inaccurate, irrational thinking we are likely to misperceive reality; create unnecessary distance and conflict between ourselves and others; prevent the accomplishment of our own goals; experience more inner turmoil, sadness, or anger than we can manage; avoid expressing opinions, feelings, and preferences; avoid acting on many of our personal rights; or neglect to respect the rights of others.

Rationalizations vs. Rational Thinking

Many people have the unfortunate tendency to substitute rationalizations instead of rational thoughts for irrational thoughts when they try to alter their thinking. For example Greg, who went for an important job interview and felt extremely upset when he didn't get the job, initially thought: "I blew the whole thing! Gosh, how can I face Jennifer and the kids? Maybe mother was right, I *am* a failure." When he realized how very upset he was, he tried to talk himself out of his anxiety and alter his catastrophic thinking by saying to himself, "Who wants that job anyway. Everything's going to work out just fine. I feel lucky. I bet I'll get a much better offer in no time from some other company." Greg might very well get "lucky" and do just fine in getting another job, and saying this probably did help him to feel a little better at the time. But such "power of positive thinking" wears thin after a while if things do not work out or get better. Such platitudes as "It'll all work itself out in the end," or "Things happen for the best," or "Every day, in every way, I'm getting better and better" just may not be accurate, and when they aren't, it's very easy for the person thinking these simple positive thoughts to fall back into irrational thinking when the positive thoughts don't hold up. In contrast, more rational thinking might be something like, "I *am* disappointed that I didn't get the job. *Maybe* I'll get a better offer soon. I can plan and work toward making that happen. If it doesn't happen soon, it'll be a real hardship, but I *can* live with it."

Rationalizations seem to be a way to con or convince ourselves that we shouldn't feel badly at all about things and that we should always "keep the sunny side up" even to the point of denying reality. Rational thinking, on the other hand, also attempts to alter *excessive* emotional reactions (rage, depression, anxiety) but does so without making believe that "everything's coming up roses." Life not only is *not* always a bowl of cherries; it doesn't *have* to be. Rational thinking does not reject negative thoughts out of hand, nor is it simple positive thinking. Rather, rational thinking looks for what is accurate, accepts it as accurate, and thereby frees us to make every possible effort to improve upon the situation. Rational thinkers do *not* passively sit around accepting life's grim realities. By accepting what is true and not agonizing over it, we are freer to act on whatever intelligent plans we have available, even when they may be meager or not the most preferred options. Figure 9 contains examples of irrational and rational thinking and rationalization. After you have looked at these examples, try Exercise 7. It will help distinguish the three kinds of thinking.

Exercise 7   Differentiating Irrational, Rationalized, and Rational Thinking

The purpose of this exercise is to give you some practice in telling the difference between rationalized, rational, and irrational thinking. It is often difficult to clearly tell if a particular thought is irrational, rational, or rationalized. Sometimes there are elements of more than one type of thinking in a particular inner dialogue, and sometimes we unknowingly rationalize. For example, one person might think, "I'd better not bring this up now. It's just not a good time," and actually be excessively fearful of rejection. Someone else might be thinking exactly the same thought but be doing so because he has reasonably assessed the situation and judged it to be untimely yet does so without any great fear of rejection.

On page 110 is a sample situation with fifteen possible inner dialogues. Read the responses and select those which

Figure 9 Irrational Thinking, Rational Thinking, and Rationalization

Irrational Thinking (excessive concern and inaccurate perception of reality)	Rational Thinking (honest, appropriate concern and accurate perception of reality)	Rationalization (denial of concern and inaccurate perception of reality)
I *must*. . . . I've *got* to. . . . What if. . .that would be awful, terrible, unbearable, horrible. I couldn't stand it if. . . .	I would like very much to. . . . If I am liked/competent, that's great. If I am not, that's unfortunate but I can live with it. I will do everything I can to. . . . If I am treated unfairly, I might be angry, but I do not have to overreact. If things do not go the way I want, I might be disappointed, but I do not have to become excessively depressed, angry, or anxious.	I feel lucky. . . . It'll all work out by itself. It doesn't bother me that. . . . No sweat. . . . Everything's fine. . . . I didn't want ___ anyway. It wouldn't have done any good anyway, if I. . . .

Exercise 7   Differentiating Irrational, Rationalized, and Rational Thinking (continued)

most closely reflect your own reactions. Also note the classification of that reaction. For each of the four following situations there are listed some brief inner dialogues that might occur in that situation. Read each dialogue and decide whether you think it is *mostly* irrational (I), rational (R), or a rationalization (Z). This may be more difficult than making decisions about your own inner dialogues because you may have no sense of the feelings or motives behind these thoughts. For this exercise, then, you may have to make certain assumptions and make your choices based on those assumptions. There are no single right answers. We have listed the choices we made at the end of the exercise. We picked the category that we believed most represented the thought, but we did not indicate our own assumptions due to space limitations. Develop your own choices and state why you believe they fit into the category you chose.

Sample
Situation: A woman is thinking about telling her lover what she does and doesn't enjoy in their sexual relations.

Alternative thoughts:

1. What if he thought I was a brazen hussy? He might think I was putting him down and trying to threaten his masculinity. What if he got really mad? What if he started losing his erection! That would be awful!
    Irrational

2. It's really not that important anyway. I can get along without enjoying sex as much as I'd like to. It's not that big a deal. It doesn't really matter.
    Rationalization

3. If he really loves me, he should know what I enjoy.
    Irrational

4. I do want to tell him what I enjoy. If he gets mad or embarrassed, I can deal with that and try to assure him that I am not putting him down. If he keeps being defen-

sive and even threatens to leave me, that would be very
sad, but I can live with that. We are both likely to feel a
little uncomfortable at first, but we can both get over that.
Rational

5. If I did tell him, I'd probably feel so awkward that I'd
   sound really foolish. What if he made fun of me? I'd be so
   hurt. Besides, he might get embarrassed and upset. I might
   blow the whole relationship.
   Irrational

6. It will be good for him to hear this. I'm really only doing
   this for his benefit. He'll thank me for it later, I'm sure.
   Rationalization

7. If I don't tell him, I'll be breaking my vow to be assertive.
   I've got to tell him. I can't back out now. What would my
   friends think?
   Irrational

8. What if I tell him, and don't get really turned on by it?
   Irrational

9. If I do tell him right now, he is likely to be very upset. I do
   want to tell him, but I'm not willing to do it at a time
   when he is not likely to listen as well. I will talk with him
   within the next week at a time that's more appropriate.
   Rational

10. What if I tell him and he can't or he won't do it?
    Irrational

11. He would be a bear to live with. (Your past experience
    indicates that this is true.)
    Rational

12. He would be a bear to live with. (You simply want to
    avoid confronting him.)
    Irrational

13. I would like to enjoy having sex more often. I do care if he
    gets upset or angry, and I hope he doesn't. I'm not going

to avoid talking about it because he might get upset. I can
handle it if he does.
Rational

14. I don't give a damn what he thinks or how he reacts. I'm
going to tell him. I've got my rights; you won't see me
letting a man intimidate me.
Irrational

15. Men! They're all alike. Maulers. Never give a damn about
the woman and what she likes. Just in and out for a quick
one. Well not with me. I won't stand for it. Either he
shapes up or ships out. He gets only one chance.
Irrational

Situation 1: You have been seated with your companion at a
table in a small restaurant in your neighborhood.
Water is poured, and crackers have been placed
on the table. You do not find anything appealing on the menu, and the prices are higher than
you expected. You would like to leave after several minutes.

Alternative thoughts:

1. We can't just get up and walk out now. I'd be so embarrassed! Everyone in here would think we were rude or just
crazy. We're stuck.
Irrational

2. I don't want to eat here, and I do have a right to decide
where I want to eat. Others here might think I am rude or
cheap and that's unfortunate, but I can live with that. I
won't worry about what others *might* be thinking. I don't
have to explain our leaving. I can simply say we decided
not to stay.
Rational

3. It's probably really very good food. They wouldn't charge

such high prices if it weren't, would they? Maybe I'll like veal parmigiana, this time. Besides, we are already here.

Rationalizing

4. Boy, they have some nerve charging prices like this. What are we supposed to do now? If we walk out, they'll just think we're too cheap. What a rip-off.

    Irrational

Situation 2:   You are in a staff meeting at work, and the group is trying to decide on a policy that will affect you. There is disagreement between other members of the group. You have an opinion, and you are thinking about expressing it.

Alternative thoughts:

1. What if I do speak up and make a fool of myself? I might say something obvious, and they'll think I'm stupid.

    Irrational

2. I'd probably just confuse things even more. I'm sure it'll all work out for the best in the end anyway. They probably won't decide anything that would turn out too badly for me. There are enough people talking now anyway.

    Rationalizing

3. If I do say what I think, someone's bound to not like it. I just don't like to make waves. Bob would be offended if I agreed with the proposal, and Jane would be hurt if I disagreed. No matter what gets decided, at least there won't be any hard feelings toward me.

    Rational

4. This decision does affect me and my work. It's OK for me to have my opinions and say them without being pushy. If some people here disagree with me, that's all right. If some people feel hurt or upset because I disagreed with them, I'll care about that, but I won't take responsibility for their feelings.

    Rational

Exercise 7 Differentiating Irrational, Rationalized, and Rational Thinking (continued)

Situation 3: You find someone very attractive. You have spent some casual time together, and you want to express your feelings for that person.

Alternative thoughts:

1. But what if she just stares at me or starts acting weird and distant. I'd feel awfully stupid and embarrassed. I just couldn't stand that "let's just be friends" bit.

2. I'll bet she's really dying for me to show some interest. Go ahead. She'll love it. You've got it made.

3. She probably thinks she is too good for anybody. Well I'll show her. I can take her or leave her. She doesn't mean a thing to me. I'll just play it cool.

4. I'm anxious about saying something because I'm not sure how she will respond. I hope she feels about me the same as I do about her. If she doesn't, that's too bad, but I can live with it. If she does, I'll be glad I did speak up.

Situation 4: A person under your supervision has been generally uncooperative, doing as little as possible and often taking an excessively long time to complete work. This person tends to be indifferent and coldly hostile to you and other supervisors. You're thinking about confronting this person regarding this less than acceptable work.

Alternative thoughts:

1. What if he just acts cold and uncooperative even when I bring it up? I get so upset when he looks at me like that. I just go to pieces. I can hardly think of what to say. And

114

that would make things even worse. What a mess!
irrational

2. I don't have to take this stuff from anybody, least of all someone who works for me. The nerve of him—goofing off and then acting like he's the kingpin around here. Not any more, damn it. He's had it. Shape up or ship out.
irrational

3. I've just never had to handle people like this. I never grew up with any of them, and I just don't understand them. Every time I try to be pleasant, he acts like I'm some kind of phony liberal. He makes me so upset that I just want to crawl away.
irrational

4. I think it's important to try to get him to do his work better. If he acts nasty and uncooperative, I can say something to him about that, too. He may not get any more cooperative, but I can handle that for the moment. If he doesn't improve, I can either take steps to fire him or try other ways to get him to improve. No matter what happens, I don't have to get myself all upset. And I can be honest and direct with him, however he responds.
rational

Our Choices for Exercise 7

Situation 1
Alternative thoughts:
1. Irrational I
2. Rational R
3. Rationalization Z
4. Irrational I

Situation 2
Alternative thoughts:
1. Irrational I
2. Rationalization Z

Exercise 7   Differentiating Irrational, Rationalized, and Rational Thinking (continued)

3. Rationalization and irrational   Z & I
4. Rational   R

Situation 3
Alternative thoughts:
1. Irrational   I
2. Rationalization   Z
3. Irrational   I
4. Rational   R

Situation 4
Alternative thoughts:
1. Irrational   I
2. Irrational   I
3. Irrational   I
4. Rational   R

DEALING WITH UPSETTING FEELINGS BEFORE AND AFTER ENCOUNTERS

Before or after a difficult encounter, many people may feel very upset. Dealing with these feelings can be troublesome, but the following four-step method, Changing Inner Dialogues and Irrational Assumptions,[3] can help you:

1. Discover your inner dialogues
2. Identify the underlying irrational assumptions of the inner dialogues
3. Accept what *is* true and accurate
4. Change those thoughts and assumptions that are irrational and inaccurate and substitute more accurate, rational thoughts.

Each step will be described in order to help you apply the principles and steps to your own assertion situations. Examples and exercises are included.

STEP ONE: DISCOVER YOUR INNER DIALOGUES

Becoming Aware of Inner Dialogues

To develop more rational thinking and to alter and cope with inaccurate, irrational thinking, it is necessary to begin to become aware of the kinds of thoughts you have in specific situations, i.e., you need to start paying attention to your inner dialogues. At first it's not easy to stop what you are doing (being excessively angry, upset, or depressed) and start thinking about what you are thinking. As practice, think of a situation that occurred during the past week which you believe you didn't handle well because you got excessively angry, anxious, or depressed. Then try to recall what you were thinking before and during the time you were feeling so strongly. For example, you have been asked to represent your PTA group at the special state board of education hearing on educational improvements. You will have to make a brief statement and answer the board's questions. After you agree, you begin *thinking* about it: "Oh damn, why did I say I'd do this? I'm no good at this speech making. What if they ask me something I can't answer? I'll probably embarrass myself, my family, and the whole PTA . . . . Come on, get yourself together! So what if you've never done this sort of thing before? . . . But I do want to make a good impression. I'm afraid I'll get scared and blow the whole thing. Oh no, I can see it now. Me making a fool of myself with all those people watching me. Oh, gads!"

For the first few times all you need to do is recall your actual inner dialogue. As stated earlier, sometimes the actual words are not easy to recall, partly because the thinking occurs so quickly and subtly. If you do have trouble recalling the dialogue, recall how you were *feeling*. There are hundreds of words to describe various nuances of feelings. You might start with these basic four: mad, sad, glad, or scared. If you find yourself saying, "I felt *that* . . ." or "I felt *like* . . . ," you are probably going to express a thought, not a feeling (e.g., "I felt that he had no right to say that to me"—that is a thought, not a feeling). Try "I felt ——" and insert a "feeling" word. Then say to yourself, "I felt——*because* I thought that——" and see what comes to your mind. It probably will be something about yourself, the other person, and/or the situation. Don't stop thinking about your dialogue too soon. For example, a person whose boss was yelling at him unfairly may think, "I was extremely angry because my boss was yelling at me unfairly," and believe that that was all there was to it. Actually, if he was extremely angry (as opposed to only being irritated or annoyed), he was probably thinking much more like, "How dare you speak to me this way! I didn't do anything to deserve this! I won't stand for it! You can't treat me this way; I'll get you, you bastard!" or "Nobody can speak to *me* like this in front of all these people! I'll show *you* who you think you can push around! I can be a hell of a lot tougher than you think! I'll show you who's a man or a mouse around here, buster!"

You may discover that some of your inner dialogues are about the feelings you are having and are afraid to express, e.g., "I'm so mad; she'll be devastated if I tell her how mad I am. What if I explode; what if I break down? That would be humiliating!" Holding back strong feelings of affection, caring, love, or pleasure may involve thinking: "Maybe she doesn't feel like I do"; "Maybe I won't say it right"; "What if they all act like I'm weird"; "What if I get it screwed up—I'd be so embarrassed"; "What if they think I'm just weak and mushy." All of these thoughts are related to irrational ideas about rejection, respect, and competence as a person. Holding back expressions of caring or of annoyance can be changed in the same manner as any other behavior (i.e., being indirect, sarcastic) that is based on irrational beliefs and fears.

Using Feelings to Cover Up or Avoid Other Worse Feelings

It can be more difficult to get at underlying feelings and the irrational thinking when you use your feelings (and thoughts and behaviors) to avoid other feelings. For example, Elmer's wife would occasionally correct him for making a mistake or ask him to change his behavior. She was assertive and did this infrequently, yet Elmer always reacted angrily, criticizing her for something else or accusing her of nagging. If taken at face value, Elmer's A-B-C's might be presumed to be:

A	B	C
Being criticized by his wife	Thinking: She can't treat me this way. I'm not a child!	Feeling: Angry and resentful Behavior: Yelling and criticizing her

At first it might seem that Elmer gets angry because of absolutistic thoughts ("She can't—— She mustn't——") about being unfairly treated. However, his feelings of anger and resentment are actually covering up other, less acceptable (to Elmer) feelings, namely hurt and vulnerability. Thus his A-B-C's for this situation are more A-B-C-B-C's (see Figure 10).

Figure 10 Elmer's A-B-C-B-C's

A **Activating Event**	Being criticized by wife
B **Thinking**	I've failed her; she's rejecting me because I've failed; I can't stand it!
C **Feeling and Behaving**	Hurt and vulnerable Pausing briefly
B **Thinking**	I have to stop this "threat," but I *cannot* show that I am hurt and vulnerable; I *must* be strong now.
C **Feeling and Behaving**	Outwardly angry and resentful Criticizing wife about something else

Elmer first irrationally turns constructive criticism into personal failure and rejection and then, perhaps unknowingly, goes on to cover up these feelings because he irrationally believes that he *must* be strong. He chooses defensive, counter-critical behaviors to get the focus off himself, keep his wife off balance, and get himself in a stronger position. Elmer's anger was a coverup for his irrationally based feelings of hurt and vulnerability.

Sometimes we use our feelings to keep other less desirable feelings from occurring. For example, Martha felt depressed, but she believed that her depressed feelings, although undesirable in themselves, were better than experiencing the fears of taking risks with people. Thus, she maintained her feelings of depression because they "saved" her from her fears. By recognizing this function of her depression and working successfully on the irrational bases of her fears, she started to take risks with people and became happier.

Avoiding one's true feelings, consciously or not, is not always inappropriate. A woman who is attempting to be warm and pleasant with visitors while feeling extremely sad at the very recent death of her husband is acting reasonably, not irrationally. Her underlying sadness and grief are reasonable and normal emotions. To keep her grief to herself and to attempt to get over it is not the same as Elmer's self-defeating, fearful behavior.

Excessive Feelings

When a person is experiencing excessive anxiety, anger, or depression, it is very likely that he is also engaging in or about to engage in some type of nonassertive or aggressive behavior. The word *excessive* should not be confused with the term *intense*. Intense feelings can be quiet, appropriate, self-enhancing, and compatible with assertive behavior. Intense love or intense sadness or even intense anger or frustration may follow from rational thinking in highly stimulating situations and may not get in the way of clear thinking and assertive behavior. However, it is important to distinguish between those feelings that result from rational thinking and facilitate assertive behavior and those excessive feelings that result from absolutistic, catastrophic, inaccurate thinking and become barriers to assertive behavior. Thus the best way to determine the propriety or desirability of your feelings is to identify the thoughts that prompted the feelings, check them for irrational components, and assess whether your feelings are barriers to more assertive behavior. If the feelings are inappropriate or undesirable, you will have several ways to alter them by changing how you think about them.

Mild feelings of being embarrassed, helpless, vulnerable, afraid, weak, bored, sad, frustrated, timid, or hurt can also be inappropriate or incompatible with assertive behavior even though they are not intense. That is, in a specific situation these feelings might be the result of inaccurate thinking that leads to self-defeating behaviors and thus would be undesirable and incompatible with assertive behavior.

As you probably can tell by now, behavior, even your own behavior, isn't necessarily what it seems to be. You need to carefully analyze your thoughts and feelings as well as your actions before and after a problematic situation.

The purpose of Exercise 8 is to give you practice in being able to identify the A-B-C's in your own assertion situations. The next two sections of this chapter will then help you identify the inaccurate parts of your thinking and how to control, alter, and change them.

Exercise 8   Becoming Aware of the A-B-C's of Your Inner Dialogues

At some convenient time during the day—at lunch, just before dinner, driving home, or at night—think about one incident that occurred during the day. Think about your own inner dialogue before, during, and after the incident. The incident itself might be a pleasant or unpleasant experience. It does not have to be one with lots of dysfunctional thinking. Take the time to write down what you thought to yourself at the time: (1) about yourself, (2) about others, and (3) about the situation. Be sure to try this exercise systematically for at least a week, if not longer.

For example, Art could have listed a situation (A) when he and a colleague co-led a workshop on assertiveness training that did not go as well as hoped. Art wanted to state his opinions, which included criticism of his colleague's work on the assertiveness workshop.

Exercise 8 Becoming Aware of the A-B-C's
of Your Inner Dialogues (continued)

Situation	Thinking	Feelings and Behaviors
A	**B**	**C**
Criticizing a colleague's work	**About self:** I'm not good at this. What if I say it wrong? I probably did some lousy things, too. Who am I to criticize him? Nobody's perfect. Forget it. **About other person:** What if he gets mad or hurt? I don't want to lose him as a friend. He's really hard to talk to about things like this; he gets so defensive. He'll probably just start a fight. He really can't take it. **About situation:** Why did this whole thing have to happen? I should just work alone. Now I probably have a bad reputation with these people.	Anxious and angry Talked about other topics Didn't say what I wanted to
A *upset @ Jeremy's internet habits*	**B** **About self:** *I'm not good enough for him* **About other person:** *He's a man; he doesn't think there's a problem* **About situation:** *I shouldn't even think about it. Snoop.*	**C**

Exercise 8 Becoming Aware of the A-B-C's
of Your Inner Dialogues (continued)

Situation	Thinking	Feelings and Behaviors
A	B	C *Act on it;*
Matt revealing his feelings for me.	**About self:** *I can't believe it; guilt*	*discussed it first;*
	About other person: *Must be joking*	*felt very safe, and*
	About situation: *I've wanted this for years... shocked*	*that I was doing the right thing.*

STEP TWO: IDENTIFY
THE UNDERLYING IRRATIONAL
ASSUMPTIONS OF INNER DIALOGUES

The first step of this method helped you identify your inner dialogue. The second step involves identifying the basic irrational ideas or assumptions that underlie your dialogue. Dr. Albert Ellis has identified ten basic ideas that underlie most irrational thinking in most situations.[4] Not all of them are operating all the time, but it is helpful to know what they are because you are likely to be thinking one or two of them when you get excessively angry, anxious, or depressed or when you behave nonassertively or aggressively.

The first four ideas are the most important and the most common. People seldom state these ideas as part of their actual inner dialogues because they are the underlying assumptions that lead to a particular dialogue in a specific situation. These irrational assumptions and some common resulting behaviors are listed below. Though changing irrational assumptions is not explained until Step Four, some possible rational alternative thoughts are listed at this time. You may wish to make up your own rational alternatives and compare them.

Ten Basic Irrational Ideas
and Possible Rational Alternatives

Irrational Idea Number One: You must—yes, must—have sincere love and approval almost all the time from all the people you find significant. People who think that assertiveness will result in disapproval are likely to seldom express their opinions; avoid conflict even when others violate their rights; and rarely express personal desires, preferences, or feelings. And, of course, this kind of nonassertion doesn't make things better and often makes them worse.

Some rational alternatives to an excessive need for approval are:

1. I would *like* to be approved of by every significant person, but I do not *need* such approval.
2. If I am not approved of by someone I would like to have like me, I can try to figure out what it is that person does not like about the way I behave and decide whether or not I want to change.
3. If I decide that this rejection is not based on any inappropriate behavior on my part, I can find others I can enjoy being with.
4. I can determine what I want to do rather than simply adapt or react to what I think others want.

Your rational alternatives: _It's almost an insult for certain people to admire you_

Irrational Idea Number Two: You must prove yourself thoroughly competent, adequate, and achieving, or you must at least have real competence or talent at something important. This form of absolutistic thinking has led some people to be extremely anxious, to the point of being unwilling to make a presentation at a conference; prefacing almost every task that requires some skill with profuse criticism of external influences that make the accomplishment of the task less likely (and thereby not one's own "fault"); avoiding social interaction for fear of having nothing worthwhile to say; and having difficulty accepting criticism without getting defensive (because one should be perfect).

Some rational alternatives to counteract the need to be perfect are:

1. I would *like* to be perfect or best at this task, but I do not *need* to be.
2. I'm still successful when I do things imperfectly.
3. What I do doesn't have to be perfect in order to be good.
4. I may be happier if I am successful, but success does not determine my worth as a person unless I let it.
5. I will be happier if I attempt to achieve at a realistic level rather than a perfect level.
6. I still want to achieve and to be successful. If I am, I will likely be happier, and if I am not successful, I probably will be unhappy, but I do not have to be depressed and miserable.
7. It is impossible for anyone to be perfectly competent.
8. Above all, if I *demand* that I be perfect, I will always be pushing or worrying so that I will slip; instead, if I do what I want and what I enjoy as well as I can, I'll feel happier and perform better.

Your rational alternatives: <u>People don't hate me for</u>
<u>not being perfect</u>

Irrational Idea Number Three: You have to view life as awful, terrible, horrible, or catastrophic when things do not go the way you would like them to go. When people act on this irrational assumption, they whine or bemoan their "tragedy," withdraw into isolation, speak extremely bitterly about others, or act helpless and destroyed. They feel and act like victims.

There are rational alternatives to feeling victimized. You can tell yourself, "This person has really treated me badly, and I don't like the situation or that person's behavior. I can help myself by asking myself what I can do to change either. If I can't change either, it is frustrating but not the end of the world. I can begin to make plans for making my life as desirable and as enjoyable as I can."

Your rational alternatives: _A year from now it won't matter._

Irrational Idea Number Four: People who harm you or commit misdeeds rate as generally bad, wicked, or villainous individuals, and you should severely blame, damn, and punish them for their sins. People who act on this belief may constantly criticize others for their incompetence, lack of sensitivity, or their ignorance; constantly question the motives of others or excessively berate persons who have been unfair; treat others as worthless individuals who deserve damnation because they don't raise their children properly, drink too much, have not succeeded in their careers or education, or do not do their work efficiently or effectively. Often people not only turn this severely critical thinking on others but may also turn it in on themselves. When they fail at a task, are rejected by a significant other person, or treat someone else unfairly, they then damn themselves for being bad or wicked persons.

Some rational alternatives for dealing with misdeeds are:

1. I can tell people firmly and directly how their behavior has negative effects on me, and I don't have to go so far as to personally punish them for their behavior. I may feel irritated or hurt, but I don't have to berate that person.
2. When I do punish someone, it costs me too in energy, and it seldom facilitates correction or change.
3. Just because I think something is wrong doesn't automatically mean it is wrong.
4. I (or others) may have behaved obnoxiously, unfairly, or incompetently, but that does not mean that I (or others) *always* will.
5. I can recognize and admit my own (or others') wrong acts, and I can work hard to correct or have others correct this misdeed or its future occurrence.

Your rational alternatives: _They may have positive traits as well._

Irrational Idea Number Five: If something seems dangerous or fearsome, you must become terribly occupied with and upset about it. This irrational idea leads to unrealistic anxiety

126

instead of reasonable concern and fear (the kind of fear that keeps people from playing on freeways and exposing themselves to other real dangers). Unrealistic anxiety leads to preoccupation, which actually interferes with the clear thinking that would lead to control of a dangerous or fearsome situation.

Some rational alternatives to dealing with danger are:

1. It's impossible to prevent a bad event from occurring by worrying about it; instead of worrying, I can think constructively and problem-solve.
2. In all likelihood that event will not be as bad as I fear. Even if it is bad, I don't have to crumble. I can stand it though it will be uncomfortable.

Your rational alternatives: _What will be will be._

Irrational Idea Number Six: People and things should turn out better than they do, and you have to view it as awful and horrible if you do not quickly find good solutions to life's hassles. People who behave under this assumption may continually search for perfect solutions to interpersonal problems and feel very inadequate when they cannot find them.

The following is a rational alternative to this kind of thinking. There may not be any perfect solution to this problem; in fact there may not be any solution. However, I can work toward improving the situation. All I can do is the best I can do, and if that is insufficient, it's OK for me to accept that reality. I can determine my priorities and accomplish what I can by assertively communicating my limits to others.

Your rational alternatives: _Live with it._

The final four irrational ideas represent four distinctly different beliefs; however, holding these beliefs is likely to result in some form of passivity and reluctance to take responsibility for one's own behavior.

Irrational Idea Number Seven: Emotional misery comes from external pressures, and you have little ability to control

your feelings or rid yourself of depression and hostility. Rational alternatives include:

1. I can stand it when things go wrong; I can choose to stand it if I want to; feeling uncomfortable or upset doesn't mean I'm not standing it.
2. I do have quite a bit of control over how I react to a situation, though I may not immediately realize it; others also have choices in how they react to me.
3. I am responsible for my own behavior and can accept reasonable consequences; as long as I respect the rights of others, I do not have to take 100 percent responsibility for others' reactions.

Your rational alternatives: _One can be proactive about their own life_

Irrational Idea Number Eight: You will find it easier to avoid facing many of life's difficulties and self-responsibilities than to undertake more rewarding forms of self-discipline. Rational alternatives include:

1. Even though I get immediate relief when I avoid a disturbing situation, I feel unfulfilled, and that is often as frustrating as confronting the problem.
2. What I am avoiding will probably not be as awful as I convince myself it is.
3. Avoidance does not ultimately lead to pleasure.

Your rational alternatives: _What am I missing?_

Irrational Idea Number Nine: Your past remains all-important and because something once strongly influenced your life, it has to keep determining your feelings and behavior today. The following is a more rational alternative. Although my past does exercise considerable influence, my thoughts, feelings, and behaviors are not fixed. I can change. It is possible to learn new behaviors in the present just as I learned old ones in the past.

Your rational alternatives: _I can change my behaviors_

Irrational Idea Number Ten: You can achieve happiness by inertia and inaction or by passively and uncommittedly "enjoying yourself." Essentially this form of irrational thinking is a "rationalization" to cover fear of some activity.

Some rational alternatives are:

1. Lots of inactivity will simply isolate me from people and activities.
2. Though inactivity may reduce the threat of taking risks at meeting people and trying out new activities, it doesn't produce feelings of pleasure and happiness.
3. Simply "enjoying myself" eventually will decrease my enjoyment of myself and of life because enjoyment and a personal sense of accomplishment come from making commitments and putting some effort into activities and people who are important to me.

Your rational alternatives: _What am I missing?_
I will still be unfulfilled.

These ten irrational ideas are the most common ones; you may have recognized others by now. Exercise 9 will give you practice in recognizing different kinds of irrational ideas.

Exercise 9   Identifying Irrational Ideas

Below are three situations and three dialogues (much of which, but not all, are irrational) that might occur in those situations. Write in the basic irrational assumptions that might be underlying each dialogue. Several irrational ideas might fit each dialogue. The possible answers are on page 131.

Situation 1:   You are a part-time employee, and you are finding that you are working more hours than you are paid for. You have made an appointment with your boss to ask for a raise, and you are in the outer office thinking about it.

Exercise 9 Identifying Irrational Ideas (continued)

"I haven't slept for three nights just thinking about going in there. He's so touchy that anything might set him off. He gets me so upset every time he comes around; I just fall apart. He's so intimidating. And what if he just ignores me or laughs me off and sends me away? I'd be so embarrassed! If I could only think of a way to get on his good side! But I've racked my brain, and nothing would work for sure. I'm so nervous that maybe I should just forget the whole thing. I could slip out before he's ready to see me. Oh no, the door's opening . . . ."

Basic irrational assumptions: _Absolutism / catastrophizm, evidence?_

Situation 2:   You just got off the phone with your mother, who told you how terrible she thinks it is that you are planning to get divorced. She is trying to make you feel guilty, irresponsible, and immature. You are thinking about what she was saying.

"Maybe she's right. I guess I decided to leave purely for my own interests. Maybe we could have worked it all out if I had stayed. I thought I really tried, but I guess I just wanted too much for myself—all that 'career' stuff and wanting friends of my own. Maybe I am just too self-centered. Maybe I can't give enough to someone else. Mom's probably right. If I had just stayed at home and raised a family and been supportive of Tom, I could be very secure today. Now I'm living alone, and I'm scared. What if I never fall in love or marry again! Mom's right, I failed again. I guess I'll get what I deserve."

Basic irrational assumptions: _Self-deprecation, catastrophizm_

Situation 3:   You are having a disagreement with your spouse, and you make a particularly direct, honest statement in an assertive manner. You have been non-assertive in past similar situations. Your spouse responds with "Oh, trying to use that assertive trick on me, eh!" You think . . . .

130

Exercise 9   Identifying Irrational Ideas (continued)

"I knew it wouldn't work. He can see right through me. I just can't do it. Why don't I just admit it. I've always been weak, and I guess I always will be. Even when I try to be assertive, I mess it up. And darn him, why does he have to pick on me like that right away. He doesn't even give me a chance to be assertive. He gets me so upset I couldn't be assertive even if I wanted to."

Basic irrational assumptions: _Self-deprecation, projection, evidence?_

Possible Irrational Assumptions for Exercise 9

Situation 1:   Irrational assumptions 1, 3, 5, 6, and 8

Situation 2:   Irrational assumptions 1, 2, 3, and 4

Situation 3:   Irrational assumptions 2, 3, 4, 6, 7, 8, and 9

STEPS THREE AND FOUR:
ACCEPT WHAT IS TRUE AND ACCURATE
AND CHANGE INACCURATE INNER DIALOGUES
AND UNDERLYING IRRATIONAL IDEAS

Now that you have identified your inner dialogues and the irrational assumptions they are based on, the next step is to analyze the *accuracy* of the thoughts you have.[5] You need to accept those thoughts that are accurate and place them in a reasonable perspective. Once you have done so, you need to challenge inaccurate thoughts and irrational assumptions and replace them with more accurate, rational statements. When more rational, logical inner dialogues are substituted, you are more likely to be in control of your thoughts, feelings, and behavior and thus act more assertively. While these two steps— accurately identifying your feelings and challenging them—are distinct, they are so related that we will explain them together.

131

Some people make the mistake of thinking that this process is "intellectualized" and is therefore distant or removed from oneself and one's "real" problems. In fact, when you are in touch with your inner dialogues and are able to alter the irrational thoughts that lead to self-defeating feelings and behaviors, you probably will experience a greater sense of wholeness. People often experience a sort of emotional relief and clarity after altering their inaccurate thinking, and their thinking, feelings, and behavior make more sense and fit together more congruently. They seem to be untied from restrictive cognitive and emotional binds and are freer to act in more self-enhancing ways. The purpose of this process is not to intellectualize your world until all emotions and sensory awareness are eliminated. Rather, it is a process that can foster the emergence of self-enhancing feelings and minimize the negative impact of irrationally based, self-defeating feelings that are incompatible with assertive behavior. You may want to verify the accuracy of this "sorting" process by trying it yourself: Separate your self-enhancing feelings from those that are self-defeating. The latter will usually be associated with the violation of your own personal rights or the rights of others through some type of non-assertive or aggressive behavior, while the self-enhancing feelings probably will be associated with self-regard, intimacy, honesty, directness, potency, and assertive behavior.

The process of becoming more aware of your feelings, thoughts, and behaviors and then taking greater control of them can be exciting and enjoyable. However, challenging, changing, and taking control of inaccurate thinking is often difficult to do, though it is easy to understand in principle. For this reason two detailed examples of how people have worked through this process for themselves will be presented.

The Case of Chris's Anxiety

Chris purchased a new dresser on sale. She hoped to save the $12 delivery charge by asking a casual friend, Bill, to help her by using his van to pick up the dresser. After Bill picked up the dresser, she took him and his friend (who had helped) to lunch and asked Bill how much he wanted for the use of his van. When Bill said $20, Chris paused and then readily agreed to pay him the next day. For three days Chris avoided him and was depressed and extremely angry with herself and Bill.

When recalling this situation in an assertiveness training group, Chris began to explore some of her thinking before she actually practiced how she would have preferred to respond to Bill. She recalled that her inner dialogue went something like this when she asked Bill to help her: "This is great. I'm really saving a lot of money. Maybe Bill will even do it for free. I'd better not bring up money. He might be offended. I wouldn't want to make him mad." Later when she offered to buy lunch, she thought, "If I buy Bill and his friend lunch, that will surely be a nice gesture and I'll still save some money." And when she asked Bill how much he wanted, she thought, "Well, I guess I *should* go ahead and ask just to be polite, but I'm sure he'll refuse any money after lunch and all." And when Bill asked for $20, she thought, "What! You bastard! How could you! What are you trying to do, rip me off? I blew it! How could I be so stupid and not see this. What can I do now? What if I make a big deal about it? He'll probably tell all my friends about it, too. You always do this to yourself, damn it—save some money on something and then blow it. You really are a jerk!" The group leader also asked Chris to think about any underlying irrational assumptions; three emerged:

1. If I spoke up and offered a specific amount, Bill might not like it, and he would then avoid me and possibly tell others how "cheap" I am and that would be awful because I must be liked and respected by others.
2. Bill treated me unfairly, and that was intolerable because I must always be treated fairly. (Note that Chris was able to get very angry and upset by herself but not directly toward Bill because she wanted to be liked and she feared losing his friendship.)
3. Both Bill and I acted wrongly and therefore deserve to be blamed and punished. (Bill gets his by delaying payment beyond the next day as agreed, and I get mine by being upset, depressed, and miserable.)

With this background Chris challenged and altered her

thinking. First of all, and possibly most importantly, Chris learned the A-B-C's and was willing to try out the notion that she could influence, even control, the way she thinks, feels, and behaves, and that there is no "magic" about these three components of herself.

Chris then assessed what parts of her thinking were reasonable and accurate and what parts were not. Going back over her inner dialogue, Chris made the following decisions: "When I first asked Bill, it made sense to hope he *might* do it for free, but I should not have expected it. It did *not* make sense to avoid bringing up money for fear of offending him. If he was offended by my asking him if he wanted any money for the help, I could have dealt with that. Even if he got mad, I could have tried to get along and let him know that I hadn't intended to offend him. I liked buying Bill and his friend lunch. I could have made it clearer that I considered lunch to be payment for his help, instead of assuming that he understood this. I also could have offered him a few more dollars instead of asking what he wanted. I guess on that last point I got trapped by my desire to "look good" in his eyes. And when Bill did ask for $20, it was OK for me to think that his request was unfair. I could have told him I thought it would be lower and that the company charge would have only been $12. I could have made a counteroffer. I guess I was so worried about losing his friendship and being thought of as "cheap" that I never even considered the possibility of making a counteroffer. Realistically, though, his thinking I'm cheap doesn't make me cheap, and it's OK for me to want to save some money. I could live with his thinking I was cheap if I couldn't change his mind directly. I could even live with his spreading the word that I am cheap. Actually my real close friends understand how I like to save money. Last of all, I am *not* a jerk. I can control how I think and how I feel; I don't have to feel good about everything, but I don't have to get depressed either."

What Chris did was to figure out what part of her dialogue was already accurate and accept that part. She altered parts that were inaccurate or exaggerated by stating them reasonably. Particularly, Chris changed from thinking she *absolutely* needed to keep Bill happy and maintain their friendship to believing that she would very much prefer to maintain the friendship but not at the cost of giving up her personal right to be assertive about her own feelings and preferences. The process of changing from believing one *needs* or *must* have something or somebody to believing one strongly prefers that thing or person is often a significant step in altering inaccurate inner dialogues and opening the way to assertive behavior. Compare Chris's original inner dialogue with her new, altered dialogue and speculate on how she would likely feel and behave after each series of thoughts (see Figure 11, page 136).

Chris's self-analysis illustrates how inner dialogues can be "dissected" and reassembled so that more reasonable and accurate thinking occurs. Obviously, when you are in the middle of a situation, you won't have time to do such a detailed analysis. However, three points are worth noting. First, your brain works extremely fast, and you *can* very quickly think about what you are thinking without distracting yourself, especially if you give yourself permission to take time to think and do not respond immediately to others. As you get more experienced, you will recognize even faster what you are saying to yourself, what is accurate and inaccurate about it, and what are the underlying irrational beliefs. Since some of the same irrational ideas will emerge in a variety of situations, you will be able to recognize them even more readily. Second, even if you don't assess your thoughts at the time, it can be very valuable to go back over difficult situations, as Chris did, recall your thinking, and then alter it. Although the actual situation is over, you might find that you have similar dialogues in other situations that are likely to occur again, and it is very good practice. As you get better at assessing your thinking in retrospect, with systematic practice you can make your assessments sooner and sooner after the actual situations. Third, doing this type of analysis is particularly valuable when you know in advance that you want to assert yourself and are feeling very anxious or already angry about the situation. Had Chris focused on her inner dialogue and assessed it before she asked her friend for help, she could have assertively and directly dealt with the money issue before he delivered her dresser. If they had been unable to come to a mutually satisfactory agreement on the

Figure 11   Chris's Irrational and Alternative
           Rational Thinking

Irrational Thinking

1. I'd better not bring up money, he might be offended. I wouldn't want to make him mad.

2. I *should* go ahead and ask just to be polite, but I'm sure he'll refuse any money after lunch and all.

3. What, you bastard. How could you! What are you trying to do, rip me off?

4. I blew it! How could I be so stupid and not see this!

5. What can I do now? If I make a big deal he'll probably accuse me of being cheap.

Alternative Rational Thinking

It's OK to want to know what this will cost me. There's no evidence that Bill is likely to get mad. And if he does, I don't have to fall apart. I can explain that I hadn't meant to offend him.

I'm not being impolite by being direct about my own preferences for payment. I can say that I want to reciprocate the favor by lunch and a few dollars.

Maybe he's trying to rip me off; maybe he really thinks that's what his services are worth; I really don't know what his motives are. What *I do know* is that I think that's too much (at least more than I planned to pay and can afford). I don't like what he's said, but I don't need to get outraged.

Just because I didn't see this coming doesn't mean I'm stupid. What it does mean is that I need to stop making hidden bargains with people and that money is a sensitive issue for me. I didn't handle this as well as I would have liked, but that doesn't make me stupid either. I do not have to berate myself because I made a mistake. I can figure out what I did and change what I want.

Simply saying that was more than I was prepared to pay and telling Bill how much the company delivery would have cost is *not* making a big deal. If he accuses me of being

Irrational Thinking	Alternative Rational Thinking
	cheap, I can restate my opinion and I can handle his putdown. If he becomes intimidating, I can ask him to stop it. Even if Bill thinks I'm cheap that doesn't make me cheap.
6. He'll probably even spread it around to my friends.	Actually he doesn't know most of my friends. My close friends understand my feelings about money. If he does spread the word, I can ask him to stop and tell him how I feel about his behavior. My friends may or may not agree with him, and I can live with that. I do not have to run out and defend myself to them.
7. You always do this to yourself, damn it; save some money on something and then blow it. You really are a jerk!	I do not always do this. I don't like it when I do, but I don't have to get down on myself. I can work to change. I am *not* a jerk! I am a person who sometimes makes mistakes.

money issue, she could have found some other options, i.e., asking someone else for help, having the company deliver the dresser, etc. Figure 12 (page 138) gives self-assessment questions you can ask yourself. Whenever you assess your thinking, these questions may help you change your faulty thoughts.

The Case of Bert and Anger

Bert is a young political scientist who lives with Carla, a microbiologist. Both have Ph.D. degrees, and in addition to their full-time positions—Bert's at a major university and Carla's at a renowned research institute—they engage in several additional professional projects like writing and consulting, which take up at least four evenings a week and some weekends. The following is Bert's description of the situation.

**Figure 12 Self-Assessment Questions
for Challenging Inaccurate Thinking**

1. What is actually true about this situation?
   What facts might I be forgetting or ignoring?
2. What is *not* true? Especially, look for "musts," "shoulds," "need to's," and "awfulizing." How might I be exaggerating my thoughts and feelings by catastrophizing and thinking absolutistically?
3. What's the worst thing that could happen?
   How likely is that to happen?
   How awful is that worst thing?
4. What *is* probable or likely to happen?
5. How could you handle the worst possible response the other person might make?
6. What specific thoughts do you need to think to yourself to reduce and cope with the excessive feelings you have in that situation? Are those thoughts direct, rational counters to the irrational, upsetting thoughts, or are they just rationalized coverups or avoidances of the original upsetting thoughts?
7. How do I want to act and feel in this situation, and what do I need to keep thinking in order to be that way?
8. What can I think to myself that will help reduce the excessive feelings (anxiety, anger, depression)?
9. What can I think to myself to keep from deprecating myself if I'm not handling the situation as well as I'd like?
10. How might I be overly focusing on self-deprecating or negative thoughts?

It was Carla's birthday on a Friday, and I would have gotten her a present, but I didn't have a free day or evening for over two weeks. I was heavily involved in writing a federal grant that was due in a few days. Besides, Carla had to work all day Friday and most of that evening. We did have a quick dinner together on Friday, and I brought Carla some flowers and some special candies she liked. We agreed that Saturday afternoon would be a great time to really celebrate her birthday. Carla had to go to a professional conference Saturday, but she said she would be back about four in the afternoon and we could do something then.

As I thought about it, I realized we really haven't been spending as much time together as we have in the past, and I got really excited thinking about going out and getting Carla some special

138

presents. So I spent practically all day Saturday going to stores and getting some really great things. All day I kept imagining how pleased and surprised she'd be. I didn't just spend a lot of money; I also picked things that were unique or special. When I got home, I hid all the presents around the house in places where Carla would easily find them so she'd be surprised over and over. I even baked a cake and put candles and a "Happy Birthday Carla" on it. I was so excited by the time four o'clock came that I was almost like a kid.

But Carla didn't show up at four. And she didn't show up at five or six. First, a lot of the excitement went away, and then I started getting real disappointed, almost depressed. Then I started getting mad. We've had so little time together, and she was ruining the precious time we did have. It was really crazy because I worried, too, that something might have happened to her. I had all these feelings going on, and they just seemed to get worse and worse. At six-thirty Carla finally came in, and I really blew it. I made some nasty crack about hoping she had as lousy a day as I did. She snapped back at me, and we yelled at each other a few more times about how crabby and inconsiderate the other person was. And then we both went to "neutral corners" of the house. We both spent most of the rest of the night sulking. What I hoped to be a really special evening turned out miserable. I love Carla very much, and she loves me. We have gotten along great, so we're not incompatible, but this time everything went wrong.

Your first reaction might be, Can this relationship be saved? The situation, though, is not as serious as it might seem. Bert shared this incident in an assertion training group. Before practicing how to discuss this incident with Carla, he recalled his inner dialogue at various points during that day. When he was shopping, he was thinking, "Wow, will I surprise her with this present. I can hardly wait. I'll even bake her a cake. This is really fun, just like it was before. Since we've taken on these grant proposals and the extra classes, we hardly see each other anymore. We'll have to talk about that; it seems like we've gotten caught up in our work with all these new opportunities." In the group Bert decided that these thoughts were logical and accurate and that he felt warm and caring toward Carla, excited about the birthday, and reasonably concerned with their work-loads. Later, though, Bert recalled thinking, "Well, we may be overworked, but *this* is going to be *our* special day. We won't have a lot of time together, but it'll be great!" Bert decided that these thoughts were reasonable but that they were the beginning of his putting a great deal of time pressure on this upcoming few hours to make up for much lost time.

More important was Bert's thinking between the time he expected Carla and the time she arrived. He reported the following dialogue: "Where *is* she? It's well past four. Damn it, she said she'd be back at four! Everything's ready. She knew we would do *something*. What a drag! I'm not even as excited as I was before. Where the hell is she!" A bit later: "Some damn birthday surprise this is. I can't understand her. Maybe she doesn't care that much about being together. Maybe she's working so hard just so she can be away. I can't believe she'd be so thoughtless. She's probably sitting around with all those damn scientists. Well, if that's what she prefers, the hell with it. Some surprise! (pause) Hey, maybe something's happened, and I'm getting angry while she's hurt or something. What a jerk." And even later he thought, "This is crazy. The whole damn thing is ruined. If she walks in that door soon, she's going to get a piece of my mind. No wonder we've been spending so little time together. Well, if being with me on her birthday means so little to her . . . ."

By the time Carla did return home, Bert had worked himself up into such resentment, hurt, anger, and worry that it was highly unlikely that much of anything could happen besides the conflict that did occur. In an assertion group, Bert reassessed his thinking and made the following changes:

1. He convinced himself that these hours together were overly important when, instead, he could have been excited about it without letting the time pressure be so important. He could have thought: "I would really like to spend this time with Carla, and I'm excited about it. If it doesn't work out, I'll be disappointed, but I can live with it. We'll have to talk and plan how we can make more free time for ourselves so that the time we do spend together isn't so pressured."
2. He told himself that it was all her fault and that she was a bad person and deserved his anger and resentment because she didn't return on time. He changed that thinking to:

"I'd like you to be here. When you do arrive, I'll want to know what kept you, but I don't have to be accusing. If you were held up for a "good" reason, I'll still be disappointed, but not hurt or angry. If you didn't come back because you decided to spend time with others, I probably will be very disappointed and irritated since we agreed to get together at four. Either way, I don't have to get terribly outraged and upset."

3. Bert recognized that his exaggeration about Carla's working and her lack of interest in him was inaccurate and improbable since there was ample evidence that both cared a great deal for each other. He therefore changed that thinking to: "It's true she isn't here when she said she would be. She may even prefer to be with someone else. That's unlikely, but if it is true, I can ask her and we can talk about our relationship and what other relationships she has. Even if she did prefer to spend some time with someone else, that doesn't mean that she cares less for me. If she did choose to be with someone else, I would be irritated that she broke our agreement to meet at four. But I don't know yet if that's true."

Bert changed his thinking in three ways:

1. He no longer made this limited and special time into something crucial.
2. He stopped prejudging and blaming Carla for her irresponsibility and unfairness at not returning on time.
3. He stopped agonizing over the possible meanings of her lateness.

The fact was that Carla was late because she returned with a colleague and her family. The conference was in a mountain resort area, and when coming back from the conference, one of the infant children got carsick several times. The cleanups and having to wait until the infant seemed better caused the delay. When Carla returned to a fuming Bert, it is not surprising that she was equally angry at his anger and outrage.

It is important to note, however, that any of Bert's worries were "possible." The point is that the *way* Bert agitated himself when considering these possible concerns was to assume the worst ("What if we don't get to be together this afternoon . . . ; What if Carla's with someone else . . . ; What if she doesn't care for me anymore . . . .) and to answer each assumption with: "It would be awful, unbearable, horrible, the end of the world!" Admittedly, some of these concerns, if true, are serious and might involve losing Carla, which would be very sad. Even when Bert worried about Carla being in an accident, he assumed the worst. The fact is that even if the worst possible thing happened, Bert still was being premature. That is not at all to say that he should not have any feelings at all about any of these concerns. Thinking rationally about these possible explanations leads one to feel concerned, irritated, sad, or anxious, not extremely angry, excessively anxious, or severely depressed. Look at Figure 13. Compare Bert's original inner dialogue with his new, altered dialogue.

Bert then went on to practice how he would talk with Carla about this incident. If he had not made this analysis of his thinking, you can imagine how difficult it would have been for him to practice behaving assertively in such a situation. He would probably either just have gone through the motions mechanically or would have had a difficult time suppressing all those feelings of resentment, rage, jealousy, and worry. After dealing with his thinking, Bert no longer simply "held back" those feelings, he actually changed them.

But caution is in order here. It is very easy to develop a whole set of irrational thoughts about becoming more rational or more assertive. For example, some people mistakenly say to themselves, "What's wrong with me? I blew it again! Why can't I control my thinking just like it says in the book! I must be a real jerk"; or "From now on, I've *got* to be assertive. I don't care who it is. Damn it, I'm never gonna let anybody take advantage of me again. They'll see!"; or "Gosh, what if I can't even do all this changing your thinking stuff. Maybe I'll never stop being so nonassertive."

Of course it is desirable for people to make serious commitments to being more assertive; however, the problem is that people sometimes become absolutistic ("I must . . .") or exces-

142

**Figure 13 Bert's Irrational and Alternative
Rational Thinking**

Irrational Thinking	Alternative Rational Thinking
1. Damn it! She said she'd be back at four. She's ruining everything! Where is she?	Carla did say she'd be back by four, and it's well past that now. I'm really disappointed, but I don't have to get myself upset. Maybe she is being thoughtless. I don't like that at all, and I can find out if it's true. If it is, I can let her know I'm angry without blowing up or trying to make her feel bad or guilty.
2. Maybe she doesn't care any more. Maybe she'd rather be with those other people.	It's possible that she does prefer to be with them, that we have become more distant. I can talk with her about it; if it's true we can plan ways to get together again. If she chooses not to I'll be sad, but I don't have to make myself upset now.
3. Maybe something's happened to her and here I am getting mad.	Although it's unlikely, it's possible that something has happened to Carla. It makes sense to be concerned, but I don't need to upset myself about that possibility. It's also OK for me to feel disappointed (and irritated) right now. If it turns out she was late because of problems out of her control, I can accept that and still be disappointed.
4. The whole damn thing is ruined. If she walks in that door, she's going to get a piece of my mind.	The afternoon is shot. Carla may have been thoughtless, but I don't know that yet. Things don't always *have* to go my way. I'm very disappointed, but it's really not awful. Even more important, I don't need to blame Carla or berate her. If it turns out that she *was* being thoughtless, I'll be angry, but I don't have to punish or berate her.

sively alarmist ("What if . . .") in their thinking about becoming more assertive. It is not awful if you are not *always* assertive, and while it probably would be better to be assertive fairly often, it makes sense to decide what *you* want, assess the likely consequences, and act accordingly. And when you don't act assertively, even when you wish you had, it is not awful. It is merely inconvenient and unfortunate and you can think about how you kept yourself from acting assertively and work to change those barriers if you decide you want to do so. Exercises 10, 11, and 12 will help you identify irrational thoughts and assumptions and develop alternatives to them.

Exercise 10 Challenging and Changing Irrational Assumptions

1. Think of a situation that has been difficult to handle asser- tively or where you've gotten excessively angry, anxious, or depressed. Think about what you say to yourself that leads to these feelings and behaviors. Write down your inner dialogue, especially noting what you are thinking (1) about yourself, (2) about others, and (3) about the situa- tion. Fill in the A-B-C's for this situation:

Situation	Your Thinking	Your Feelings and Behaviors
A	B	C

2. List your underlying irrational ideas that support your inner dialogue.
3. Challenge the accuracy of the inaccurate ideas and accept in a realistic manner those which are true (e.g., "I didn't get the job; I don't like that at all; it was OK for me to feel nervous during the interview and to feel disappointed now"). Then change those statements that aren't accurate ("It is not awful and I am not a failure; I haven't gotten this job, and I can continue to do all I can to succeed in what I choose in the future"). Write down the new, rational alternatives.

Exercise 10   Challenging and Changing Irrational Assumptions (continued)

4. Practice saying the more rational thoughts over and over. Each time an inaccurate one comes up, restate a rational alternative. Notice how you feel when you are thinking in self-enhancing, rational ways and when you are thinking with lots of inaccuracies.
5. Use these steps for as many other assertion situations as you would like to improve.

Exercise 11   Analyzing Your Thinking and Behavior

1. Think of a recent incident in which you behaved assertively and recall what you were thinking before, during, and after you acted assertively. Write down the actual thoughts, putting words to the ones that seem a bit vague.

2. Think of how you could have altered your thinking so that you would be nonassertive *or* aggressive. Pick the way you would be more inclined to act if you had not been assertive. Write down the thoughts that would have led to nonassertive or aggressive behaviors.

Exercise 12   Identifying Types of Irrational Assumptions

Read Ellis and Harper's *New Guide to Rational Living.** This book, written for the lay person, describes the ten irrational assumptions in greater detail and cites many excellent examples of how people apply the irrational ideas to specific situations and how you can change your inaccurate, irrational thinking and substitute more rational thoughts.

A New Guide to Rational Living by Ellis and Harper. © 1975 by Institute for Rational Living. Published by Prentice-Hall, Inc., Englewood Cliffs, New Jersey.

COPING WITH UPSETTING FEELINGS IMMEDIATELY BEFORE AND DURING ENCOUNTERS

This chapter has presented one method for dealing with upsetting feelings: analyzing and altering inner dialogues and irrational assumptions. That method is most useful for dealing with upsetting feelings that occur sometime before or persist after difficult encounters with other people. For constructively coping with feelings that occur during encounters, just before, and immediately after, a less time-consuming method is needed. The last part of this chapter discusses such a method: the coping self-statement method.[6] When the two methods—analyzing and altering inner dialogues and irrational assumptions and the coping self-statement—are used together, they can make a powerful combination for dealing with feelings which interfere with the ability to act assertively.

Even when you have analyzed and altered your inner dialogues, know *what* you want to communicate, and *how* to get your message across, it is not uncommon to feel some degree of apprehension or irritation as you approach the situation and then to have emotional reactions to these feelings. For example, some people get even more upset when they realize that they are anxious in the first place ("Oh, my heart's going a mile a minute! I know I'm going to blow it! What's wrong with me! Oh, now my stomach's churning. I can't stand this! If I feel this bad now, and I haven't even opened up my mouth, what'll happen to me when I do start speaking up for myself!"). It is important to have a readily available method for dealing with these emotional surges. A quick method for dealing with increased anxiety and anger is particularly needed *during* the encounter itself, especially when the other person does not immediately comply with what you want, is irritating, attempts to make you feel guilty, or acts in threatening ways. Afterwards, you may feel upset if it did not go as you wished. When the encounter does go well, it is important to know that sometimes people feel guilty or scared instead of pleased—even though they have done nothing wrong—particularly when they have broken some long-standing internal rule that forbids them to be assertive. You can cope with these feelings by using the analysis method and/or the coping method. Or you can get reassurances from a friend that you did nothing wrong, that you did your best, and remind yourself that you have the right to be assertive.

The Coping Self-Statement Method

The coping method involves internally giving yourself instructional statements that will enable you to better cope with upsetting feelings as they occur. Examples of some self-statements are shown in Figure 14 (page 150). These are given *when* you become aware that you are experiencing distracting or upsetting feelings or when you are aware that you are starting to have irrational thoughts. The following case illustrates how one person used both the analysis and coping methods.

> As Dick started walking to his boss's office, he felt anxious. As he noticed his stomach beginning to churn, he immediately instructed himself, "Relax—take a deep breath—OK. I *can* handle this." When they finished their initial discussion, and Dick's boss asked what he had wanted to talk about, he could feel an instant rise in his anxiety. He dealt with these feelings by giving himself a self-instructional statement: "OK—I'm tense; take a deep breath—I don't have to say it perfectly—. Just say it—go." He immediately felt better as soon as he told his boss that he wanted to talk about getting a raise.
>
> As the salary discussion proceeded, Dick periodically felt surges of anxiety and irritation. As he noticed these feelings, he coped with them by giving himself a constructive instructional message: "OK—slow down. Take it step by step." When he successfully managed his feelings, he immediately said "good" to himself. The salary discussion ended with his boss saying that she would think about it and get back to him. As Dick walked out of the office, he was aware of feeling very upset.
>
> Taking out fifteen minutes for himself, Dick took a close look at what he told himself and realized that he had been upset mainly because he told himself that he should/ought to have been able to have gotten an immediate yes answer out of his boss and that he was a failure because he didn't get it. Upon reanalyzing it, he decided that it was OK to feel disappointed, that he hadn't failed in his objective to discuss the salary issue assertively, and that he wasn't a

147

failure; as a matter of fact, he had "done good." He felt better after coming to these conclusions. During the rest of the day, when he periodically found himself feeling upset and his mind drifting to the discussion, he coped with his feelings by giving himself another instructional message: "Stop! You did well in there. You're not a failure; she just failed to give you an immediate answer. Not getting an immediate answer doesn't mean no."

Using the Coping Method: Three Steps

The first step when coping is to have a cue that will remind you to turn on your particular self-instructional statement. The two most commonly used cues are visceral emotions (e.g., tense or irritated feeling or tightened stomach, throat, and facial muscles, etc.) and specific overt behaviors (e.g., fidgeting, drooping, lurching forward). Instead of using these reactions as cues to turn on panicky thoughts (e.g., "Oh I'm really getting mad! I'm going to blow my stack now any minute!"), use them as cues to turn on constructive, self-instructional thoughts (e.g., "I'm getting mad; that means slow down, breathe. Just state your case and don't get personal"). One woman found that whenever she started to clench her teeth and felt her face and stomach muscles tightening that she was likely to act aggressively. She used these signals to instruct herself ("Relax—let go of your stomach. You don't have to win in order to be OK") with the result that she felt less defensive and didn't respond aggressively. Sometimes people are so aware of their inner dialogues that they can use the presence of irrational thinking as a cue to turn on self-instructional statements (e.g., "What if she gets mad? What if I can't say anything when I walk in there! Stop! These thoughts are just getting me scared. Take a breath—Think of what you're going to say—I want to talk about getting a raise— Good!").

The second step is to develop internal statements that can help you cope with upsetting feelings. The same internal statement probably will not be equally helpful for all people, but Figure 14 shows some self-statements that have been successfully used by other people. Though any of the statements could be used, those on the left side may be more helpful for dealing with irritation and possible aggressive reactions; those on the right side can be used to cope with anxiety and possible non-

148

assertive reactions. Circle any statements that strike *you* as particularly helpful. If none seem suitable, experiment with creating your own self-instructional statements. The statements seem to be more effective when they are reasonably brief and simple. It is very important that they are genuine (not rationalizations) and feel right for you. Some people have found that simply reminding themselves of their rights is effective (e.g., "Relax—you *do* have the right to say no"). In other cases, the process of analyzing and altering inner dialogues and irrational assumptions helps people discover particular rational thoughts that they can use as self-instructional statements to cope with upsetting feelings (e.g., "It's OK for me to want to save money; I'm not selfish just because I want to save some money").

For people inclined to behave nonassertively, self-statements that help them to simply relax are often helpful (see Appendix A). For people who are inclined to behave aggressively, the self-statement usually needs to do more than simply instruct the person to stop what he is doing or is about to do; a "go" instruction, which tells the person what to do instead, is also often needed (e.g., "Stop jumping to conclusions—check out your assumptions"; "Take it step by step"; "Remember, there's no need to make a fight out of this"; "Remember you don't have to win in order to be OK"; "Take a moment to look at it from the other person's perspective"). The reason for this is that simply giving oneself "stop" messages may result in nonassertive behavior for those who are inclined to act aggressively.

Using self-critical or self-deprecating thoughts as self-instructional messages (e.g., "You're acting like a chicken; get in there and speak up for yourself"; "Quit getting so hysterical and grow up!") usually do not help people cope. Most important, even when threat and guilt are successful in getting people to act assertively, self-deprecation is not worth the price. The coping self-statements offered in Figure 14 can produce the same assertive behavior while still respecting your own dignity as a person.

The third step is to praise yourself when you successfully cope with your anxiety (e.g., "Good for you!") not only during the process but also right after. It is important that the praise be genuine: You should not kid yourself by saying "good" when

149

Figure 14 Coping With Feelings

Anger	Anxiety

Preparing for the Confrontation

What do I have to do?	What do I have to do?
This is going to upset me, but I know how to deal with it.	This is going to upset me, but I know how to deal with it.
There won't be any need for an argument.	Just think about what you have to say. That's better than getting anxious.
Try not to take this too seriously.	No cutting yourself down; just think rationally.
Relax—take a deep breath.	Relax—take a deep breath.
Easy does it. Remember to keep your sense of humor.	Stop worrying; you *can* do it.

Coping When Feelings Start to Build

My muscles are starting to feel tight. It's time to relax and slow down.	My muscles are starting to feel tight. Time to relax.
My anger is a signal of what I need to do. Breathe—you don't have to win to be OK.	My anxiety is a signal of what I need to do. Breathe—you don't have to be perfect to be OK.
Let's take the issue point by point.	You *can* meet this challenge.
Let's try a cooperative approach. Maybe we are both right.	One step at a time; you can handle the situation.
Negatives lead to more negatives. Work constructively.	Don't think about fear; just think about what you have to do. Stay relevant.
He'd probably like me to get really angry. Well, I'm going to disappoint him.	Relax; you're in control. Take a slow, deep breath.

Coping When Feelings Start to Overwhelm

As long as I keep my cool, I'm in control.	You can expect your fear to rise. That's OK.

150

Figure 14   Coping With Feelings (Continued)

Anger	Anxiety
Think of what you want to get out of this.	When fear comes, just think of what you want to say.
You don't need to prove yourself.	Label your fear from 0 to 10 and watch it rise. I'm at 7 and I need to take a deep breath.
Don't make more out of this than you have to.	It's OK to be afraid; you *can* handle it.
There's no need to doubt myself. What he says doesn't matter.	Keep the focus on the present; what do you have to do? Take a deep breath.
Look for the positives. Don't assume the worst or jump to conclusions.	I can handle this; just get the tension down a little bit.

Coping When It's All Over

These are difficult situations and they take time to straighten out.	You didn't get what you wanted; that's OK. You tried and that's all that counts.
Don't take it personally.	You did the right thing for yourself even if the other person is a little angry. It's not your fault.
That wasn't as hard as I thought.	That wasn't as hard as I thought.
I'm doing better at this all the time!	I'm doing better at this all the time!
I can be pleased with the progress I'm making!	I can be pleased with the progress I'm making!

Source: Reprinted by permission of the publisher, from *Anger Control* by Raymond W. Novaco (Lexington, MA: Lexington Books, D. C. Heath and Company, Copyright 1975, D. C. Heath and Company).

Source: Donald Meichenbaum, *Cognitive Behavior Modification.* © 1974 General Learning Corporation (General Learning Press, Morristown, NJ). Reprinted by permission of Silver Burdett Company.

you did not successfully cope with your feelings. If the encounter with the other person didn't go as well as you had hoped, it also is important to use some coping statement to deal with your disappointment (e.g., "So it didn't go like you hoped. That's OK, you can feel good about how you carried your end of it!").

SUMMARY

You are not a robot. You are a living, breathing, feeling, thinking being. No one can begin acting assertively simply by learning a prescribed set of responses and then doing them. Assertive behavior is influenced by your belief system of personal rights *and* by your ability to tell the difference between nonassertive, assertive, and aggressive responses. Equally important is the impact of what you think about yourself, others, and the situation at issue. These thoughts make up your inner dialogues, some of which are logical, reasonable, and accurate and some of which are irrational and exaggerated or based upon irrational assumptions or ideas.

Hopefully the two methods discussed in this chapter—recognizing and challenging your assumptions and making coping self-statements—will help you use these inner dialogues to your advantage. Learning to use these two procedures takes practice and continued effort. Many people try once or twice, get discouraged, and give up, but people who stay with these methods get better and better at recognizing and changing their thinking. While you probably will not miraculously change your life, you will gain more control over your thoughts and actions.

You may never get rid of all your irrational behaviors. In one sense that probably is a good sign. To occasionally think and act irrationally is a kind of human right. The methods described in this chapter—or the reasons for acting assertively—are not intended for suppression or denial of these feelings. Rather these feelings are part of your real self, and learning to recognize them is a matter of self-knowledge and self-acceptance. Ellis's list of irrational behaviors deserves repeating here:

1. You must—yes, must—have sincere love and approval al-

most all the time from all the people you find significant.

2. You must prove yourself thoroughly competent, adequate, and achieving, or you must at least have real competence or talent at something important.
3. You have to view life as awful, terrible, horrible, or catastrophic when things do not go the way you would like them to go.
4. People who harm you or commit misdeeds rate as generally bad, wicked, or villainous individuals, and you should severely blame, damn, and punish them for their sins.
5. If something seems dangerous or fearsome, you must become terribly occupied with and upset about it.
6. People and things should turn out better than they do, and you have to view it as awful and horrible if you do not quickly find good solutions to life's hassles.
7. Emotional misery comes from external pressures, and you have little ability to control your feelings or rid yourself of depression and hostility.
8. You will find it easier to avoid facing many of life's difficulties and self-responsibilities than to undertake more rewarding forms of self-discipline.
9. Your past remains all-important and because something once strongly influenced your life, it has to keep determining your feelings and behavior today.
10. You can achieve happiness by inertia and inaction or by passively and uncommittedly "enjoying yourself."

Once you can recognize these behaviors, you can be well on your way to gaining better control of your behavior.

NOTES

1.   Mahoney, M. *Cognitive and behavior modification.* Cambridge, MA: Ballinger Publishing Company, 1974. Meichenbaum, D. H. *Cognitive behavior modification.* Morristown, NJ: General Learning Press, 1974. Meichenbaum, D. H. Self-instructional methods (How to do it). In A. Goldstein & F. Kanfer (Eds.), *Helping people change: Methods and materials.* New York: Pergamon Press, 1975.

2.   Ellis, A. *Reason and emotion in psychotherapy.* New York: Lyle Stuart, 1962. Ellis, A. *Growth through reason.* Palo Alto, CA: Science and Behavior Books, 1971. Ellis, A. *Humanistic psychotherapy: The rational-emotive approach.* New York: Julian Press, 1973. Ellis, A. *Disputing irrational beliefs (DIBS).* New York: Institute for Rational Living, 1974. Ellis, A. & Harper, R. A. *A new guide to rational living.* Englewood Cliffs, NJ: Prentice-Hall, 1975.

3.   This model is based on the work of: Ellis, A., & Maultsby, M. Jr. *More personal happiness through rational self-counseling.* Lexington, KY: published by the authors, 1971. Ellis, A., & Maultsby, M. Jr. Systematic written homework in psychotherapy. *Psychotherapy: Theory, Research, and Practice,* 1971, *8*, 195-198.

4.   Ellis, A., & Harper, R. A. *New guide to rational living.* Englewood Cliffs, NJ: Prentice-Hall, 1975. Ellis, A. *Reason and emotion in psychotherapy,* 1962.

5.   Much of this challenging and altering step is the outgrowth of the work of Albert Ellis, Maxie Maultsby, and Donald Meichenbaum.

6.   Meichenbaum, D. H. Cognitive factors in behavior modification: Modifying what clients say to themselves. In C. Franks & T. Wilson (Eds.), *Annual review of behavior therapy: Theory and practice.* New York: Brunner/Mazel, 1973. Meichenbaum, D. H. The cognitive-behavioral management of anxiety, anger, and pain. In P. Davidson (Ed.), *Behavioral management of anxiety, depression, and pain.* New York: Brunner/Mazel, 1976. Also see: Ellis, A. *Growth through reason,* 1971.

6
Basic Types of Assertive Messages

There are many different ways to act assertively. Depending on what your goal is in a particular interaction—maintaining your relationship with the other person, achieving your objective, or maintaining your self-respect—one alternative may be more effective than another. The case of Fred and Paula shows the different assertive alternatives that can be used to approach a problem. Paula had agreed to talk with their son, Ronnie, about his low grades, but she didn't carry through on the agreement she made with Fred.

Option 1:   "Last week you said you'd talk to Ronnie about his low grades. I know you've been busy, yet I do think it's important that you talk to him. What do you think about doing it after dinner tonight?"

By using this assertive alternative, Fred is stressing the importance of their earlier agreement, making his request a little stronger by suggesting a specific time for the talk. With Option 2 the emphasis is a little different:

Option 2:   "I'm a little annoyed that you haven't talked to Ronnie like we agreed. Each day that goes by with no mention of his grades means another day lost for him to improve on his studies, and I'm very worried about that."

Here Fred is stressing his feelings in the situation: annoyance and worry. With Option 3 there is yet a different emphasis:

Option 3:   "I've been thinking about Ronnie's low grades. When we talked about it last week, the best idea seemed to be for you to talk with him because I get a little hot under the collar when I talk to him. But I get the impression that it's not so easy for you to talk to him either. Would you rather we worked out some other way of handling it?"

With the third alternative Fred stresses his understanding of Paula's feelings and his willingness to problem-solve and think of other alternatives.

Option 4:   "Honey, about Ronnie's low grades. I know you agreed that you're the best person to talk to him, yet I can see that each day something comes up so you don't get to it. What's making it hard for you? I'd like to help if I can."

In this case he is stressing his willingness to figure out what the problem is that's stopping his wife from carrying out her agreement.

These options give you an idea of how many different ways there are to approach a problem. Which option you choose depends on your goals and your assessment of what is most appropriate in your particular situation. Sometimes it is more productive to focus your assertiveness on devising other alternatives and figuring out what the problem is. It may be less disruptive to a relationship to emphasize your desires or wants rather than your feelings. In other situations, expressing your feelings of annoyance may be preferable so that you can clear the air and let the other person know that you want your feelings considered and what your limits are. (For example, "Frank, this is the second time in the last week that you've called to cancel a date simply because you've changed your mind. I feel hurt and very irritated about your doing this. I enjoy your company and would like to continue seeing you. But if it's going to go on like this, that's another matter entirely.")

This chapter presents six basic types of assertive messages.

These assertions represent only half of communication: sending your message to the other person. The other half of communication takes place when the person responds to you. The other person may do what you want, refuse, attack, deny, counter-complain, raise other issues, or express her own wants and feelings. Chapter 7 discusses how to listen to others when they send their messages back to you and how to problem-solve conflicts. Chapter 9 discusses how to persist, cope with aggressive communications, and deal with your own aggressive tendencies.

SIX BASIC TYPES
OF ASSERTIVE MESSAGES

I Want Statements

You use I Want statements when you say, "I want to do *this*," or "I want you to do *this*," while referring to a specific behavior. Also included in this category are "I'd like you to do this," "Would you do this?" "How about doing this," and "I'd appreciate it if you'd do this" statements. Here are some more examples:

- I do want to know what I did that made you angry but I don't want you to call me names.
- Yes, I'd like to get together for dinner tonight, but I don't want to go any place where I have to get dressed up.
- I'm in a hurry and would like to get served as quickly as possible.
- I want you to check with me first before you ask other people to join us for dinner.
- I'd like to think about your question and then get back to you.
- I'd like you to come on time for our dates.

Effects. I Want statements help you to clarify to both yourself and others what you really want. It gives the other person information which is necessary to know *how* to fulfill your wants. If the other person chooses not to fulfill your wants, at least you are relieved of the conflict of wanting, being afraid to ask, and worrying whether or not the other person will

157

do what you want. When the other person has his own wants that conflict with yours, the two of you can openly problemsolve the conflict and try to negotiate mutually agreeable compromises, figure out some other ways of getting what both of you want, or learn to live with it.[1]

Guidelines for Using I Want Statements. Sometimes people misinterpret a simple expression of preferences or wants as nonnegotiable demands. There are at least three ways in which you can reduce the likelihood of this misunderstanding occurring. A *first* way and probably the simplest is to ask the other person about her preferences or willingness to do what you want. Some examples follow:

- I'd like some encouragement on my work. Would you be willing to tell me about the good things you see in my work?
- Instead of going to that party, I'd just like to stay home and cuddle with you. What do you want to do?
- I want to drop a letter off at the post office before we go clothes shopping. Is that OK with you?

A *second* way is to quantify your wants on a verbal scale of "slightly"—"moderately"—"greatly"—"extremely," or on a numerical scale of 0 to 10.[2] By quantifying your wants, you can communicate more precisely how mild or strong your desires are, thus reducing the likelihood of others mistaking a minor want for a very strong one or vice versa. Some examples are:

- I want you to stop pressuring me about getting a new job; that's a 10 on a scale of 10!
- I'd like to eat Chinese food tonight; it's not a strong preference—about a 2.
- I very much want to work on this assignment alone and then give you a call if I run into a problem I can't handle.

A *third* way is to clearly state what your I Want statement means and what it doesn't mean. For example:

158

- I'd like you to stay overnight with me; that doesn't mean I expect you to nor that you must. I'd just like it if you would.
- I'd like to get together this week. That's just for information; no pressure if you can't make it.

I Feel Statements

These statements take the form of "When you did *that thing,* I felt *this way,*" "I liked it when you did *that,*" "I didn't like it when you did *that.*" *That thing* is a behavior that the other person did, and *this way* is your specific feeling.[3] Some examples are:

- When you touched my cheek at the dinner table, I felt really close to you.
- When you told our friends how we're pinching pennies to send Marcie to college, I felt embarrassed.
- I didn't like it just then when you told me to go on a diet.
- I feel sad when you talk about how you don't trust people to care about you.
- I liked it when you helped with the dishes without being asked.

Effects. I Feel statements help you express your feelings without attacking the self-esteem of the other person. They clarify for yourself and for others just precisely what you feel; this may reduce misunderstandings about the nature of your feelings. For example, when you feel disappointed, other people may assume that you feel angry. By describing the specific behavior you like or dislike, you give other people specific information that they can take into consideration when they make decisions about how they will act.

Guidelines for Using I Feel Statements. Consistently using only one feeling word to describe most of your feelings (e.g., "I'm upset") does not accurately convey your feelings to others, and it may keep you from discovering how you actually do feel. One woman consistently said that she was anxious virtually anytime she experienced an upsetting feeling; it took her some time to realize that at times she felt irritated (as opposed to anxious) or sad or lonely.

Instead of making a general statement about how you feel, specify the degree of the feelings you experience. For example, there are degrees of anger starting from a little annoyance all the way through to boiling mad. By quantifying your feelings, you can communicate them more accurately and thus reduce the chances of being misunderstood. This is particularly important when expressing annoyance. Other people may assume that your saying, "I'm angry," means you're *extremely* angry, when you actually mean "I'm a little irritated." [4]

When expressing irritation, it generally is a good idea to first describe the specific behavior you find offensive and then express your feeling. The reason for this is that many people get scared and immediately disoriented and defensive when the first words they hear are "I'm angry with you."

Mixed Feelings Statements

These statements take the form of naming more than one feeling and explaining where each is coming from.[5] Some examples are:

- My salary increase is a good one. I feel good that my work this year has been noticed, and I appreciate your going to bat for me. At the same time, I feel very disappointed that my raise still puts me below the male supervisors who've put in the same number of years I have. What can be done to put me at the same pay level as the rest of the staff?
- Vic, I've got some mixed feelings about what you just said. I'm thankful that you are willing to play handball with a raw beginner and that you pass on some tips about how I could improve. Yet I didn't like the *way* you told me. The extra comments about what a rotten player I am—that's unnecessary, and I found it irritating.

Effects. When people have mixed feelings, sometimes they say nothing. For example, a female supervisor might have felt that she couldn't express her disappointment about a salary increase because she also felt glad about getting a large increase,

160

even though her salary still was below that of male supervisors. When you can communicate both positive and negative feelings in response to the same situation, your ability to communicate is greatly improved. Moreover, the other person knows that his actions were neither all pleasant nor all unpleasant and is given clearer information about which parts of his behavior are acceptable and unacceptable.[6]

Guidelines for Using Mixed Feelings Statements. Although the two examples of Mixed Feelings statements showed the speakers expressing their feelings in one single communication, sometimes it is more appropriate, as well as effective, to allow the other person to respond to one set of feelings before introducing the second set. For example, it may have been better for the female supervisor to have first expressed her good feelings about the salary increase and allowed her boss to respond to that before saying that she also felt disappointed about still being paid less than the men who had the same experience and qualifications that she had.

Empathic Assertion

Often you want to do more than simply express your wants or feelings. At times you may also want to convey some sensitivity to the other person, especially when you are concerned that the other person might feel offended or put off by your assertiveness. In such cases the Empathic Assertion can be used.[7] It consists of a two-part statement. The first part states your recognition of the other person, recognizing one or more of the following:

- his situation (e.g., pressures, difficulties, lack of awareness)
- his feelings (e.g., sad, mad, glad, scared)
- his wants (e.g., to get a higher grade, to discuss a topic)
- his beliefs (e.g., that he's been unfairly treated).

Recognition does not mean sympathy (unless you are sincerely sympathetic) or agreement (unless you really do agree). A recognition statement simply indicates that you see, hear, acknowledge, realize the situation, feelings, wants, or beliefs of

161

the other person.

The second part of the Empathic Assertion is describing your situation, feelings, wants, or beliefs. Some examples are:

- I realize that you don't want to intrude on me or crowd my emotional space, yet I feel crowded.
- I know it's hard to say exactly when the truck will come, yet I'd like a ballpark estimate of the arrival time.
- I can see you're upset with me and in no mood to talk right now; I would very much like to talk it over when you're ready.
- I know that many of you would like to discuss this topic further in class today, yet I think we need to move on so that we can cover the material for today.
- Sounds like you're real disappointed and think that because you tried hard you should have gotten a higher grade . . . . Where I'm at is that even though you did try hard, your performance in class has not been at the minimal passing standards.

Effects. Many people find that they feel more comfortable acting assertively when they have first recognized the other person. Since it is necessary to take a moment to think about the other person's situation from her perspective before you express yourself, this type of assertion can help you keep yourself in perspective because it reduces the likelihood of your losing sight of the other person and reacting aggressively. Empathic Assertions are particularly helpful when the relationship with the other person is important and when you want to reduce the chances that the other person will become defensive or feel hurt. Very importantly, other people are more likely to hear your assertive message when they know that their message has been recognized first.

Guidelines for Using the Empathic Assertion. You should try to keep the empathic recognition part of your statement reasonably short. When it is very long, you possibly will become so involved in the other person's feelings or wants that you will lose sight of your own.

The empathic recognition statement shouldn't label or evaluate the personhood of the other or include derogatory phrases (e.g., "I realize that you've been goofing off all semester and now want me to ignore my integrity as a teacher and give you a higher grade than you deserve"). Such expressions are aggressive.

Avoid the gimmicky phrase, "I understand how you feel." This rarely demonstrates understanding and usually feels insincere to the other person. Describe what you understand; for example, "I understand *that you feel hurt about my criticism.* I don't want to hurt you, yet I think it's important that I let you know what I think you should improve on."

Often it is helpful to bridge your recognition statement and the statement of your wants with the words *and*, or *and yet.* You can also simply pause between the two statements. Bridges like these communicate that you consider both your recognition statement and the statement of your wants to be of equal importance. Bridging with the words *however* or *but* puts the emphasis on your wants and lessens the importance of the recognition statement. Compare these two communications: "I like you, and yet I find your smoking annoying" versus "I like you, but I find your smoking annoying." *But* lessens the weight of the previous statement; *and yet* gives both parts roughly equal weight. Of course at times you may want to place more importance on the statement of your wants. When that is what you want to do, you can say something like, "I realize you think I shouldn't be concerned about the fact you are married, but I am, and I'm not going to start a dating relationship with you."

Confrontive Assertion

The Confrontive Assertion is appropriate when there are discrepancies, for example, when the other person's words contradict her deeds, when there is a difference between what your friend said he'd do and he did do, or when there is a conflict between what a job description reads and what you are asked to do in a job.[8] The Confrontive Assertion has three parts:

1. Objectively describing what the other person said would be done

2. Describing what the other person actually did do
3. Expressing what you want.

The following are examples of Confrontive Assertions:

- I was supposed to be consulted before the final proposal was typed. But I see the secretary is typing it right now. Before she finishes it, I want to review the proposal and make whatever corrections I think are needed. In the future I want to get a chance to review any proposals before they're sent to the secretary.
- I thought that we had agreed that you were going to be more considerate towards students. Yet I noticed today that when two students asked for some information, you told them that you had better things to do than babysit for kids. As we discussed earlier, I see showing more consideration as an important part of your job. What is making it hard for you to carry that out?

Effects. In contrast to assertive confrontation, aggressive confrontation involves judging other people and trying to make others feel guilty, rather than describing their behavior. When discrepancies are confronted by simply describing them, it is much easier to deal with conflicts. The other person is also less likely to react defensively because he is not being personally attacked. The Confrontive Assertion is particularly helpful when you have previously asserted yourself and the other person has agreed to change his behavior, but has not carried through with the agreement. Thus the Confrontive Assertion is a good followup assertion to use.

Guidelines for Using the Confrontive Assertion. When using the Confrontive Assertion, you point out the *discrepancy* rather than confront the *person*. Contrast the impact of these two thoughts: "I'm going to confront *Sally* with her behavior," versus "I'm going to confront the *fact* that we made an agreement and Sally's not carrying through on it."

When there is a discrepancy between what a person said she would do and what she did do, avoid jumping to conclusions and assuming the worst possible motives. Find out what happened. Simply describe what you see in terms of specific behaviors. Quite often the problem lies with the original understanding, which may have been unrealistic or unclear and interpreted differently by the two parties.

Since the types of assertion presented in this chapter are not techniques but rather principles to guide your assertive behavior, the different types of assertion can be combined. For example, a combination of Confrontive Assertion, Empathic Assertion, and I Feel statements would produce a statement such as "I realize you've been very busy this week, and yet we did agree to talk about our vacation plans this weekend. The weekend's almost gone. I'd like to take out at least a half hour to talk. How does that sound to you? I'm afraid that if we don't do it this weekend, we'll never get plans going, and we'll miss out on renting the best resort cabins."

I Language Assertion

I Language Assertion is a particularly useful guide for expressing difficult negative feelings.[9] It involves a four-part statement in which you:

1. Objectively describe the other person's behavior or the situation that interferes with you
2. Describe how the other person's behavior or the situation concretely affects your life, for example, in terms of additional time, money, or effort
3. Describe your own feelings
4. Describe what you want the other person to do, for example, provide an explanation, change behavior, apologize, offer suggestions for solving the problem, give his reaction to what you've said.

The following are situations in which I Language statements can be helpful.

Nancy understood her friend Ann's desire to take advantage of an opportunity to date a man she liked, yet Nancy also felt irritated when Ann cancelled plans they'd made together so that Ann could go on a date. However, Nancy didn't feel that

165

she had the right to express her irritation to Ann. When she figured out the *concrete* or *tangible* effects that Ann's behavior had on her, she felt OK about expressing her irritation, realizing that her irritation didn't stem from jealousy or possessiveness but rather from the concrete effects. This is what Nancy finally said:[10]

> When you cancel a date with me so that you can go out with a man and I just get a few hours notice, *I don't have enough time to make other plans and I'm left with an empty evening.* I feel irritated about that and I'd like to work out an understanding with you about changing plans that we've made together.

Maria was upset about her boss's reports. She wanted him to write the reports in dark pencil, and at first she couldn't figure out a way of gracefully getting this across to him. Before talking to her boss, she wrote down the four parts of the I Language Assertion. She then decided to skip the feelings part, figuring that in this case she'd get her point across better without it. She also decided to include an Empathic Assertion to make it less likely that her boss would get offended. Here's what Maria eventually said:

> You're probably not aware of this, but when you turn in reports for me to type that have been written in light pencil, it takes me twice as long to complete them. I'd really appreciate it if you'd write them in dark pencil.

Effects. When you are able to specify concrete or tangible effects that another person's behavior has upon you—such as money, time, or effort—your I Language Assertions are likely to be more effective in making a positive impact on others since most people do not knowingly want to have their behavior result in tangible negative effects on others. When you are not able to specify such concrete effects, the effectiveness of your assertion depends on three factors.[11] One, you are more dependent on the degree to which the other person values your relationship or your feelings, as in the following cases:

When Harvey told his wife that he felt unloved and hurt when she wouldn't talk to him in the morning until after her first cup of coffee, she made a conscious effort to change her ways because she valued the relationship and the cost of changing herself was more than offset by the warmth she received from Harv in return.

Mrs. Cooper, a junior high school teacher, used the following I Language statement, which did not specify any concrete effects in terms of energy, time or money: "When you turn in themes that have a lot of bad grammar, I feel bad because then I think I'm not a good teacher. Please take more time with your work." As it turned out, one of her students did not value the relationship. As a matter of fact he thrived on knowing that he upset his teacher. He felt over-controlled by her persistent demands and criticism. Upsetting her was a way he used to get back at her.

Two, the effectiveness of I Language statements also depends on the degree to which the other person isn't engaged in a power struggle with us. Iola's problem is an example:

Iola wanted her teenage son to keep his room neat. She worked full time and did all the household chores with very little help from her son. Iola figured that the least her son could do was to keep his room really clean. This was her symbol that he cared for her and appreciated all the work she did.

Her son, on the other hand, believed that his room was his own territory; it was his symbol of his own growing independence as a young adult. When Iola insisted that he keep his room clean to her standards, she met with little success because they were both involved in a power struggle. She needed to problem-solve with him so that they would come to some mutually satisfactory compromise rather than to continue simply giving him I Language statements.

Three, the effectiveness of I Language statements depends on the degree to which the other person doesn't have a strong investment in continuing the objectionable behavior:

A college dean circled any errors in red ink, including minor typographical ones, in the reports completed by departmental chairpersons. Even though she knew that using red ink resulted in extra work for the secretaries and irritated everyone, she continued doing it. She was very angry with the smallest mistake made on reports and had a strong investment in using this method to show her disapproval.

Guidelines for Using I Language Statements. The most important part of the I Language statement is specifying the concrete or tangible effects. However, this is the most difficult part to describe, and some situations do not have such effects. Keeping the following examples in mind may help you specify the concrete effects in your I Language statements:

- When you are constantly interrupted and asked new questions, you may give incorrect information to the other person.
- When clothes are left on the floor, they have to be washed more frequently.
- When bills are not paid on time, misunderstandings arise.
- When employees take long rest breaks, the work piles up.
- When employees are late to work, the supervisor has to take extra time to reorganize others' schedules.
- When you're overworked, important details may skip your attention.
- When the stereo is on loud, it's harder to carry on a telephone conversation.
- When repair people don't keep appointments, your time is wasted.
- When people make commitments for you without checking with you first, you may have already made prior conflicting commitments and you're put in an awkward position.

To help yourself become more comfortable with I Language statements, it is often helpful to write out the four parts so that you can spend more time identifying the concrete or tangible effects.

168

SUMMARY

As you probably know only too well, two situations are almost never the same. Similarly, there are many different ways to assertively approach the same situation. Depending on the circumstances, one approach may be more effective than another in maintaining a relationship, achieving an objective, or maintaining self-respect. It will be helpful to restate the six basic types of assertive messages that were discussed in this chapter. They are:

1. I Want statements
2. I Feel statements
3. Mixed Feelings statements
4. Empathic Assertion
5. Confrontive Assertion
6. I Language statements.

Of course these messages represent only half of the communication process: sending messages to others. The next chapter discusses the other half of communication: receiving messages from others.

NOTES

1. In *Talking It Out,* Dr. Joseph Strayhorn, Jr., describes an I Want statement that he based on the work of Virginia Satir. See: Satir, S. *Conjoint family therapy.* Palo Alto, CA: Science and Behavior Books, 1967. Dr. Strayhorn also discusses the I Feel statement, based on the work of Thomas Gordon, and the Mixed Feelings statements. We appreciate his permission to use his definitions for these types of assertive messages.

2. Strayhorn, J. M. Jr. *Talking It Out.* Champaign, IL: Research Press Co., 1977.

3. Strayhorn, J. M. Jr., 1977.

4. Strayhorn, J. M. Jr., 1977.

5. Strayhorn, J. M. Jr., 1977.

6. Strayhorn, J. M. Jr., 1977.

7. The Empathetic Assertion and Cognitive Assertion were originated by Patricia Jakubowski-Spector. See Jakubowski-Spector, P. *An introduction to assertive training procedures for women.* Washington, DC: American Personnel and Guidance Association, 1973.

8. Jakubowski-Spector, P., 1973.

7
Effective Listening and Conflict Resolution

Expressing our wants, feelings, and opinions is an important part of being assertive. However, it's only half of communication and interpersonal effectiveness. The other half is listening and making a genuine effort to understand what the other person is communicating back to us. Listening skills are essential to constructively resolving conflicts between what we want and other people want.

EFFECTIVE LISTENING

If you lack effective listening skills, you are much more likely to misinterpret what others say, jump to conclusions, and inappropriately interrupt them. You are more likely to be preoccupied with your own assertive objectives and be blind to the legitimate points that others make. Instead of listening to others, you are likely to engage in self-listening (i.e., listening to only a little of what the other person is saying and thinking about what you are going to say, thus anticipating what the other person is actually saying rather than really listening).[1] In contrast, by using effective listening skills you can help others share their real needs and feelings with you. This is especially important when you are trying to discover why others persist in acting in ways they know are objectionable to you.[2] When other people have strong, negative reactions to your assertiveness, good listening skills can help clarify their feelings and clear up misunderstandings. Taking a few moments to put yourself in another's shoes and understand his point of view can reduce your impulse to immediately respond aggressively. Listening to others tends to encourage them to reciprocate and listen to you.

Effective listening is not the same as agreeing. Instead, it is taking time and leaving room for others while still reserving the right to disagree, make the final decision, or express your feelings and viewpoints.[3] If you do not have the time to listen or are preoccupied with your own problems or thoughts, it is usually better to be honest and tell the other person that you cannot listen at that moment, perhaps by saying, "Right now I've got several things on my mind that make it difficult for me to listen. I'd like to be able to give you my full attention, so I'd like to talk with you later. Is that OK with you?"[4]

Silent listening is using body language to communicate attentiveness while saying nothing except for "I see," "Go on," which lets the other person know you are listening. Though this communicates interest in what the other person is saying, it does not let the other person know that you are getting her message accurately, nor does it allow you to check out the degree to which you have accurately heard the other person. For this you need to use active listening by which you paraphrase or feed back the content of what the speaker said, the feeling behind the communication, or both in order to make sure that you have heard correctly.[5] Either kind of paraphrasing helps you avoid distorting others' statements and can help the speaker express herself more clearly. Also the paraphrasing process is very important during heated discussions. It gives both parties time to slow down and reason, rather than simply responding reflexively and thoughtlessly.[6]

When you paraphrase content, you use your own words to describe the speaker's basic message. Some examples of paraphrasing are:

- Then as far as you are concerned, you still want me to raise your grade, even though you realize that you have had C's on all your tests?
- Are you saying that you would like me to be less dogmatic when I give opinions?
- In other words, you would still like me to come to work on time, even though I take shorter lunch breaks and skip the coffee breaks entirely.
- What I am hearing you say is that my inviting friends over

without checking with you first is definitely not OK with you.

Often it is helpful to use lead-in phrases to paraphrase content. Some examples of such phrases follow:

- From your perspective . . .
- The way you see it is . . .
- Your point of view is . . .
- It seems to you . . .
- What you'd like me to know is . . .
- I guess what's important for you to get across to me is . . .

When you paraphrase feelings, use a feeling word such as sad, glad, mad, scared, happy to describe your perceptions of the speaker's state. The following are examples of paraphrased feelings:

- So you're really upset with me.
- Looks like you're feeling real proud of what you accomplished.
- That really made you feel good, huh?
- You sound like the more you think about my advice the more unsure you feel.
- I get the impression that you're irritated with what I just did. Am I right?[7]

Two Conversations

Calvin and Vivian work in the same school and are friends. In the following conversation, Calvin used simple assertiveness to defend himself against what he thought was unfair criticism.

Vivian: I've been concerned that you're getting selfish because of all the self-growth you've been going through lately.

Calvin: I don't think that I'm getting selfish. Sure, I think about myself and am absorbed in my work, but that's not the same thing as being selfish. (pause) Any other questions on that score?

Vivian: Well, what can I say?

Calvin: OK, I'm glad we settled that one . . . . What's been happening with you lately?

Vivian: Not much. How about you?

In the next conversation, he listened and used paraphrasing skills as well as assertiveness.

Vivian: I've been concerned that you're getting selfish because of all the self-growth you've been going through lately.

Calvin: I don't think that I'm getting selfish. Sure, I think about myself and am absorbed in my work, but that's not the same thing as being selfish. (pause) I am surprised to hear you say that. Have you seen me do something selfish?

Vivian: Well, not exactly. But I have been concerned about it.

Calvin: *Not exactly*. Have I done anything toward you that you felt was selfish?

Vivian: Well, last week you said that you were too tired to have dinner after work.

Calvin: You were very disappointed with me then?

Vivian: Yeah, it was like you were taking our relationship for granted and . . .

Calvin: And there's something else?

Vivian: Yeah, and it was my birthday.

Calvin: Oh, so you felt doubly hurt by me. Did you think I knew it was your birthday and didn't care?

Vivian: I could tell that you didn't realize it was my birthday.

Calvin: You're right. If I had known, I would have made a special point of being available that night. I'm sorry that we had that misunderstanding and that you've been feeling bad all this week. I didn't mean to do anything that would hurt you.

Vivian: Well, OK.

Calvin: I get the impression that you're not very satisfied with my apology. Am I right?

Vivian: I just think that as a friend you should have figured out when my birthday was so I wouldn't have to tell you. I've checked around and found out when *yours* is.

Calvin: Sounds like one of your definitions of friendship is that friends find out things even if they're not told. They figure out what the other person wants without having to be told.

Vivian: That's right.

Calvin: Vivian, I realize that you'd try to figure out what I want before I even say it and then do it for me. And I guess that's the way you try to show caring. For me, that's real scary because I don't think I can always know what's on your mind. It also means that I'm definitely going to guess wrong sometimes, like about dinner last week and your birthday.

Vivian: Mmmmm.

Calvin: It just occurred to me that maybe we've been doing a lot of guessing wrong. Like a couple of weeks ago during spring break, you kept calling early in the morning to make sure that I was working on that project I was having trouble with. Were you doing that because you guessed that I needed the help and you were going out of your way to "help" me even though I hadn't asked for it?

Vivian: Yeah, didn't that help?

Calvin: I wasn't straight with you at the time. Actually, I found the calls annoying, but I was trying to "help" you by letting you do that because I guessed that you needed to "help" me. I can see where each of us guessing about what the other person wants has led to some misunderstandings. I'd like to change that and be a lot more clear about what I want and stop my own guessing and making assumptions about you. Would you be willing to do that in return for me?

Vivian: I guess you've got a point there. But I have to do some more thinking about that. I don't like people doing things for me just when I ask them to.

Calvin: Are you saying that you need some time to sort this out?

Vivian: Yeah, I know we could talk more about it now, but

175

I'd like to figure it out alone.

Calvin: That's OK with me. I'd still like to celebrate your birthday. When can we do it?

Vivian: How about Friday night?

Calvin: Great!

Calvin and Vivian's second conversation shows how combining listening skills with assertiveness increases the ability to discover the source of misunderstandings and clarify problems so that conflicts can be resolved.

Listening to Others

Though listening to others has many advantages, some people fear that if they listen to other people, they won't get a chance to present their views. It is important for such people to identify the source of their fear and to develop some methods for protecting themselves and reducing their fear. Exercise 13 gives examples of common fears and provides you with space to identify your fears and ways you can cope with them. Exercise 14 can help you paraphrase and detect others' feelings.

Exercise 13   Protecting Yourself

Fear	How Can I Help Protect Myself?
I won't get a chance to present my views.	After a reasonable interval, I will paraphrase what the other person said and then state my own views. I can interrupt if the other person goes on endlessly. When possible, I will arrange discussions so that there is sufficient time for both of us to express ourselves.
I'll be seen as weak.	I will reduce head nods that may give the impression that I agree with the other person. I will remind myself that it

Exercise 13   Protecting Yourself (continued)

Fear

How Can I Help Protect Myself?

takes strength to listen and keep open to the legitimate points of others and that the other person will discover soon enough that I can assertively state my views as well as listen to hers.

I might make a fool out of myself if I paraphrase wrong.

I can give myself permission not to berate myself if I guess wrong about what the other person has communicated. The only thing that is likely to happen is that the other person will tell me that I'm wrong and will explain himself so that I will understand better. If I consistently paraphrase incorrectly, this will give me information that I need to listen more closely.

I might find out that I was incorrect in the position I've taken if I listen to the other person.

I can give myself permission not to berate myself and not to have to be perfect and always right.

I'll be swept away by the other person's feelings or arguments and will lose my ability to act assertively.

I can remind myself that I can listen, hear the other person, and still react to what I hear. I can think and feel at the same time. I can give myself permission to spot weaknesses and illogic in the other person's position. I can use coping skills to cope with my own feelings. (See Chapter 5.)

Exercise 13 Protecting Yourself (continued)

My Fear	How Can I Help or Protect Myself?
1.	1.
2.	2.

Exercise 14 Detecting and Paraphrasing Others' Feelings

In the blank spaces, write in the feelings the person is expressing and a sentence that paraphrases the feelings, content, or both.

1. "Now I've been a parent for years and I've had lots of experience in these matters. You're just letting your kids get away with murder. You're entirely too permissive."
   Feelings:

   Paraphrase:

2. "What do you expect anyway? I've got the house to run, kids to clean up after, and now you're mad because I forgot to tell you your boss called!"
   Feelings:

   Paraphrase:

3. "I had a dream last night. I dreamed the grandchildren came over to visit their old grandad. But that's dreams for you. Nobody comes over to see me anymore."
   Feelings:

Exercise 14   Detecting and Paraphrasing Others' Feelings
  (continued)

Paraphrase:

4. "If you take a job, it'll just ruin our marriage. There's no way I'm going to start washing the dishes and cooking food—that's your job!"
   Feelings:

Paraphrase:

5. "Why should I clean up my room? It's *mine*, and I'm perfectly comfortable with it. You're just too picky."
   Feelings:

Paraphrase:

6. "For heaven's sake, why would you want to go Dutch treat on this date? After all I invited you out for dinner."
   Feelings:

Paraphrase:

7. "I just can't seem to get along with my roommate. Sometimes I don't know what to do."
   Feelings:

Paraphrase:

8. "I've worked in this department for ten years. And now this new manager comes in and acts like he knows everything. If I disagree with him in any way, he just blows his stack. Oh what's the use."
   Feelings:

Paraphrase:

9. "How could you even think of taking a job when your

child is so young?"
Feelings:

Paraphrase:

10. "Do you think I should complain about my salary? Won't
that just make my boss upset?"
Feelings:

Paraphrase:

___

Key

1. Feelings: Confident that speaker has the answer, worried
   Paraphrase: "The way you see it, the problem seems like a
   simple one, and you're confident that you have
   the answer."
   "I guess you're worried about the kids and
   think I'm doing a bad job of raising them."

2. Feelings: Misunderstood, irritated, overwhelmed, guilty
   Paraphrase: "It's clear to me that you're irritated with me."
   "I guess you'd like me to realize that you're
   only human and can't be expected to take
   care of everything."

3. Feelings: Lonely, unloved
   Paraphrase: "Feeling lonely and a little blue?"
   "Are you saying you would like to have the
   family visit you more often?"

4. Feelings: Worried, angry, determined
   Paraphrase: "I guess that the very thought of my taking a
   job really upsets you."
   "Sounds like you're worried about how things
   might change around the house, and you're

real determined that there's no way you'll change anything that you do."

"I'm getting the message that you're assuming that as soon as I take a job, I'll try to stick you with all the jobs I hate. Do I understand you correctly?"

5. Feelings: Picked on, irritated
   Paraphrase: "So from your point of view, you're satisfied with the room and see no problem."
   "Feeling irritated with me?"
   "As far as you're concerned, I'm just being too tough on you."

6. Feelings: Surprised, embarrassed
   Paraphrase: "I guess that really came as a surprise to you."
   "Did I embarrass you by saying I'd like to go Dutch?"
   "As far as you're concerned, I shouldn't even have considered going Dutch, huh?"

7. Feelings: Discouraged, worried
   Paraphrase: "Sounds like the roommate situation is really getting you down."

8. Feelings: Discouraged, irritated, tempted to give up
   Paraphrase: "You sound discouraged."
   "Sounds like you just don't know what to do with him."

9. Feelings: Surprised, shocked, displeased
   Paraphrase: "I guess it's hard for you to understand how I could do that."
   "I guess that really comes as a surprise to you."
   "Sounds like you really disapprove of women with young children working."

10. Feelings: Worried, unsure, scared, uncomfortable
    Paraphrase: "I guess the thought of raising the salary issue with her scares you."

> "Sounds like you're not sure that's a good idea."
> "I get the impression you're not too sure you want to risk it."

Using Door Openers

When you assertively refuse a request, give criticism, or express your feelings or opinions, the other person may hesitate to directly express his negative reactions. Instead he may act sullen, hurt, or hostilely silent and simply clam up, especially if you have power over him, if he is having difficulty handling his feelings about the situation, if he thinks he "shouldn't" have, or if he is afraid that you will ridicule his true feelings. When a person clams up, misunderstandings or breakdowns in communication cannot be openly dealt with. This has especially important consequences in work and personal relationships. Since people sometimes need time and emotional space to sort out their reactions before sharing them, ask for reactions in a nondemanding, nonjudgmental way. There are several ways to do this.

Asking for Reaction. The simplest way to ask for a reaction is to do so straightforwardly. The following are examples:

- What's your reaction to what I've said?
- How do you feel about my saying no?
- What do you think of what I've said?
- It would help me if you would tell me what reaction you have.

Asking for the other person's reaction relieves you of the pressure of guessing and worrying about what's going through her mind. It shows that you value her reactions and that you assume she has a reaction that she is entitled to express. It communicates your willingness to hear her side of the story and consider what she has to say, and it demonstrates that you really believe that effective communication is a two-way street.

Asking for Message Received. People often have negative reactions to a message because they have received it incorrectly. There are many reasons for not "getting the message." The receiver may receive our communication through a distorting filter, hearing suggestions as personal criticism, hearing requests as demands, or hearing lack of agreement as personal disrespect. Sometimes the speaker doesn't communicate the message clearly. The husband-wife exchange in Figure 15 (page 184) demonstrates the problems that can be caused when the speaker does not communicate clearly.[8] Their encounter shows how important it is to ask for information about the specific message the other received, for example, saying:

- I sent you a message; what message did you think you got from me?
- I've been talking for a while; what's the basic message you've gotten from me?
- What's the message you think I'm trying to get across to you?

When the message received is different than the one intended, it is important to clarify what you meant to communicate, for example, saying:

- I didn't mean to imply that you're stingy. What I meant to say was that I don't understand why you don't want to spend money on fun things and instead want to put it into savings.
- So you thought I was criticizing you for not doing the assignment the way I asked. Actually, I wasn't feeling at all critical but instead was thinking that you were showing good initiative for figuring out how to do it another way.
- I'm glad you told me the message that came across to you. That gives me a chance to clarify what I really meant to say.

When a discussion gets very heated, as in the husband-wife con-

Figure 15 Communicating Clearly

Husband Unspoken Intent or Impact (He thinks)	Spoken Message	Spoken Message	Wife Unspoken Intent or Impact (She thinks)
She's got a new sweater. I wonder if it is new. She looks good in it.			
	Is that a new sweater?	I got it on sale!	He thinks I'm a spendthrift!
Boy, is she nasty. Well, I have been denying myself a new pipe, sticking to our budget.	Where did you buy it?		
			I'm not putting up with this third-degree police investigation!
		None of your business!	
I'll show her.	I'm going to buy a new pipe. I'll show you whose business it is!		
		I don't care what you do.	He certainly is childish.

From *A Couple's Guide to Communication* by J. Gottman, C. Notarius, J. Gonso, & H. Markman. Champaign, IL: Research Press Co., 1976. Used with permission.

flict, these steps can be taken to stop the cycle:

1. Call for a Stop Action, which means stopping the interchange and focusing on the process of the discussion itself, e.g., asking how the other person feels, commenting on how the discussion has gotten heated, etc.
2. Ask for information on the message that was received.
3. Identify the source of the misunderstanding.
4. Clarify what you meant to communicate.[9]

Figure 16 (page 186) presents the husband-wife interchange with the Stop Action technique.

Asking for the specific message the other person received is a powerful way of clearing up misunderstandings. Also everyone has idiosyncratic ways of expressing himself. Checking on what actually was communicated can help you understand your own peculiarities of expression and avoid those behaviors that cause communication breakdowns and misunderstandings.

Asking for Reaction Based on Body Language. Often it isn't what a person says but what she does that leads us to misinterpret her reaction. Asking for a reaction based on body language simply means asking for an interpretation of those gestures that led you to think that the other person was reacting strongly to your statement, describing your feelings (optional), and requesting that the person express her reactions directly.[10] You might ask one of the following questions:

- Your tone of voice leads me to believe that you are upset with me. I'm interested in hearing what is on your mind. Would you be willing to share that with me?
- As we have been talking, I've noticed a kind of wry smile on your face like you were thinking what is this jive I'm giving you. Would you tell me what's been going through your mind as I've been talking?
- I'm concerned. You're frowning and I'm not sure if that means you don't understand what I've said or that you disagree. It would help me if you would tell me what your frown means.

Figure 16   Stop Action Communication Technique

Husband Unspoken Intent or Impact (He thinks)	Spoken Message	Spoken Message	Wife Unspoken Intent or Impact (She thinks)
She's angry. I wonder where we missed each other. What did I say that made her angry?	Hey, wait a minute! Stop the action! How are you feeling now?		He cares about me. He senses something has gone wrong.
		I am feeling accused of spending too much money.	
Where did she get that? I didn't say that.	What did I say to give you that feeling?	It was your questioning me about the sweater. The way you kept asking questions.	Maybe he didn't mean to accuse me.
And I thought I was going to compliment her. But she was so nasty.	I liked the way you looked in it and I just wondered if it was new.	I guess I was too sensitive to your questions.	
I'll check Intent/Impact.	I don't think you've been a spendthrift if that's what you felt I was saying.	I misunderstood then. I'm really glad you like my new sweater.	

From *A Couple's Guide to Communication* by J. Gottman, C. Notarius, J. Gonso, & H. Markman. Champaign, IL: Research Press Co., 1976. Used with permission.

Asking for a reaction based on body language tends to make it more likely that the other person will respond to your question than if you were more global and said, "You seem angry." People tend to feel less defensive when specific body language is noted than when general feelings are attributed to them.

Another alternative is to use an Empathic Assertion, saying, for example:

- I guess you are probably feeling under pressure and would rather not talk about how you feel. Yet I would appreciate it if you would.
- Right now you are glaring at me. Yet when I ask what's wrong, you shrug your shoulders and say nothing.
- I have no idea what's bothering you or what I have done to upset you, so I'm at a loss as to what to do.
- I feel really unhappy when you are silent. I don't want to crowd you if you need some time and emotional space to sort out your feelings.
- I do want to hear what is on your mind. Would you be willing to talk about it? If not now, when would be a good time?
- If we talk it over, I'll make every effort to work out a mutually satisfactory compromise.

These kinds of questions can help create a positive atmosphere for discussion and solving problems.

NEGOTIATING AGREEMENTS

In varying degrees all relationships hold the potential for satisfaction, fun, support, and warmth, as well as for conflict, disagreement, and opposition. In the best of relationships there are times when you can become disappointed, scared, hurt, or irritated by the other person. Inevitably there are times when someone does something that prevents, obstructs, or interferes with your actions. You may disagree about goals and ways of reaching those goals, or your needs may differ. Very often, two people have conflicting expectations about how each should act toward the other.[11] A key to relating more satisfactorily with other people—and thus increasing your sense of personal fulfillment and control over your life—lies in how you handle the conflicts that come up in relationships. Effective listening skills are an important part of this process, and so is the ability to give and take when confronting a problem.

Many people incorrectly believe that a conflict automatically must be their fault or that they should be able to handle a conflict so well that the problem never recurs. Other, similar kinds of misconceptions include:

- You must win the conflict in order to be OK.
- Any sort of compromise means losing and forever being less powerful than the other person.
- Conflict should be avoided at any cost.
- Your solution is the only worthwhile one.
- All conflicts must be resolved.
- Compromise inevitably leads to bad feelings.
- Long-enduring or important conflicts can be handled easily in one discussion.
- There is one party who is right and one who is wrong in any conflict.
- The party who is in the right must/shall get what he wants.
- To be unsuccessful in resolving a conflict means being inadequate.

Such thinking is dysfunctional and needs to be challenged and changed because it can interfere with your ability to constructively resolve conflicts.

Some conflicts can be resolved by simply explaining how you feel or what you want. Some can only be resolved by persistently assertive behavior, for example, by repeatedly refusing an unreasonable request or by returning defective merchandise to the seller and insisting on a refund. In yet other situations, it is more appropriate as well as effective to discuss and *problem-solve* the conflict rather than to continually repeat wants or feelings. This is often the best way to deal with an ongoing conflict that hasn't been resolved because what we want interferes with the other person's felt needs or goals.

188

A Problem-Solving Model

To successfully solve problems and negotiate agreements both parties can live with, it is important to negotiate the conflict on the basis of what objectively makes sense—taking into consideration the needs and feelings of both parties—as opposed to who is the most powerful or the most right. The most common model for problem solving and negotiating has been popularized by Dr. Thomas Gordon.[12] It involves these six steps:

Step One: Defining the problem
Step Two: Generating possible solutions
Step Three: Evaluating the solutions
Step Four: Making the decision
Step Five: Determining how to implement the decision
Step Six: Assessing the success of the solution

Step One. The first step in problem solving is recognizing that there is a problem, not just admitting that a problem exists, but defining it in terms that are clear to both parties. The discussion between Linda and her mother is an example.

Mom: I'm really upset with how dirty your room is. I realize that you're entitled to your privacy, and yet when I walk into the room and see dirty dishes around and candy wrappers and clothes on the floor, I feel irritated. I'd like us to figure out an agreement that would be acceptable to both of us. What do you think of that?

Linda: It's my own room, and I don't think it should upset you.

Mom: That's the bind I feel I'm in. On the one hand I realize it is your own room, and you're a young adult and are entitled to keep it the way you want to. On the other hand, I'm worried that we'll get bugs because of the food and dirty dishes. Also when your clothes are left on the floor and chairs, it makes extra work for me in ironing and washing. And I feel embarrassed when relatives visit and see your room.

189

Linda: Oh, Mom, really. I feel like a kid when you check up on me.

Mom: OK, so you don't want me to check up on you. I have the impression that it also irritates you to have to put your plates in the dishwasher immediately after your snack. And I can understand that you don't like to hang up your clothes right away. Am I right about these things?

Linda: You got it.

Mom: OK, so those are your needs, and mine are to not have bugs, not be embarrassed, and not have to wash and iron so often.

Step Two. The second step is identifying possible solutions.

Mom: What ideas do you have on how we can solve this problem? Let's just say everything we can think of and not judge the ideas until they're all out. OK?

In the discussion the following solutions were generated:

1. Keep door closed so that Mom doesn't see mess and won't get upset.
2. Buy bug spray.
3. Linda will take dirty dishes out of her room before she goes to bed.
4. Hire someone to clean up the house.
5. Mom will clean up Linda's room.
6. Linda will wash and iron her own clothes.

Step Three. Once all of the possible solutions have been identified, they can be sorted out.

Mom: Let's take a look at the list and see what we think of them and which ones we like and don't like.

Linda: I don't really like the one about your cleaning up the room for me. I just said that as a joke. Actually if you did that, I couldn't find some of my things that way.

190

Mom: OK, let's scratch that one. I don't like the one about just closing the door and leaving the room as it is because that doesn't take care of the bug problem and extra washing and ironing work for me.

Mom and Linda continued discussing the solutions until they arrived at a solution.

Step Four. Once you feel that you have reached a solution, state it clearly. You may want to revise it.

Linda: OK, so we agree that I'll keep my door closed and you won't invite any relatives in to see the room. I'll empty out the dishes from my room before I go to bed, and you'll make sure that the clean dishes are out of the dishwasher. I'll pick up my clothes off the floor before I go to bed.
Mom: That sounds like a good solution, but before we decide for sure, how about if I picture walking past your room with the door closed and see how that feels. You picture yourself at 10:30 at night and you're ready to go to bed, and it's time to pick up your clothes and put away the dishes. (pause) How does that feel? Is it realistic?
Linda: Feels like too much work!
Mom: So that didn't quite work out for you; it was OK for me to have your door closed.

They discussed this and arrived at the solution that Linda would put away the dirty dishes and food in her room every day. She would be responsible for her own clothes and whether or not she picked them up. Mom would continue washing the clothes but Linda would do her own ironing. Every Saturday Linda would pick up her clothes and straighten her room.

Step Five. When you have agreed on a solution, establish when it will go into effect.

Mom: When do you want to start this? How about today?

Linda: OK with me.

Mom: How shall we do it if I forget and complain about your room or you forget to straighten up on Saturday?

Linda: OK, if you complain, I'll remind you of our agreement, and if I forget, you remind me.

Mom: And you'll do it without complaining?

Linda: As long as you don't complain but just remind me in a nice way.

Mom: OK, it's a deal.

Step Six. Mom and daughter agreed to reevaluate the solution in three weeks to see how it is working.

Considerations in Using the Model

Defining the Problem. It is important not to state the conflict in terms of nebulous gripes that both parties have with each other, as for example, in the case of Bob and Karen:

Bob: You're inconsiderate.

Karen: I am not. You're too demanding!

There are several better ways to state the problem causing the conflict. One is to clearly describe specific objectionable behaviors, their effects, and/or give a positive suggestion. For example, Bob and Karen might approach their disagreement in this way:

Karen: When you come home from work and immediately ask to see the mail and read the newspaper and won't talk to me, I feel unimportant. I would appreciate it if you would ask me about my day and spend about 15 minutes talking with me before you read.

Bob: Well, what I object to hearing is complaints about how the kids acted and the washing machine breaking down the first thing I walk in the door. It just overwhelms me. I'd like you to leave me alone until supper and then discuss problems or whatever later in the evening.

192

In this case, the conflict is that Karen would like to talk about the day, which may include complaints, and Bob would like to withdraw and talk later.

If the other person globally complains about your behavior, you can help him become more specific by asking questions, for example, "What do I do that feels inconsiderate to you? Can you give me an example of when I've done that recently? What specifically do I do that bothers you?"[13]

Another alternative is to state the problem in terms of unmet needs rather than positive suggestions or solutions to meet these needs.[14] This approach tends to open up more possibilities for meeting these needs. The discussion between Linda and her mother (see page 189) illustrates how helpful it can be when both parties to a discussion focus their attention on unmet needs (e.g., not to worry about the bugs, not to have to immediately pick up clothes) instead of focusing on competing solutions to the needs (e.g., Linda to clean up the room to Mom's standards versus Mom to totally ignore the state of the room). This led to a more creative solution than if either had continued to push for the other person to accept her particular solution.

Generating Possible Solutions. The key to resolving a conflict is to have both parties brainstorm a variety of solutions and to resist the temptation to evaluate them at this point. Some possibilities include:

- What are some of the possible solutions to this problem?
- Let's see how many ideas we can come up with.
- What are some things we might do?
- There must be a lot of different ways we can solve this problem.
- What ideas do you have for solving this problem?
- What are some solutions we might try?[15]

Evaluating the Solutions. It is at this step that the solutions are critically examined. It is important that all parties assertively express their feelings about the proposed solutions, being clear which ones are unacceptable. In rejecting a particular solution, it's a good idea to briefly explain what the negative effects of the solution are, why it does not fulfill your needs, or why it seems unfair. The process of evaluating the solutions may be started by saying:

- It seems like we have generated all the solutions we can think of. Let's take a look at them now, and see what we think of them.
- Are any of these solutions unacceptable to you?
- Which of these solutions would best help us both to meet our needs?
- Which ones do you like best? Which ones do you like least?

The goal of this process is to identify a solution that meets the needs of both parties. If either party has strong objections to a particular solution, it should be eliminated.[16]

Making the Decision. When a solution has been identified as the one that's satisfactory to both parties, it is a good idea for both people to picture how it will be carried out, for example, by saying:

- If we accept this solution, what do you think the effect will be?
- We seem to agree on this one; do you think it would solve our problems?
- Where could we fail?[17]

If the parties can't find any mutually satisfactory solutions, another brainstorming session or an alternative strategy may be needed. (Alternatives to assertion are discussed later in this chapter.)

Determining How to Implement the Decision. Problem-solving efforts may lead nowhere when the decisions do not get implemented.[18] Sometimes the parties never specify when the decision will be implemented, who shall do what, or how failure to adhere to the decision shall be handled. These matters must be defined and understood clearly if the solution is to be suc-

194

cessfully implemented.

Assessing the Success of the Solution. In their desire to resolve the conflict, people sometimes underestimate their needs or agree to solutions which are unrealistic for them and then have a hard time carrying out the agreement. It's a good idea after a reasonable length of time to check how satisfied both parties are with the agreed-upon solution. For example, you might say, "Are you satisfied with the way the solution is working out?" or "Do we need to make any modifications in our agreement?" If the person has not carried through on the agreement, it is good to discuss what happened and to find ways of dealing with the obstacles that made it hard for her to live up to her part of the agreement.

Overcoming Blocks to Negotiating Agreements

Clamming Up or Refusing to Discuss the Conflict. The door openers discussed earlier can be used when the other person clams up. Listening and paraphrasing can also be helpful, as in George and Jack's disagreement:

George: I just don't want to discuss this anymore. It's a waste of time as far as I'm concerned.

Jack: So you're skeptical about the whole thing and a little irritated that I want to talk about the problem again.

George: Yeah, I'll say that. What's the use? We've been over this again and again, and we never seem to get anywhere.

Jack: I can see that you're discouraged. I've been discouraged, too. I think that one of the things that's gone wrong in the past when we've tried to discuss this problem is that I, for one, have tried to convince you that you were wrong and I was right. I'm not going to do that anymore. This time I'd like to see if we can find a solution we can both live with, and I'll stop selling my one solution. Are you willing to give it another chance?

Selling a Solution and Not Listening. When the other person tries to sell you on his point of view, you can give feedback about the message that is coming across. For example you might respond, "The message I'm getting is that there's only one solution for this problem and that's yours and that you're not interested in what I have to say. I want my views considered too." Or your response might be empathically assertive: "I realize that your solution is very important to you, yet if I'm to have an investment in working out the conflict, I'll need to have my desires heard and considered, too."

Summarizing Self. Each person simply keeps restating her position.

Mary: I want you to spend more time with the kids.
Tom: I work hard at the office, and I need to relax. The kids sure aren't relaxing to me.
Mary: The kids need a father.
Tom: No one appreciates how my work drains me, and the kids just get on my nerves.
Mary: Sure the kids are draining. They get on my nerves, too, yet I don't give up being a mother. They need a father, not just a mother.
Tom: If I didn't have to work outside of the home on this job, I could do the parenting bit better. But frankly, I just get home exhausted. Do you realize what I have to put up with at work?

When a disagreement reaches this kind of impasse, it's as though each person thinks that *if only* the other person would understand how logical his point is, there wouldn't be any problem. The result is that neither person is listened to, and both feel misunderstood. One antidote to this problem is following the Stop Action technique outlined earlier (see page 185).[19]

Cross-Complaining. With this kind of problem, every time one person brings up what she thinks is a reasonable issue, it is met by a stronger countercomplaint that makes it impossible to resolve either issue. This discussion between Alice and Fred is an example:

Alice: I want to talk with you about your giving me more help with cleaning up the kitchen after we eat.

Fred: I should give you *more* help? What about all the times I have to drive you places. Just why won't you learn how to drive?

Alice: Helping me clean up has nothing to do with driving. Besides, I do all the cleaning of the apartment, too.

Fred: And that brings up another thing. You keep this place so perfect that I'm afraid to sit in the front room. Why do you have to be such a perfectionist!

Alice: I'm a perfectionist? What about you and the car? If you want to know why I don't drive, it's because you're constantly criticizing me!

Even though cross-complaining feels like a "tit for a tat" and the person is often countercomplaining in order to defend himself and attack the other person, the complaints are often *legitimate* ones. One way out of cross-complaining is to paraphrase the content of the complaint and the feelings of the other person, list the complaints that both parties have with each other, and make an agreement to deal with one complaint at a time during the problem-solving discussion session.[20]

ALTERNATIVES TO ASSERTION

Sometimes listening skills are ineffective. Knowing precisely what the problem is only causes frustration because you cannot negotiate it. In some situations you can't be assertive. When it is not appropriate to be assertive, the risks of assertive behavior are too great, or assertive communication efforts have not produced positive changes in the other person's behavior, you still have at least two sets of alternatives: you can change the environment or you can change yourself.

Changing the Environment
When assertive behavior isn't effective or appropriate, you can sometimes change the physical surroundings. This means

197

doing such things as "child-proofing" your home so that you won't have to constantly reprimand or limit a young child's behavior; getting a second TV set when there are frequent arguments about which program the family will watch; modifying courses when students' disinterest is partially caused by an inadequate curriculum; or enriching the jobs of workers who aren't motivated to use their abilities.

Changing Yourself

Alternative A: Developing Other Ways of Taking Care of Yourself. In some cases you can develop ways of taking care of yourself and meeting your needs which do not require other people to change to accommodate you. This means figuring out how you can get your major needs met without support, change, or input from others.

Gloria requested a job transfer within a large company to another state so that she could be closer to her family. Being a new employee and unfamiliar with the project that was assigned to her, she was eager to do a good job and learn the project as quickly as she could, but she wasn't getting enough assistance from her boss. She became frustrated to the point that she didn't want to go to work. She believed that her boss had an "attitude" against her and that he was purposely frustrating her efforts to do the best job she could. Gloria initially focused her efforts on changing her boss's attitude, but realizing that this was going nowhere, she decided to see what behavior of hers she could change.

The first thing she did was to closely observe her own feelings at work, become more aware of her boss's actions towards her, and more particularly, become aware of her reaction to him. After some self-observation, she was able to pinpoint specific things that she did not like about her boss, two of which are described here.

(1) My boss is very unorganized; because of this he cannot set priorities. He is constantly giving me work with the impression that it is very important to get it done as soon as possible. When I ask him to set priorities on work that he has already given me (while stressing

the fact that it is impossible for me to do everything at once), he won't. He responds by saying that everything he gave me is important to do and to work until I get it done.

She asked herself the following questions:

- *What do I want?* "Information on which work priorities to fulfill."
- *What makes this want important?* "Without this information I may be working on the wrong set of priorities and be subject to criticism by my boss because I haven't fulfilled the priorities he considers important."
- *How am I currently trying to get this want fulfilled?* "I ask him to tell me which priorities are important, and he won't give me this information."
- *How is this method working out?* "Poorly."
- *What are some things I could do to fulfill this want?* "I could use my own best judgment in establishing my work priorities. Periodically, I could tell or advise my boss about the ones I've established and see if he has any reaction to my judgments. Alternatively, in the absence of negative reactions from him I could assume that my judgments are good ones."

Solution: I now set my own priorities concerning my work assignments. I make the decisions on what I think is most important to get done first. My decisions are sound, based on my previous working experience at the company in another city. I keep an accurate daily log of work assignments, work completed and when, and decisions that I made and why. In case my boss or someone else (like his boss) questions my reasons for making certain decisions, I can go back to that day and see why I made a particular decision. This makes me feel more relaxed. I feel that my judgment is good, and I am able to get my assignments done fast and efficiently.

(2) My boss is an egotist and resents anyone who knows more about a particular portion of a project than he does. Consequently he does not inform his employees of everything they need to know to do their assignments correctly. He even neglects to tell us about important changes that have been made in the project that we need to

199

know to get our assignments done. He normally volunteers the information once he knows that we are having problems completing our assignments. This can be very frustrating when we do something that does not work correctly only because we don't have the correct information to get the assignments completed.

Again she asked herself the following questions:

- *What do I want?* "Information about the job I'm supposed to do and information about any important changes that have been made."
- *What makes this want important?* "I waste time and energy doing things that do not work correctly only because I didn't have the correct information."
- *How am I currently trying to get this want fulfilled?* "Ask him and he won't tell me—even when I point out the tangible effects on me."
- *How is this method working out?* "Rotten."
- *What are some things I could do to fulfill this want?* "I could check out everything the boss tells me to do with other people. If it looks to me that doing something the way he tells me to do it will not work, then I'll find another way to do it. If it seems to me that I'm lacking a certain piece of vital information to do the job, I'll ask him directly instead of waiting, or I'll ask someone else in the department."

Solution: I do the above things and just show him the results. I don't tell him that I never did the assignment the way he wanted me to do it, and usually all he wants to see are the results anyway!"

Gloria reported that she feels much better about going to work now. As she said, "I know what the problems are and I have been able to change my behavior to counteract these problems. In so doing, I have saved myself from worry and frustrations. I have even won respect from my boss, and he shows confidence in my abilities!"

A fifty-eight-year-old grandmother suffered from high

blood pressure and was so worried about family problems that she felt the need to take tranquilizers daily in addition to her hypertension medicine. She kept an A-B-C behavioral chart to help her identify her worries and the results of her actions.

A. What happened just before she got upset; i.e., what she was thinking, what she and other people were doing.
B. What she did; i.e., what she said, actions she took, etc.
C. Consequences or results of her actions on herself and other people.

Keeping this chart of all significant events that led to her feeling upset and worried brought her to these observations:

> I worry about my husband, who is recently retired, and the drinking he does every day at a local bar, visiting old friends (what happened before I got upset). I've tried talking to him, asking him not to do it, crying, begging, yelling (what I did). Consequently, I feel upset and he continues to drink, something that he's done for years (what the consequences were).
> I worry about my daughter, whose husband has moved out of state for a job. She spends far too much time in bars, dancing, and associating with unmarried women friends. I've tried talking to her, and she just laughs in my face or else we get into an argument.

As a result of her self-observation she realized that she was going to stop worrying herself to death over things she had no direct control over. As she put it, "The people I worry about will still be doing the same thing when I am dead, so why should I worry myself sick about them. They know how I feel about what they're doing, and I realize how they feel. No one is willing to change, so rehashing the same thing over and over again isn't getting me anywhere except closer to the grave. I need to do something else with my life than play watchdog for the family." As a result of her observation she joined Weight Watchers and started losing weight. Though she got no encouragement from her husband, she did get encouragement from friends and club members. She joined a church group and her grandson's PTA. She also located a nursery for the younger grandchildren and told her daughter that she was unwilling to babysit any longer. The nursery was close to her home so that she could pick up the children at the end of the day; however, she decided that she could do without the money and hassle that occurred with her daughter when she babysat the children. After several months her blood pressure returned to normal, and she stopped taking the tranquilizers.

Alternative B: Reanalyzing the Problem and Determining Whether You Are Protecting Others from the Consequences of Their Behavior. When people are protected from the natural consequences of their behavior, they have little motivation or reason to change. Acting on this alternative does not mean supplying new negative consequences for the undesired behavior but rather simply letting others experience the natural consequences of their behavior. Going out of your way to punish someone's undesirable behavior can be effective in decreasing unwarranted behavior. However, this is an alternative to be used with considerable caution since it may produce undesirable side-effects. It can arouse many emotions, such as anxiety and aggression on the part of the other person. If she is strongly motivated to continue the undesired behavior, she may continue it as soon as the punishment is discontinued, especially if she doesn't have any more constructive behaviors to replace it with.

Beth worked with a fellow social worker, Eugene, who was frequently gone from the agency and wouldn't tell anyone how he could be reached or when he would return. When his clients called, Beth listened to their complaints, "covered" for Eugene, and ended up taking care of his clients. This took a lot of extra time and subjected her to unnecessary stress in dealing with the clients' irritation. When Beth complained to Eugene about his behavior, he laughed it off and refused to cooperate. When Beth complained to their supervisor, he just responded with, "Well, what can you do with Eugene?"

As long as Eugene was not experiencing the consequences of his own behavior, that is, dealing with his own clients' complaints, he had no real reason to change. Even though Beth and the supervisor occasionally complained, Eugene had learned to let their complaints run like water off his back. Finally Beth calmly informed Eugene that she would no longer lie to his clients about his whereabouts, nor would she do his work for him. She would, she said, tell his clients the truth—that she didn't know where he was, that he had not left word, that she didn't know when he would return, and that she would advise them to take up the matter with him. During the next few days, Beth didn't go out of her way to be friendly or unfriendly; she simply kept up the usual social courtesies. The results were that, after a few days of alternatively sulking and calling her names, Eugene changed his behavior, staying at the office more often and leaving explicit information when he left.

Alternative C: Reanalyzing the Problem and Determining Whether the Person Has the Skills to Engage in the Desired Behavior. Sometimes people are unresponsive to assertive communications simply because they are unable to do what someone wants them to do. If they do not, you will need to redirect your efforts.

A bank employee left his desk several times a day and didn't arrange for anyone to cover his responsibilities. Consequently, bank customers and officials couldn't get needed information. Though his supervisor repeatedly asked him to arrange for a replacement and the employee said that he would, he never did. As the supervisor reanalyzed the problem and asked, *"What stops this person from doing what I want,"* that is, arranging for others to cover his desk, several things became clear: (1) the employee continually underestimated the length of time that he would be away from his desk; (2) he lacked the assertive skills to ask for help; and (3) he was afraid that the other workers would think that he wasn't doing his job. Upon obtaining this information, the supervisor redirected his efforts to having the employee keep a record of how long he estimated he would be away from his desk and how long he was actually away, helping him practice asking for help, and lastly the supervisor spoke to the other workers in the area and made it clear that he wanted them to help fill in when needed.

In another case, a student counseling service receptionist

203

kept interrupting the psychologists' counseling sessions with calls from clients. Staff members' requests to hold all but emergency calls did not result in any changes. Upon reanalyzing the problem, one of the psychologists, Jim, realized that the receptionist had not always had trouble discriminating which calls were emergencies. In fact, the problem had started about a month previously. When Jim asked himself, *"What other things were happening about the time the problem started?"* he remembered that the receptionist's father had taken ill with terminal cancer and was in the hospital dying for the last month. Most likely the receptionist was not able to discriminate who needed immediate help and who didn't at this time. Many calls probably sounded like they came from desperately ill people. Realizing this, staff members redirected their efforts to sympathizing with the receptionist's current state of mind and arranging to have another person screen client's requests to talk to the psychologists when they were tied up in private sessions.

Alternative D: Reanalyzing the Problem and Determining Whether Assertive Expressions of Irritation are Actually Increasing the Undesired Behavior. In some cases assertive expressions of irritation actually make the problem worse rather than better. This is particularly true when the other person gets a kick out of seeing you upset, irritated, or thrown off balance. For example, when students act up in order to irritate the teacher, the teacher's irritation can be a kind of reward or reinforcer. In such cases it is more effective to ignore (or extinguish) the undesired behavior (assuming that the undesired behavior is not dangerous or of such a nature that it must be responded to) and catch the person at being good instead of at being bad. One caveat, however: When you ignore or extinguish the other person's behavior, that behavior usually gets worse for a while before it gradually becomes more acceptable.

One mother got caught in what has been called the Criticism Trap.[21] She was fooled into thinking that criticism worked because the criticized behavior stopped for a bit, when in fact the behavior was being strengthened in the long run. Each time her five-year-old son, Mike, misbehaved, she criti-

204

cized him. He stopped misbehaving but after a few moments did something else that was objectionable. In the long run her assertive expressions of irritation were making the problem worse. The way out of the Criticism Trap is to redirect your efforts to assertively praise desired behavior more and to be less critical.

One mother had a continuing problem with her five- and seven-year-old children. She constantly reminded them to do such things as make their beds, pick up their toys, and brush their teeth, with the result that there was a hassle nearly every morning. After discussing the problem with the children, she realized that they needed more praise and something more concrete than a simple "that's good" when they did what she wanted. She set up a star chart, and each morning after the children brushed their teeth or made their beds, they pasted a star on the chart; the stars were traded in for little special privileges. This system caused fewer hassles, the children upset her less, and she was now in a position of being able to make positive comments instead of negative ones. The children felt proud of their increasing ability to take care of their responsibilities without reminders; eventually they got into a positive morning habit and no longer needed the star system.[22] The following example deals only with extinction.

A woman took a job selling Cadillacs, a job formerly held only by men. As is often the case, the male salespeople had to go through a readjustment, and in the readjustment process quite a few teasing, sexual, and sexist remarks were made—some meant in earnest, some in jest, and some just because the person didn't know what else to say. Using no judgment and responding to each of these with assertively expressed irritation actually worsened the woman's situation. By passing over all but the most blatant comments and maintaining some perspective, she found that the problem gradually became less severe.

Alternative E: Using Listening, Understanding, and Discussion. As indicated earlier in this chapter, sometimes simple listening and increased understanding of other people is more effective and a better alternative to standing up for yourself.

A young woman received a lot of criticism when she joined a previously all-male staff. The most vehement comments came from a particular man who strongly believed that women should stay at home. By listening and engaging him in discussion so that she could gain a better understanding of his point of view, she accepted him as an individual, and he gradually stopped viewing her as a threat. When they both accepted each other, they were able to discuss rather than debate their differences.

Alternative F: Using Empathy. Another alternative is to express empathy rather than irritation.

A man who was shopping for shirts was served by a very brusque and irritating clerk. He chose to be empathic and inquired: "You seem to be having a hell of a bad day. Is something wrong?" The clerk disclosed that his wife was in the hospital and that he was worried about her. He expressed sympathy and asked whether the clerk would care to say what was ailing her. They discussed her illness for a few minutes, in the process of which the clerk felt better. The customer left the store with a good feeling that his behavior had brought comfort to a fellow human being while enabling him to still purchase the exact shirt he was looking for.[23]

SUMMARY

As we have mentioned many times in this book, acting assertively doesn't mean riding roughshod over others. Assertive behavior is good communication, an important part of which is effective listening. Effective listening makes it possible to know precisely what the other person's viewpoint is. When you know that, you can usually negotiate a mutually agreeable solution. Effective listening skills also are helpful in handling situations that can't be negotiated, for even though you aren't able to approach the other person assertively, you can control your life by changing your environment or adapting to the situation.

206

NOTES

1. Farrell, W. *The liberated man.* New York: Random House, 1975.

2. Gordon, J. *Parent effectiveness training.* New York: Wyden Books, 1970.

3. Paulson, T., Thorn, R., & Kormondy, L. Assertive management. *Assert 19,* April 1978, 1-2.

4. Becvar, R. J. *Skills for effective communication.* New York: John Wiley and Sons, 1974.

5. Gordon, J., 1970.

6. Strayhorn, J. M. Jr. *Talking It Out.* Champaign, IL: Research Press Co., 1977.

7. Strayhorn, J. M. Jr., 1977.

8. Gottman, J., Notarius, C., Gonso, J., & Markman, H. *A couple's guide to communication.* Champaign, IL: Research Press Co., 1976.

9. Gottman, J., Notarius, C., Gonso, J., & Markman, H., 1976.

10. Becvar, R. J., 1974.

11. Johnson, D.W. *Reaching out.* Englewood Cliffs, NJ: Prentice-Hall, 1972.

12. Gordon, J. *Teacher effectiveness training.* New York: Wyden Books, 1974.

13. Gottman, J., Notarius, C., Gonso, J., & Markman, H., 1976.

14. Gordon, J., 1974.

15. Gordon, J., 1970.

16. Gordon, J., 1970.

17. Gordon, J., 1974.

18. Gordon, J., 1974.

19. Gottman, J., Notarius, C., Gonso, J., & Markman, H., 1976.

20. Gottman, J., Notarius, C., Gonso, J., & Markman, H., 1976.

21. Becker, W. C. *Parents are teachers.* Champaign, IL: Research Press Co., 1971.

NOTES (continued)

22.   Setting up such systems requires information that is beyond the scope of this book. Interested readers may consult the following: Becker, W. C., 1971. Patterson, G. R., *Living with children*. Champaign, IL: Research Press Co., 1968.

23.   Lazarus, A. A. On assertive behavior: A brief note. *Behavior Therapy*, 1973, *4*, 697-699.

8
Handling Tender Feelings, Requests, and Anger

How do you pay a compliment or express affection? How do you react to others' compliments or expressions of affection? How do you make a request, or refuse one, or ask someone to change his way of doing something, or express anger? This chapter will discuss these kinds of behaviors and the different kinds of self-defeating beliefs that you need to deal with to act assertively. The guidelines included in each section should help you handle these situations assertively.

GIVING COMPLIMENTS
AND EXPRESSING TENDER FEELINGS

Why give compliments and express tenderness, appreciation, and affection towards other people? First and most simply, it feels good. It feels good to express positive feelings, and other people like to hear good words even when they act embarrassed or respond in other awkward ways. Expressing positive feelings, particularly in personal relationships, tends to bring you closer to others.

Everyone needs positive feedback, whether it is about their work or their personal behavior. Giving positive feedback makes it more likely that others will continue to act in ways which you want. Positive expressions make others less likely to resort to trickery and deception to get what they want, for example, getting sick to receive some tenderness; making mistakes to get some attention, even if that attention is negative; or starting arguments to get the affection associated with "making up." Lastly, when you have expressed your positive feelings toward others, you are less likely to feel like an ogre when you finally are critical or express your annoyance. Likewise, when other people's efforts have been praised and they know they are appreciated, it is much easier for them to accept constructive criticism and to take your criticism than if their efforts have been taken for granted.

As you go through the day, you are likely to have many positive thoughts and feelings about others. You may notice their clothing or special abilities. You may appreciate a favor they have done—completing a rush piece of work, taking time to listen to a complaint, or raising a question that helped you tackle a problem more clearly. Or you may just feel a pleasant rush of positive feelings toward someone you value. Yet many times you don't express your positive reactions. Some common ways in which people stop themselves from expressing tender feelings towards others are summarized in Figure 17.

Guidelines for Expressing Compliments and Tender Feelings

The most important part of expressing compliments and tender feelings is that they are said sincerely and reflect your personality. There are, however, some guidelines you can use in expressing yourself.

Statements that praise the whole person (global praise) often fall flat because people realize that generalizations about their whole character or behavior don't fit. When praised, they may feel guilty or suspicious instead of complimented. Compare these two expressions of positive feelings, the first of which praises the whole person while the second praises specific behavior:

(Global praise) "What a grownup boy you are. You are such an angel."

(Specific praise) "Tommie, you are such a good helper to me. You set out the glasses and cereal bowls and filled them without spilling anything. Thank you!"[1]

When Tommy received the global praise, he cringed a little; he is a little worried about being a grownup, and he knows he's not

Figure 17 Thoughts That Stop People from Expressing Positive Feelings

Dysfunctional Thoughts	More Accurate Thoughts
He already knows these positive things about himself, so why say anything?	He may or may not know it. He may or may not know that *you* recognize these qualities in him. Even if he does know, a kind word goes a long way.
She knows I love her, so why say it?	She'll feel good to hear it again and to *know* rather than assume that your love and affection continue.
I might embarrass him.	Chances are that *even if* he's embarrassed, he'll secretly like hearing your positive feelings.
I like her a lot, and she may not feel the same way about me.	If she doesn't feel the same way, you both can deal with it. You can survive the fact that you feel differently about each other. What really creates problems is when your expression of positive feelings carries the message—or is interpreted as meaning—that the other person *must* feel the same way and to the *same* degree that you feel.
What I'm really trying to say won't come out right; I'll embarrass myself.	You don't have to say it in some perfect way. The most important thing is that you are sincere. Your sincerity comes through to others *even if* you're ill at ease while expressing yourself.
The other person may make fun of me.	If he does, you can tell him in I Language terms about the effects on you.
I'll show I'm a weak, sentimental old fool.	More accurately, you'll show that you're a sensitive, caring person who has enough courage to show your tender side.

an angel. He was more pleased to receive the behaviorally specific praise because he could see for himself that he had done a good job of setting the table. Thus the praise felt real to him. To reduce the chances of having the other person reject your expression of positive feelings, you can simply describe or praise the specific behaviors that please you rather than give global praise. Other examples of praising specific behaviors follow. Several of these examples show how to express tender feelings by describing the tangible effects of the behavior. Other examples show one simple but often overlooked approach: Go right ahead and straightforwardly describe your feelings.

- I can see that you put a lot of effort into organizing this report so that it could be easily read by the staff. I appreciate your thoroughness.
- I appreciate the way you spend time answering my questions; it has helped me do my work much more easily.
- I just want to tell you how much your encouragement has meant to me. It has helped me feel more confident of myself, and I'm taking risks that I wouldn't have dreamed of taking six months ago. Thanks!
- When I hear you laugh, a warm tingle goes through me!
- I love you.
- I never knew I could have so much fun just throwing around a frisbee. Being with *you* makes the difference. Even little things come alive when I'm with you.[2]

When giving compliments and expressing tender feelings, you should also think about the following: (1) giving a gigantic expression of your feelings once a year is less meaningful to the receiver than giving lots of little compliments and positive feelings over a stretch of time; (2) limiting your praise to those times when you're also criticizing creates resentment; (3) pairing praise with a request (e.g., "You've done such a good job of heading up the charity drive, I'd like you to do it again this year ") is often experienced as manipulation by the receiver; and (4) going on and on with your positive feelings with shy people may make them feel so uncomfortable that they avoid doing the things you've complimented.

212

Exercise 15 will give you practice in expressing positive feelings.

Exercise 15   Expressing Positive Feelings

For each of the following situations, consider how you could express your positive feelings.

Situation: A friend has unexpectedly dropped off home-grown vegetables (your favorite kind and just the right amount).

You say: _____

Situation: You've been feeling very upset about some work (or a personal problem) and a friend has been listening and helping you sort out your feelings. You're feeling much better now after talking to him for a while.

You say: _____

Situation: The secretary has just completed a rush piece of work you've been worried about getting done in time for the meeting.

You say: _____

Situation: Your daughter calls long distance to say that she's just won a $400 award for being the best art student in the junior class.

You say: _____

Situation: You and a friend have just played a fast handball game. You've really enjoyed your friend's company, and you're thinking about how good you feel about your friend.

You say: _____

NEGATIVE REACTIONS
TO WELL-MEANT COMPLIMENTS

Sometimes people react quite negatively, even angrily, to well-intentioned compliments. This can happen when your compliment accidentally hits a sensitive spot and sets off a series of incorrect thoughts or assumptions.

Compliment	Receiver's Thoughts
You have lots of potential.	That's what I've heard all my life. It's always *potential*! Nobody ever says I'm doing good now. I'm sick of hearing about my potential.
Your accomplishments are really impressive.	So what! I'm *only* valued for my accomplishments. That's all anyone cares about. Won't somebody just like me for me?
You are so beautiful.	That's all I ever hear, my looks. Buster, I've got brains too.
You are a sensitive person.	What does she think I am, some kind of a twerp? Sensitive my eye; I'm as strong as they come!

Though you cannot be responsible for others' incorrect thinking, you can be sensitive to the impact you have on others and try to pick up the pieces afterwards. These two possibilities are certainly worth trying:

1. Restate your intent and try to find out how the person "took" your compliment. For example, you might say, "That didn't come across like I meant it; where did I go wrong?" or "I didn't mean to turn you off; how did I do that?"
2. Try to find out what the receiver wanted to hear instead. For example, you might say, "I can see I really turned you

off with what I said; what would you rather I'd said?" or "I get the impression that you would have liked me to say something about your talents rather than your looks. Am I right?"

Either of these approaches can lead to a discussion that increases each party's understanding of the other.

Accepting Compliments and Tender Feelings
Most people want others to notice their efforts and to be liked. Yet when they get compliments, they often become embarrassed and act in ways that turn others off.

Denying. "Gosh, who me? It was nothing." You may want to be modest. However, your embarrassed reaction often leads the other person to feel sorry that she said something nice to you. She may then try to protect you by promising herself that she won't express her positive feelings about you in the future.

Rejecting. "You like this rag? I've had it for years and it's way out of style. Actually I look like a wreck today." Though you may sincerely believe that you don't deserve the compliment, rejecting it tells the other person you think he's stupid for saying something nice.

Returning the Focus Immediately. "Oh, I like *your* shirt, too!" Once again you may only intend to be modest or pleasant, but the other person is likely to think that you thought his compliment was insincere. When the focus is immediately returned, what starts off as a nice compliment ends with the whole exchange feeling phoney.

Joking Sarcastically. "Boy have you got some taste! Where did you ever get your judgment?" Though you may only intend to be funny, sarcastic remarks put down others. Making sarcastic comments or demeaning yourself punishes the other person for her thoughtfulness.

There are several reasons why people may have difficulty

accepting compliments. Some people feel that if they accept the compliment, they will be conceited. There is a big difference between conceit and healthy self-affirmation. Conceit tells the other person that she is a fool for saying anything nice to you because you know you're superior and don't need to be reminded (e.g., *"Of course* I did a good job on the speech; I always do well!"). Accepting a compliment with healthy self-affirmation sends the message that you are pleased that the other person noticed and that you want to share your good feelings with her (e.g., "Thank you, I feel real good to hear you say that"). By accepting compliments and others' positive feelings, you are giving part of yourself back to others by letting them know that their comments have brought you pleasure.

Some people think that openly showing that they are pleased with compliments is weak and unmanly. Openly showing pleasure has nothing to do with your sexuality or virility. More realistically, it can take courage to openly show that you care about other people's reactions and that you can be touched by people. Such behavior shows your humanity, vulnerability, and willingness to value other people's comments.

GUIDELINES FOR ACCEPTING COMPLIMENTS AND OTHER POSITIVE FEELINGS

Accepting sincere compliments and positive feelings can be done on two levels. The first level, *externally* accepting them, is the easiest one. This can be done by simply saying, "Thank you," and/or smiling or giving a hug. You can describe your positive feelings and share them (e.g., "I feel really good when you tell me you respect me." Or "I'm happy with the way that flower arrangement turned out, too. Thank you for noticing!"). Saying why you value the compliment is an especially meaningful way of showing your appreciation (e.g., "I especially value what you've said because you mean a lot to me." Or "I'm glad you like it because I felt like I took a big risk in painting the walls that shade of green"). When it is hard for you to accept a sincere compliment, just saying so can be freeing (e.g., "I have trouble accepting compliments, but I do appreciate what you've said"). The key here is not to worry so much about saying the

216

right words with the right degree of enthusiasm. That can make you become stiff and unnatural. Instead give yourself permission to feel whatever you feel. A quiet thank you and a smile may be closer to the real you.

The second level, accepting the compliment *internally*, is much more difficult to master. People quite often can gracefully accept compliments on the outside, but on the inside they completely block them off so that the impact never reaches them. This is particularly true when others say positive things that are quite personal. Though everyone has his own unique way of internally tuning out others' positive feelings, Figure 18 (page 218) shows the more common ones. By internally denying compliments and affection, you deny yourself the right to feel good about yourself. You can help yourself internally accept compliments by becoming aware of what stops you from accepting others' genuine positive reactions to you, assessing the inaccurate components in your thinking, and finally developing more accurate messages to give yourself.

These guidelines will help you respond to sincere compliments you don't agree with. If you cannot or do not wish to simply thank the person, you can simply express your disagreement and still thank the person. For example, you might say, "I don't feel the same way, but thank you," or "I'm not sure I agree, but I do appreciate your thoughtfulness," or "I wasn't as satisfied with my own performance, but I'm glad that you liked it."

REFUSING REQUESTS

Refusing is an affirmative act of choosing priorities and identifying yourself as an *individual* who has limits. Refusing enables you to have time and energy to put into activities and people of your choice. When you can give yourself permission to decide which requests you will grant and which you will refuse, you also are usually better able to accept others' refusals. Negative repercussions often can be avoided if the refusal is done assertively, for many people do not object so much to the no itself but rather to how it's said.[3]

Affirming your right to say no and to refuse requests bene-

Figure 18 Thoughts That Stop People from Internally Accepting Others' Positive Feelings

Dysfunctional Thoughts	More Accurate Thoughts
I don't deserve this compliment because I don't do this all of the time. I'm not always this way.	Even though you don't do it all of the time, you deserve it for the times you do do it.
If I accept this compliment, then I'll always have to act this way or I'll disappoint people. I can't do that so I won't let myself accept what he's said.	Nobody acts one way all the time. You don't have to be perfect. You will be accepted even though you're imperfect. By accepting others' good feelings, you've not signed a contract forever binding you to one way of acting.
If they really knew me, they wouldn't say that nice thing about me.	Maybe, maybe not. Chances are that you are harsher on yourself than other people are with you. It's OK for you to accept yourself even if you do some thoughtless things sometimes.
What does he really want from me?	Just because people may have manipulated you in the past doesn't mean that this person is doing that. It's OK to accept the compliment even if the person is trying to manipulate. You can let yourself feel good about the compliment and not get trapped by the manipulation.

fits you directly and can also indirectly benefit others too. Deciding to refuse makes it less likely that you will feel irritated by others and disgusted with yourself. And, refusing can indirectly protect others from accidentally taking advantage of you and later being subjected to the resentment that usually comes out in indirect and offensive ways.

Without the ability to assertively refuse, you become governed by other people's priorities. You are at their beck and call—a truly unhappy and unsatisfying way to live. Not refusing can distract you from what you really want to accomplish in life.[4]

Some Self-Defeating Beliefs

If I Refuse, I'm Rejecting My Friend. Refusing someone does not mean that you reject her. It simply means that you cannot or choose not to do what you have been *asked* to do. Your refusal does not mean that you are selfish; it means that at this particular time you cannot or will not do what this person wants. Refusing means that you are acting on your right to recognize and value your limits as a person.

If I Refuse, the Person Will Never Ask Me Again. What's your evidence that this is true? What can you do to reduce the likelihood of this happening? There are several possible solutions:

- You can tell him what you would like (e.g., that he ask you again).
- You can ask if your refusal has made him decide not to make requests of you in the future.
- You can express your fear that he will not ask you again.
- You can give a short explanation as to why you've refused *this* time and make it clear under what conditions you would be likely to say yes in the future.

If I Really Care For This Person, I Should Agree to Her Request.[5] It's true that caring and being a friend involve doing some things the other person wants. However, there are many

219

different ways of showing that you care, and each friend is entitled to show her friendship in ways that uniquely fit her. Yours may be the way of helping plant a vegetable garden instead of helping paint a bedroom. You may be willing to spend hours comforting a friend but really dislike house sitting her dog or loaning $400. You can be a friend and still set limits on what you are willing to do. Friendship does not mean limitless giving.

It's Less Painful to Say Yes than to Face How She Will Feel if I Say No.[6] It probably is easier, in the short run at least. One question to ask yourself is for how long will you feel uncomfortable if you refuse. Compare this with how much time and energy granting the request will take and for how long you will feel resentful if you say yes. Sometimes you exchange a five-minute period of discomfort for a two-week commitment and a year of periodically feeling resentful.

Guidelines for Refusing

There are three basic guidelines for refusing requests. The first guideline is to be direct instead of giving excuses. Pete and Mary's situation provides an example.

Pete was asked to loan his class notes a few days before an examination. Here's the indirect way he refused the request.

Pete: Well, my handwriting is really pretty bad. I don't think you'd be able to read it.

Mary: Nothing could be worse than my handwriting. I don't mind at all.

Pete: Oh, that's good . . . . But I tell you they're very disorganized.

Mary: No notes could be more disorganized than my own. Anyway, any kind of notes would help me more than the ones I'm working with.

Pete: Well, OK. But I don't have them with me. They're at my apartment, and I live clear across town.

Mary: Oh that's just fine. I don't mind driving. The night air would be refreshing.

Pete: Well, OK then.

When you don't say no but only try to talk the other person out of her request, a number of negative things are likely to happen. You may exhaust your excuses or talk yourself into saying yes. When you finally do refuse, the other person is apt to be even more irritated because the indirect refusal led her to believe that you would eventually say yes.

Excuses are different from explanations. When you assertively explain, you are giving personal information about yourself in a way that says that you feel OK about yourself and that the other person doesn't have to accept your explanation. When you give excuses, you are trying to get the other person to approve or "excuse" your behavior. These excuses often cover up your real reason for refusing. It is not necessary to explain your refusal to a stranger, but in work and personal relationships it often is more appropriate to offer some brief explanation.

The second guideline refers to the different ways to refuse a request. These are the major ways:

1. Simply say no.
2. Use an I Want statement, for example, "No, I didn't want to loan the notes out so close to the exam."
3. Use an I Feel statement, for example, "No, I'm worried about the exam and will need my notes"; or "No, I just wouldn't feel comfortable parting with them now."
4. Use an Empathic Assertion, for example, "I can see you're in a bind, yet I don't have time to baby sit tonight."
5. Use Mixed Feelings statements, for example, "Part of me would like to go to the movie tonight. And the other part's saying 'Watch it; you've just got loads of work to do tonight.' All in all that's the part I think I need to listen to even though I'd like to go with you."

Refusing need not be a total and complete no. Sometimes you may be willing to do part of what's asked or be willing to do it under certain conditions. You can set limits on what you are willing to do by saying, "I can't do _____ . I can do _____ ."[7] This approach is particularly useful when refusing requests from people who hold power over you.

The following statements illustrate the second guideline:

- I won't loan the notes. I can let you have them for two hours so you can copy the ones you need.
- I can't stay after work today. I can come in earlier tomorrow morning if you really need the help.
- Sure, I'll help you move. I can't give you a full day, but a half day would be fine.
- I'd be more than willing to cut your grass when you're out of town; I don't want to take care of your dog, though.

The third guideline, if you're in a situation where you're persistently refusing and feeling guilty about it, is to see if there is any way you can restructure the *situation* so that the other person has less of a need to make requests of you. The following cases show how this might be done.

Several times a week Mary Beth's mother called asking to visit the grandchildren. Mary Beth often refused but felt guilty, mainly because of the number of times she had said no. When she did say yes out of guilt, she felt resentful. Thinking through the situation, Mary Beth realized that she believed that her mother should see the children and that she too would enjoy her mother's visits if they were less frequent and at convenient times. Actually the only way her mother could get to see the children was when she asked; Mary Beth had not been inviting her. So Mary Beth asked her mother to visit, thus putting the power into her own hands. This enabled her to choose the times. Her mother felt less afraid that she would never get to see the kids unless she asked to visit, so she asked less frequently. When Mary Beth did occasionally refuse, she didn't feel guilty.

A professor was turning down many students' requests for independent studies work and for chairing their dissertations. He felt guilty about doing this and actually became angry, thinking that "students asked so that I had to say no and feel guilty." Finally he called a meeting and presented the problem to the staff. Together they developed a way of changing the program so that students' special needs could be met and the load of supervising doctoral dissertations could be more evenly distributed.

222

MAKING REQUESTS FOR
INFORMATION AND CLARIFICATION

Since people cannot read minds, you must tell them what you want. Poor decision making often results from a lack of necessary information, which can create misunderstandings. If you don't ask for clarification or for the information you need, you force yourself to live with more ambiguity than is necessary and this ambiguity often creates unnecessary anxiety. When you are not sure how others feel about your actions and don't ask, you have to resort to guessing—often incorrectly.

Many people tell themselves, "If I ask how he's going to repair the car, he'll think I don't trust him." You have the right to ask for information so you can make a decision and ease your mind. There's no reason to believe that asking for information will be automatically interpreted as lack of trust. A mechanic could just as easily assume that you are curious, or really concerned about your car, or have been taken advantage of in the past. A host of other reactions is equally possible.

You have the right not to trust people until you have some basis for trust. This does not mean going to the opposite extreme and assuming the worst of people until they prove otherwise. Even if the mechanic does assume that you don't trust him, he may or may not take offense. If he does take offense, you don't *have* to feel guilty or act defensively. You can use your listening skills to deal with his feelings by clarifying why you wanted the information (e.g., "I've put blind trust in people in the past, and I've been disappointed with the results").

Guidelines for Requesting Information and Clarification
If you are afraid that the other person will become defensive or misinterpret your request for information, clarifying your purpose in asking often reduces such reactions. For example:

- I want to check out something with you. How do you feel about my calling you most every night? I'm asking because I'm concerned about intruding.
- I want to be sensitive to your needs so I want to know

whether you want advice from me or if you just want to talk about your rotten day.

Consider whether or not it is better to express your question as a statement. For example, when you are fairly sure that the other person hasn't taken out the garbage, asking, "Have you taken out the garbage?" is a question to entrap her into an admission of guilt. It's more honest to make it a statement (e.g., "I want the garbage taken out before you leave"). It's better not to ask a person why she interrupts when you don't really care about her reasons but instead simply want her to stop doing it. Likewise, when you've just gotten a new haircut that you like, asking, "*Do* you like my haircut?" is asking for a critical opinion and puts the other person into a position of having to say yes or no. If he agrees that it looks good, that's great. If it doesn't happen to appeal to him and he says so, you're apt to feel disappointed and may try to convince him that his opinion is wrong. If you ask, "*How* do you like my hair cut?" your question is still asking for criticism, although it leaves the person a little more room to say what parts of the style he likes or dislikes.

Asking these questions is fine if you are really looking for criticism. However, many times you are really looking for a compliment. In that case it would be more honest to admit that you're pleased with your haircut and just show your pleasure by saying, for example, "I really got a neat haircut; I just like it so much and I wanted to show it to you!" No criticism is being asked for, and the other person is free to spontaneously say he likes it too; if he doesn't, he can say nothing or honestly share in the fact that you are happy.

Making Requests for Assistance or Help

When you don't ask for help, you can become overburdened and feel unappreciated and resentful, which is reason enough to ask for assistance. You can even ask for help when you don't absolutely "need" it; for example, you could paint your bedroom alone, but by asking friends to help you could create a painting party. Most people enjoy helping a little and don't mind being asked for help if the request gives them a choice to say yes or no and if it considers their needs and limits. They certainly prefer to be asked directly than to be held responsible for failing to offer their assistance before being asked. If the person refuses, that doesn't mean you did something wrong; it means that she acted on her right to say no.

Some people feel that if they ask for a favor, they have incurred an obligation.[8] All take and no give leads to bad relationships and is taking advantage of others. However, asking for a favor does not mean that you immediately have an obligation that must be "paid for" regardless of the circumstances or as soon as the other person asks for a favor. Just as you gave the other person a choice to refuse your request, you have the same right, and you also can return a different favor than the one that was originally given to you. It is appreciation for a favor rather than the exactness of the returned favor that is important—in other words, a matter of quality rather than quantity.

Guidelines for Asking for Help

There are seven basic guidelines you can follow when asking for help. The first is to be direct. When you indirectly ask for help, you may not be understood (for example, complaining of feeling tired rather than asking for help with the dishes).[9]

The second guideline is to make requests that give clear, specific information that will help people to decide whether to say yes or no. When the other person agrees to fulfill a vague request, misunderstandings often result. Some examples follow.

- I'm planning on putting in a garden this spring, and I would enjoy having some company and help in spading the ground and putting in seedlings. *Would you be interested?* I'm thinking of doing it next Saturday afternoon.
- I'd like to ask you for a favor. I'll tell you what it is and then see if it's something that you can do. (Describe the request.) *Are you available* to help out on this?
- *Would it be inconvenient* for you to pick up two bottles of Scotch before you come to the party?

Third, give the person some reasonable time to ask you questions and think about your request.

225

Fourth, limit your requests to specific things that you would like from the other person (e.g., "I'd appreciate it if you could glance over my lesson plans for the next week and give me your opinion as to how realistic they are. Is that something you're willing to do?"). Global requests (e.g., "I'd like you to help me with my teaching") that are said with helpless, victim-like body language sometimes result in others withdrawing and refusing to give any help for fear that you will be a millstone around their neck. Some people get aggressively angry with helplessness. Others give help because they feel guilty, but later they feel secretly resentful.

Fifth, if you are afraid that the other person will say yes when she really wants to say no and will be resentful and hold you accountable for her nonassertiveness, you can make it easier for both of you by letting her know that it's OK if she refuses (e.g., "If you don't want to do this, it's really OK." "I can understand if you'd rather not do this." "I can make other arrangements if you'd rather say no"). Such statements not only avoid unnecessarily experiencing someone else's resentment, they help the other person become more assertive and are a responsible use of your own assertive skills.

Sixth, avoid waiting until you're desperate to ask for help. Feeling desperate makes it so much harder to accept another's refusal. It also increases the likelihood of your putting unfair pressure on other people to say yes.

Seventh, be clear when you are demanding rather than requesting. In a request you are accepting the other person's right to refuse. One way you can determine whether or not your request is really a demand is by your own reaction. If you feel disappointed, chances are that the request was a true one. On the other hand, if your reaction is one of outrage or humiliation, it was really a demand and you were likely telling yourself "He should have said yes." [10]

ASKING OTHERS
TO CHANGE BEHAVIOR

Most of the time people don't deliberately try to do things that annoy others or interfere with their lives, so when you ask

226

someone to change her behavior, she may react by being startled, confused, or genuinely surprised that you find something amiss with what she is doing. This initial reaction may be followed by automatically denying that anything's wrong with her behavior and by becoming angry. [11] It's important to hear the person out if she has these reactions rather than to *immediately* come on stronger with your assertive message.

When you ask someone to change long-standing habits, it is also important to be sensitive to the fact that habits are hard to change and that people don't change overnight. Asking for smaller changes, giving a reasonable length of time for them to occur, and supporting the person's efforts will make it more likely that your assertiveness will result in positive change.

Some people tell themselves, "If I really am his friend, I should accept his behavior." It is true that in friendship we overlook a few things in a friend's behavior, yet that does not mean you have to accept discourtesy or mistreatment. Not expressing yourself can hurt friendships, and requesting that your friend change his behavior is constructive when it is motivated out of the desire to improve the relationship and is done with caring and sensitivity. [12]

Guidelines for Asking Others to Change

If possible, try to think in terms of asserting yourself to prevent problems from occurring. For example, if you're in a hurry, telling the waitress right away that you'd like your meal served quickly can prevent a problem. Likewise, when having home repair work done, using your assertiveness to check with the Better Business Bureau, getting bids in writing, and asking questions can make it less likely that you will later need to ask workers to change negative behavior.

When the problem behavior occurs the first time, a mild statement of your wants is more appropriate than making an intense statement. For example, if you don't like nurses to call you by your first name, it is helpful to simply state your preference in I Want terms (e.g., "Would you please call me Ms.——," or "I prefer to be called Ms.—— rather than by first name"), or in Empathic Assertion terms ("I imagine that you're used to calling patients by their first names, but I don't feel com-

227

fortable with that. Please call me Ms. ——").

If the problem persists, you can make your assertion more intense (e.g., "I've asked you several times to call me Ms. ——. I find it very irritating to have my preference ignored"). How to persist in your assertive message and deal with aggressive comments will be discussed in the next chapter.

Lastly, describe the specific behavior you want rather than personality traits or general attitudes. Your request should be reasonable and within the power of the other person to meet.

EXPRESSING ANNOYANCE AND ANGER

Annoyance and anger are not bad emotions, nor in themselves are they destructive. Their potential destructiveness lies in *how* they are expressed. Aggressively expressed anger attacks others' self-esteem and can be destructive, but assertively expressed anger lets others know what your feelings, wants, and frustrations are and gives them a chance to change their behavior. Harboring irritated feelings does not deal with a problem situation; in fact, the irritation is likely to grow. When feelings are not pent up, they are easier to deal with. Annoyance can be shared before it turns into anger. Simply saying that you are angry in itself sometimes reduces these feelings even if the other person does not change. When you assertively express anger, you are using your energy to deal with a situation, to clear the air, and to arrive at an understanding. Understandings may include finding out that the other person meant no harm or that you jumped to a wrong conclusion, or that you have some sensitive spots. Two last points about expressing annoyance and anger deserve attention: Feeling angry doesn't make you right. Nor do people have to change *just because* you are angry. Other people don't have the job of *making* you feel better. The source of your feelings is inside of you; you are responsible for taking care of your feelings. Others may choose to change their behavior, but they don't *have* to just because you have a *feeling.*[13]

Guidelines for Expressing Anger and Annoyance
There are several ways of handling your irritation and expressing yourself:

228

1. **I Want statements in which you simply state what you want.** You don't *have* to express your anger in order to deal with an annoying situation. For example, when you are very angry that you have sat around watching TV for a month and have not gone out, saying "I very much want to get out of the house this weekend" is an I Want statement that provides a direct way of dealing with the source of your anger. And you are less apt to receive a defensive reaction by making this kind of statement.

2. **I Feel statements.** "This is the third time I've called about being billed for a phone call I didn't make, and frankly I'm getting very irritated." This kind of statement allows you to express your feelings directly and provides a way for others to learn about your limits.

3. **Mixed Feelings statements in which you describe the feeling that is underneath the anger.** For example, "Brenda, this is the second time this week you've cancelled our lunch date. I'm real disappointed because I've been looking forward to seeing you and I'm a little irritated because I'm starting to wonder about our friendship." Expressing both sets of feelings in this way often has a greater positive impact on others than simply expressing the angry part.

4. **Empathic Assertion.** "I realize that you've got strong opinions about divorce and are entitled to your opinion, but I object to the way you are stereotyping divorced people. I have not found divorced people to be particularly unstable and definitely not immoral." This kind of Empathic Assertion makes it easier for other people to hear what we have to say about our feelings or wants.

5. **I Language statements.** "This is the third time I've brought back the car to get the windshield wiper fixed. These extra trips are taking a lot of time and are really inconveniencing me. I'm getting very annoyed about the whole situation. What I want is to get those wipers fixed properly this time and not have to come back again. Coming back again is totally unacceptable to me." When you are able to cite specific, concrete effects, people are usually more interested in changing their behavior because they realize that you are not just being a "crank."

6. **Describe the feeling and the self-defeating thoughts or interpretations that are going through your mind.**[14] "I'm irritated with your interrupting me because I interpret that as meaning you're more interested in what *you* have to say than in *me*." This type of assertion is particularly appropriate in close relationships. You take clear ownership of your feelings, and it helps the other person understand particularly sensitive areas.

When expressing annoyance and anger, you should consider the degree of anger displayed and the timing. For example, as one real estate salesperson and a prospective client walked in the open front door, the owner of the house walked down the steps and hotly announced, "I'm angry; you're fifteen minutes early." Her timing and the intensity of anger displayed were both overly strong in the situation.

Though the examples cited thus far have been about expressing annoyance to correct a situation, it is equally appropriate to express your feelings even if you know that there's no way in which you can change the situation.

A professor was irritated with a graduate student's request for a delayed grade. His irritation would in no way change the fact that the student had not completed the course work on time. Nor did the circumstances warrant denying the delayed grade request. However, he knew that if he didn't express his feelings, he'd be likely to harbor them against the student. Here's what he said:

> I just want to say that I'm pretty annoyed that you didn't finish your paper because it creates extra work for me next semester. I'll give you the delayed grade, and I won't hold your lateness against you, but I wanted to tell you that I'm unhappy with the way you didn't carry through this semester, and I wanted to get it off my chest. Now that I've said that, I'm ready to hear you out.

SUMMARY

Expressing compliments and tender feelings feels good and

can result in our feeling closer to others and other people feeling closer to us. Even though there are many benefits for ourselves and others in expressing these feelings, we often neglect opportunities to pass on good words to others. The most important part of expressing positive feelings is to be sincere and behaviorally specific.

Accepting compliments and feelings of liking and appreciation adds to the enjoyment of life. Gracefully accepting compliments is a way of showing that we value other people's comments. Internally accepting compliments and expressions of liking builds self-esteem.

Refusing requests means making choices about what we'll invest our time and energy in. Relationships do not involve limitless giving.

Making requests for information, help, or that others change behavior can also add to the enjoyment of life. This does not mean making requests without regard for the limits of other people.

Expressing annoyance and anger can be constructive if it is handled assertively. These expressions can clear the air and lead to a greater understanding of both parties' limits.

NOTES

1. Becker, W. *Parents are teachers.* Champaign, IL: Research Press Co., 1971.

2. Warren, N. J. *Measurement of positive assertive behaviors.* Unpublished Master's thesis, St. Louis University, 1975.

3. Phelps, S., & Austin, N. *The assertive woman.* San Luis Obispo, CA: Impact Press, 1975.

4. Fensterheim, R., & Baer, J. *Don't say yes when you want to say no.* New York: David McKay, 1975.

5. This dysfunctional belief was taken from: Galassi, M. D., & Galassi, J. P. *Assert yourself.* New York: Human Sciences Press, 1977. We have supplied the rationale countering the rational belief.

6. Galassi, M. D., & Galassi, J. P., 1977.

7. Herman, S. J. *Becoming assertive.* New York: D. Van Nostrand Company, 1978.

8. Manderino, M. *Effects of a group assertive training procedure on undergraduate women.* Ann Arbor, MI: University Microfilms, 1974.

9. Manderino, M., 1974.

10. Baer, J. *How to be an assertive (not aggressive) woman in life, in love, and on the job.* New York: Rawson Associates Publishing, 1976.

11. Johnson, D. W. *Reaching out.* Englewood Cliffs, NJ: Prentice-Hall, 1972.

12. Johnson, D. W., 1972.

13. For a review of the dysfunctional thinking associated with expressing anger and annoyance, see Chapter 5.

14. Rosenburg, M. B. *From now on.* St. Louis, MO: Community Psychological Consultants, 1976.

9

Handling Aggression and Persisting in Your Assertiveness

HANDLING OTHERS' AGGRESSION

Handling others' aggression means acting so that you have a constructive impact on the other person. (We are using the term *aggressive* broadly to cover putdowns, ignoring legitimate objections, and attempts to induce guilt.) How you choose to conduct yourself depends on your goal. The following are four basic, if somewhat overlapping, goals:

1. To get to the source of the problem.
2. To get your objective accomplished.
3. To have the person become aware of the aggressive behavior and its effects on others.
4. To limit the aggressive behavior.

Figure 19 (page 234) summarizes these goals and possible interventions.

The Goal: Getting to the Source of the Problem
You can use three different intervention techniques to get to the source of a problem.

Reflection and Empathic Assertion. A basic intervention technique is reflecting the content and/or feelings of what the other person is aggressively communicating. Since aggressive communication is often an indirect expression of wants and feelings, it takes a keen ear as well as some patience to understand the message the person is trying to get across. After you listen to the person and clearly understand her message, you can use the Empathic Assertion to state your limits.[1] Jim's reaction

233

Figure 19 Handling Others' Aggression

The Goal	Possible Interventions
1. To get to the source of the problem	Reflection and Empathic Assertion Asking for more specific criticism Impact of message received
2. To get your objective accomplished	Ignore aggressive comments Dismiss and redirect
3. To increase awareness of aggressive behavior and its effects on others	Question for awareness Use of contrast
4. To limit the aggressive behavior	Give negative feedback Ask for a change in behavior Treat the putdown as a neutral comment Sort the issues

to Marta's aggression is an example of how you can respond with reflection and Empathic Assertion skills.

Marta: What do you expect anyway? I've got the house to run, kids to clean up after, and now you're mad because I forgot to tell you that your boss called!

Jim: I can see that you're irritated with me. I guess you'd . . .

Marta: (interrupting) That's right. I am really irritated!

Jim: I guess you'd like me to realize that you're only human and can't be expected to take care of everything.

Marta: (a little sarcastically) I'm only human. I'm glad you realize that.

Jim: I guess I did get on your back and wasn't thinking about the fact that mistakes happen. At the same time, not getting my boss's phone call scares the living daylights out of me. It's real important to me that we figure out some way of making sure his messages get through even when you're real busy. Are you willing to do that?

Marta: Yeah, I guess I flew off the handle too. I knew you'd be upset that I forgot.

Effects: Since reflecting enables you to better understand the other person's situation, clearer communication usually results. A more positive atmosphere is usually created, and you can begin problem solving more effectively. The person who is upset usually expresses her upset feelings even more strongly after the first reflection. It usually takes two or three reflections before the aggressive person realizes that you are sincerely trying to understand and that she does not need to make her message even more aggressive in order to get through to you. The reflection process ultimately calms the person and makes her somewhat more receptive. At this point you can restate your assertive message, which may cause the listener to feel threatened and again react aggressively. Another reflection usually restores the communication. Thus the interaction process is apt to be one of defensiveness—reflection—decreased defensiveness—assertion—increased defensiveness—reflection—decreased defensiveness—assertion, etc.

Asking for More Specific Criticism. When someone uses criticism, challenges, or arguments to attack you, you're more likely to get to the source of the problem by asking your critic to give you more information and to make the criticism more specific. There are three ways[2] you can do this: (1) ask what specific behaviors the person didn't like, (2) ask what specific behaviors the person would have liked instead or would want in the future, and (3) find out what made your behavior offensive to the person. The following are some examples:

Manager: You've got to stop being so namby-pamby if you expect to get anywhere in this company.
Subordinate: What do I specifically do that you think is "namby-pamby"?

Wife: Can't you ever do something besides read the paper?
Husband: What would you like me to do instead?

Father: (belligerently) Girl, you sure use big words.
Daughter: What is it about my using big words that bothers you?

235

Effects: Asking for more specific criticism can turn a nasty or unclear comment into a helpful suggestion, and it paves the way for better understanding. Asking for more specific criticism can help the critic assertively communicate exactly what is unpleasant about your behavior, what behaviors he wants changed, and what behaviors he wants in their place. With this specific information you can do something to remedy the situation: You can decide whether or not you want to change behavior; you can bargain with the other person ("I hear you saying that you want me to do *this*. Will you do *this* for me in return if I do *that*?"); or, if you don't want to do what the other person wants, you can be open with the person about what you will do.[3]

Impact of Message Received. Letting the other person know the message that you've received may help get to the source of the problem, especially if you follow it by asking for more specific criticism. It can also lead the other person to stop his aggressive behavior.

Erica had had several dates with Dick, and one evening as they were being escorted to their table for dinner, Erica asked Dick if he'd like the window seat. Rather sharply, he responded "Sit down!" Following is their resulting conversation.

Erica: Uh . . . the message I just got is that I'm pretty stupid for asking that question.
Dick: Where did you get that impression?
Erica: From your tone of voice and the fact that I was given an order to sit down.
Dick: I didn't mean that at all. What I really meant was that we don't have to sit across from each other.
Erica: Oh good!

Aggression can also be expressed more subtly, as in the following situation.

Earlier in the week, a college professor had given the departmental secretary several technical papers filled with mathematical equations to type. She accepted the papers with a dour expression. The same

236

day, the professor suddenly found that his telephone calls were not getting through to him. Later, the papers were returned to him with lots of typographical errors. Several similar incidents also took place during the week. He could not definitely say that the secretary was deliberately doing this, but the sudden increase in the number of mistakes gave him the distinct impression that he was being punished for the distasteful work he had given her. With this in mind he approached her and said evenly: "I get the message . . . . I'm being punished for the technical papers I gave you to do." He paused for a moment and then changed the subject. Though the secretary never admitted anything, her behavior promptly changed.

Effects: Letting the other person know the impact of the message received is particularly helpful when the aggression is not so much in the words the person is using but rather in a putdown attitude communicated by body language. By letting the other person know what message you are getting you can clarify whether or not it's the message that the person intended to send you. If it wasn't, the misunderstanding can be corrected. If he did intend to send a putdown message, you can follow up with the other types of assertions to set limits or negotiate the conflict. Lastly, letting the other person know the impact of the message received may lead the person to stop his aggressive behavior.

The Goal: Accomplishing Your Objective
Once you have identified the problem, you can begin working on a solution. You can use one of the following intervention techniques to reach your objective.

Ignoring. One basic intervention technique is to ignore the person's aggressive comments and to stick to your own goal.

Vince was hired as a communications consultant for a large Midwestern company. He had just completed a six-week communications course with company employees and decided to meet with the supervisors and managers to brainstorm ideas on how the program could be improved.
  During the meeting, the top-ranking manager rose to his feet and stretching to his full height of six and one-half feet, belligerently pointed his finger at Vince and said: "There's one way this program

could be improved and that is to get a new consultant—someone who wears a suit and has his hair cut. The men need to have a consultant that they can relate to." He made a few more pointed remarks and stood waiting for Vince's reaction. Vince paused for a moment, realizing that though he could defend himself and try to convince the manager that the men could relate to him, he probably wouldn't be successful. He quickly assessed that *his* goal was to brainstorm suggestions and that taking time out to defend himself would divert him from *his* goal.

Vince reflected the content of the manager's message. This technique enabled him to get time to calm himself down and let the manager know that he heard him correctly. "So your suggestion is to hire a new consultant who wears a suit and has his hair cut short." The manager smiled, "Yup, you got it." With that Vince calmly said, "OK, that's another suggestion," and wrote it on the list of suggestions and continued the brainstorming session of ways the program could be improved.

After the meeting the manager somewhat abashedly approached Vince and said that he was surprised that he didn't get a rise out of Vince and that he didn't really mean what he had said in the meeting.

Effects: By not responding to the aggressive comments that are intentionally or unintentionally designed to upset you, you're not encouraging the aggressive behavior. Your behavior doesn't pose an additional threat to the person or give him a reason to continue being aggressive. It is much less likely that the situation will escalate into a scene if your response is goal directed. By not responding in kind to a comment and maintaining your presence of mind, you often win respect.

Dismiss and Redirect. This technique involves denying the relevance of a putdown or an irrelevant comment to the main issue under discussion and redirecting the discussion to the main issue.[4] The following are examples:

- How much I paid for the mower is beside the point (dismiss). The point is that the mower shouldn't have stopped working in a week (redirect).
- That's not funny (dismiss). I feel hurt about your ignoring me at the party (redirect).

238

- That I look pretty when I'm angry isn't the point (dismiss). The point is that I'm very irritated with your continuing to put down my work (redirect).
- As far as the other clerks also getting personal phone calls at work is concerned, I'll deal with that separately (dismiss). Right now we need to deal with *your* getting these phone calls (redirect).

Effects: By dismissing irrelevant comments or putdowns and redirecting the conversation to the main issue, you are more likely to keep the discussion on track and away from unproductive side issues. If you conduct yourself in this manner, it is less likely that your legitimate points will be ignored or passed over. However, there is a disadvantage: You may accidentally dismiss some of the other person's truly legitimate points. This is particularly true in home and work situations, where seemingly irrelevant comments have some basis in fact and deserve to be listened to and explored before deciding to dismiss and redirect.

The Goal: Increasing Awareness of Aggressive Behavior and Its Effects on Others

Questions to Prompt Awareness. Hopefully, when the other person becomes aware of her aggressive behavior and its negative effects on herself and others, she will be more motivated to change. In work and personal relationships, it usually helps if you simply describe the specific aggressive behavior and its effects and ask if the person is aware of this behavior. This can be followed by expressing your concern and asking the person to change. The following are the kinds of questions you can ask:

- Do you know that when you address customers by (describe the specific behavior), they get turned off? (Pause and wait for the person's response.) I'm very concerned about this and want to talk about it further.
- Have you noticed that when you command the kids to do something in that tone of voice, they are less likely to do it than when you ask them nicely? Something you might

want to think about.

At times you may wish to let someone know that his behavior is out of line without getting involved in an extended discussion. This is often the case when you're dealing with strangers. The following examples illustrate how questions can be used to prompt awareness in such situations.

When asked to wrap a package, the clerk said nothing but looked extremely irritated and wrapped the package in a very surly manner. The customer responded in a puzzled, nonsarcastic tone of voice, "You got mad because I asked you to wrap the package?" He then walked away, leaving the clerk to think about her own behavior.

A security officer became visibly angry when a college professor, who had forgotten her office key, asked him to unlock her door. Seeing his anger, the professor became irritated, thinking that she had not asked him to do something that was unwarranted and that she didn't deserve his anger. After a few minutes, she asked in an even tone, "Tell me, are you angry because I asked you to come down and open my door?" The officer responded with a polite but cold, "No, Madam." He paused and then continued, "Well, there are other things I could be doing besides coming here and opening up doors for teachers who don't remember their keys."

The professor paused and then assertively said, "I can see where that does get irritating. I want to tell you that I don't make a habit of forgetting my key. These papers are extremely important, and I needed them today." In this situation, each party achieved more understanding of the other's behavior and established satisfactory limits.

Effects: This tactful, nonblameful way of prompting awareness makes people less likely to become defensive about their behavior. In work and personal relationships, asking about awareness is important since people quite often don't realize their effects upon others. If the person is aware of her behavior and its effects, you can learn what she gets out of continuing the objectionable behavior.

Use of Contrasts. The contrast between your own reasonable calmness and the other person's aggression can lead the

240

other person to realize that her behavior is inappropriate.

> Jenny changed her flight plans and was at the airport ticket desk trying to get information on a variety of different routes to her destination. The travel agent was short in his replies and in general was acting in a surly fashion. Jenny first tried becoming increasingly firm in her requests for information, but each firm request was met with less thinly veiled hostility. Finally, she dropped her voice and in a polite, calm voice, slowly repeated what she wanted. The agent looked startled and immediately changed his behavior.

The Goal: Limiting the Aggressive Behavior

Though the intervention techniques discussed so far in this chapter will probably lead the other person to eventually modify or drop his aggressive behavior, at times you may wish to try to directly limit the annoying behavior itself.

Direct Negative Feedback. You can limit annoying behavior by asking the person to change or by giving the other person some direct negative feedback on his behavior. The following are some examples:

- I guess it's just a habit to call women "honey," but I would appreciate your not using that term with me.
- I find your tone of voice very offensive. Please stop addressing me like a kid.
- I realize you meant no offense, yet that comment really got on my nerves.

Effects: By providing direct negative feedback, you let the other person know exactly what behavior is annoying and you have a better chance of setting limits on that behavior by providing negative feedback. You should be aware of one potential problem: Since this approach does not deal with any underlying problems, the aggressive behavior may stop without being replaced by cooperative behavior. In work and personal relationships you may want to change the emphasis when you use this approach. If you put more emphasis on expressing your appreciation for the behaviors you like than on expressing your irritation about the behaviors you don't like, you probably will have succeeded in placing less strain on the relationship.

Treat the Putdown as a Neutral Comment. This involves treating the putdown question or comment as though it were an honest, assertive question and responding to it with a straight answer. This is particularly useful in responding to double messages on the part of the other person. The following are examples:

- What do you women's libbers want, anyway? Response: Fairness and equality.
- Boy those pants sure do fit! Response: Thank you.
- A woman was interviewed for a job, in the process of which the interviewer looked at her leeringly and said, "You certainly look like you have all the qualifications for the job." Response: (firmly but nonhostilely) I'm sure I am quite capable of doing the work here.

Effects: This approach can diffuse the aggressive behavior. Though it does not have all the characteristics of assertive behavior since it is not totally direct, it does enable you to protect yourself and to indirectly set limits. It is particularly helpful in those situations where it is inappropriate or too risky to disclose your true feelings about the putdown behavior and to discuss it with the other person.

Sorting the Issues. Sorting is another technique that often is quite effective. You can use a series of three steps to focus on the real issue or problem.[5]

The *first* step is to ask yourself, "What exactly is this person saying to me about me and my motives?" You need to determine exactly what the speaker is implying about you, for example, that you are uptight or no fun or a drag if you are not dancing at a party.

The *second* step is to sort out what is factually true from what is the other person's interpretation and judgment of what those facts mean about you. For instance, it may be true that you are not dancing and that, consequently, your date is not having as much fun. But this does *not* mean that you are uptight,

242

a drag, or a "bad" person because you don't want to dance.

The *third* step, then, is to respond to the other person by *disconnecting* the faulty assumptions the other person has just made. For instance, you might say to your date, "It's true that I don't want to dance now and you do. I am not uptight or a drag simply because I am not doing what you would like to do." If your date continues to argue that you *should* dance or that you are a bore to be with, you can very directly ask him to stop putting you down or tell him that you are annoyed with how he is treating you. The crucial step in sorting is to be able to accurately assess the implied messages expressed by the other person and to determine what is legitimate and what is not.

One faulty connection that many people imply can be seen in the phrase, "I love you, and I won't buy you a Jaguar." Some people imply "if you really like/love/respect me, you will . . . (do what I want you to do)." A neighbor with whom you've spent a good deal of time during the past two years comments about your friendliness toward a new neighbor: "Well, I guess you and Emily are really getting along lately. I suppose you and Bob will be doing something with Emily and Ralph again this weekend. Mark and I hardly see you two anymore. I guess you're just too busy."

Such a comment clearly warrants some sorting. After separating what is accurate and what has been assumed, you might make this kind of assertive response: "I haven't been spending as much time with you recently, and I have been seeing Emily quite a bit. I like both of you very much, and I do want to continue to be very good friends with you." Relatives often express this same feeling, the fear that you do not care enough or spend enough time with them. If you can recognize this implied message, you will be able to respond honestly and directly. The result often is a very satisfying exchange. In these kinds of situations, it is very important to specify what you do wish to do and what you are not willing to do with that person. (I love you, and I won't buy you a Jaguar.)

Effects: Sorting enables you to separate in your own mind the incorrect and often manipulative connections others make between your behaviors and your motives. You can then admit to the other person what *is* true and disagree with her inaccurate assumptions. Sorting prevents others from redefining either your motives or your behaviors. You can then avoid ending up feeling defensive, guilty, or "bad." Exercise 16 gives you practice in sorting out issues.

Exercise 16   Sorting Out

Below are several situations in which someone else has either *redefined* the meaning of someone's behavior or has attributed some meaning that is not true. As you read them, sort out what is factually true and what is an interpretation or an assumption. Then think of an actual nondefensive response that would clarify what is true and what is inaccurate about the situation.

1. Your boss angrily complains, "How could you not follow up on those details. I thought you realized how important this project is."

2. Your professor says, "You want to turn your project in *late*? I didn't think you were that kind of student."

3. Your teenage son (or your lover) says, "If you really trusted me, you wouldn't ask me where I've been tonight."

4. You've asked the person you are intimately involved with to listen more attentively when you are talking to him. He responds with, "I always knew you needed a lot of extra attention, but don't lay that stuff on me. I'm not going to fall all over you just because you're so insecure."

5. A relative says, "You mean you let Johnny go with those others all by himself? Don't you think about what might happen to your children when they're unsupervised?"

6. After a party, your friend snaps at you, "Why do you always get so uptight at parties. You stand around like a scared chicken. No wonder you have a lousy time! Who would want to go near you?"

7. A friend applied for a job in your department, and you were a member of the selection committee. He did not get the position, and you neglected to make a special effort to inform him of the committee's decision. He comes to you several weeks later and says, "I just want you to know that I am very angry with you. You *knew* I wasn't chosen for the job. How could you be so insensitive? You never said a word to me. I thought you really cared, but I can see friendships and people's feelings aren't very important to you."

8. John criticized his wife, Jane, saying, "You've really changed since you've gone back to school. You're a lot colder. You're hardly ever around. Maybe I don't have all the education I should. So what!"

PERSISTING
Sometimes your assertive message will meet resistance.

When this happens, the intervention techniques discussed earlier in this chapter will be helpful. In addition, you can persist in assertively pursuing your objective or making your statement. Persistent assertiveness has important ingredients. There are several things to do:

- Be clear about what your goal is.
- Respond flexibly to the other person's legitimate concerns or objections.
- Deal effectively with comments that divert you from your goal. This may involve doing such things as ignoring put-downs, dismissing and redirecting, etc.
- Know when to stop persisting.

Assertively persisting involves quickly assessing whether the other person's comments are ones that are better ignored or responded to as shown in the following two examples. The guidelines for persisting are noted in parentheses.

<u>Situation:</u>	A customer had recently purchased an expensive pair of boots. After two weeks the heels fell off.
Customer:	Excuse me, are you the manager? I'd like to exchange these boots. The heels of both boots have fallen off. (Come straight to the point; don't belabor the issue.)
Manager:	Just how long have you been wearing these boots anyway? They really look beat up.
Customer:	Two weeks—and I've worn them a couple of times. I like the style, and I would like to exchange them for another pair. (Ignore the innuendo and stick to your goal.)
Manager:	(frowning) Well, we'll take care of having the boots repaired. That's the best we can do. (This is a compromise, and it may be the best you can get.)
Customer:	I appreciate your offer to have them repaired. How-

ever, I would like to exchange them for another pair. I spent a lot of money on these shoes, and I want a pair that's in good shape, not a pair that has been already repaired.
(Acknowledge the compromise and emphasize the importance of what you want with additional information.)

Manager: But boots will be just as good with the heels repaired. Besides, our store policy is not to exchange shoes.
(The store policy is a legitimate objection that needs to be addressed.)

Customer: I see. I do think that in my case the policy would not quite apply. You see, these particular boots not only have defective heels, but the glue is also showing on the seams. From looking at the other boots in the store, I can see that's not the case with them. I strongly believe that this is one of those unusual cases where these particular boots were manufactured wrong. And for that reason I'd like to have these exchanged.

Manager: Let me take a closer look at them. Well . . . . OK, I think we can make an exception in this case.

Customer: I really appreciate that. Thank you.

Situation: Judy was at her parents' thirty-fifth wedding anniversary party. Her folks served an elaborate buffet. However, Judy was on a diet. As she got her food from the table, her father started issuing commands about what she was supposed to eat.

Dad: Judy, is that all you're eating? Hand me your plate. You can't pass up the potato salad. Your mother went through a lot of trouble to make it.

Judy: (holding on to her plate) I know Mom did, and the potato salad looks good, as usual, but I'm going to say no.

(Ignore the command and sort between Mom's work and what you want.)

Dad: If you lose any more weight, you'll look like a stick. Come on. Give me your plate like a good girl and I'll fix it up for you.

Judy: I'm just fine with what I've got. Thanks anyway (starts moving around the table).
(Ignore the putdown and command. Stick to your goal.)

Dad: Well at least try the German Chocolate cake. Mom would be hurt if you didn't eat it.

Judy: I don't want to hurt Mom, and I don't want to break my diet. Dad, it's taking every bit of willpower I've got to say no. Please stop pressuring me (said firmly).
(Sort between Mom's hurt and what you want. Express feelings and request that the offensive behavior stop.)

Dad: Well, if you insist.

Judy: Yes, thanks Dad.

Escalating Assertion

In some cases assertively persisting will mean that you will have to escalate your assertion.[6] You begin escalating your assertion with a mild assertive statement that could be reasonably expected to accomplish your goal with a minimum of effort and negative reaction on the part of the other person.[7] If, instead of responding to this mild assertion, the person continues to violate your rights or ignores legitimate points, you should gradually increase the firmness of your assertive message. In most situations, it isn't necessary to go beyond the initial mild assertion, but if necessary, you have room to become increasingly firm without becoming aggressive. The following is an example.

Situation: Magazine salesman telephones to solicit for magazines.

Salesman: Is this the lady of the house?

Tricia:	I'm the owner. Who is this please?
Salesman:	My name is Gil Savoy, and I represent the Delux Merchandising Company. We're conducting a survey in this city, and I'd like to ask you some questions about the magazines that your family reads.
Tricia:	Excuse me. Is any part of this survey going to involve a special deal if I buy some magazines?
Salesman:	You're in luck. Those people who complete the survey will be eligible for a special 30 percent reduction on the homeowners' magazine.
Tricia:	Thank you for telling me that. Actually, I'm not interested in buying any more magazines.
Salesman:	Sounds like you're already a reader of magazines. Just answer this one question, "How many magazines do you subscribe to and what are they?"
Tricia:	As I said, I don't want to buy any magazines.
Salesman:	But you don't even know what you're refusing. You haven't heard me out.
Tricia:	I *know* I don't want any magazines, and that's good enough for me.
Salesman:	OK then, good-bye.

Persistance is very important in many situations. But in many of these same situations, it is just as important to know when to stop persisting.

Situation:	A homeowner hired a man to come out and cut the grass every ten days during the summer. On the day the homeowner was scheduled to have the first cut of the season, it rained.

Homeowner:	I'd like you to come out tomorrow and cut the grass, since it rained today.
Lawn man:	I can't do it tomorrow, but I can work it in in about three days.
Homeowner:	Well you did promise to cut it today. With the rain, of course, it's impossible. But I don't understand why you couldn't do it tomorrow.
Lawn man:	Here's the situation. I've already scheduled all

249

	the lawns I can handle in one day. If I were to do your lawn tomorrow—and that's assuming that the ground is dry enough—I'd have to bump another customer I had scheduled. Now if the shoe were on the other foot, you wouldn't want me to bump you for a customer who got rained out on his day, would you?
*Homeowner:	No—but I do think you should make some kind of arrangements to handle these rain days. But that's your problem, not mine. I want my lawn cut.
Lawn man:	I know you're frustrated. I don't have the extra help, and the best I can do is squeeze it in the next couple of days.
Homeowner:	But that doesn't help me with my problem. The grass is really getting long, and the place looks like nobody lives in it.
Lawn man:	I guess we're at an impasse. You want the lawn cut tomorrow, and I can't do it. All I can say is that I'll do my level best to get it in as soon as I possibly can.
Homeowner:	OK then.

In this example, the homeowner was so focused on his goal that he stopped listening to the lawn man's legitimate objections. At the point marked by the asterisk, the homeowner would have been more responsibly assertive if he would have stopped pushing the lawn man to change and found some other way of dealing with the problem.

There are at least four times when it's a good idea to stop persisting: (1) when it's clear that neither party is willing to change position so that further persistence will get nowhere; (2) when either party starts to lose control of the situation; (3) when further persistence could have dangerous consequences; and (4) when you recognize that the real issue is that of proving who's boss rather than what's being discussed. When you stop persisting, you can leave, end the discussion, change the focus of the discussion, or move toward a compromise, or generate some other ways of solving the conflict.

Ending the Escalating Assertion

The Contract Option. If the other person is not cooperating and if you are not ignoring legitimate objections, you can use the "contract option." This involves informing the other person what the final assertion will be and giving him a chance to change his behavior before it occurs. For example, when a repair shop repeatedly refuses to settle an unreasonable bill, you can say, "I'm being left with no other alternative than to write to the Better Business Bureau and your distributor. I'd prefer not to do that but I will. I hope this isn't the only alternative I'm left with." Some people only realize that you mean business at this point. If the person refuses to change, in effect, she has decided to take the consequences of her behavior. For the contract option to be effective it must be realistic—it must be something you are willing to carry out. Also, it needs to be stated in a matter-of-fact tone of voice that simply gives information about the consequences if the situation is not satisfactorily resolved. If you say it in a menacing tone of voice, relying on fear to support your argument, you are using it as a threat rather than as a simple, factual statement of consequences. This approach usually reduces the effectiveness of your statement because threats tend to hook people into being resistant.

Process Observation. When the discussion becomes repetitious and starts running in circles, you can use process observation to get things moving again. Specifically describe what you see happening in the interaction process and open up the discussion about the process *itself*. In some cases it is appropriate to point out the problem (the process) and end the discussion, as in the following exchanges.

Situation: Marianne and Cindy are close friends. Marianne has kept pushing Cindy to agree to a blind date. Finally, Cindy pointed out what was happening in this discussion:

Cindy: In the last ten minutes I've said that I don't want that blind date, yet each time I said no, you didn't accept it and came up with another reason why I should. What's going on between us? It's so unlike you to keep pushing like that.

Marianne: Well, I guess I'm just worried about you. Every since you and David broke up, you've been so sad, and I really thought a date would help.

The discussion then shifted to Cindy's sadness and what she was already doing to help herself. The outcome benefited both Cindy and Marianne. Cindy gave Marianne better information about her feelings and what she might be able to do to help with her sadness. Thus, Cindy kept a friend who was truly concerned about her welfare and also got the kind of help she really needed.

Situation: Willie worked as a supervisor of tellers at a local bank. One of the tellers, Gaylen, asked to not work the day before and after Thanksgiving. Willie refused, explaining that this was a busy period for the bank and that the teller's services were needed. The discussion continued and started to become circular until Willie used the process observation:

Willie: Gaylen, have you noticed that this talk has gone in circles? You keep asking for the holiday and come up with reasons why that's important to you. I keep saying no and coming up with reasons why not. I don't think either of us is going to change our feelings about it, so I think we might as well stop it here. What do you think?

Gaylen: I suppose you're right. I'll come to work, even though I'm not happy about it.

HANDLING YOUR OWN AGGRESSION

Getting Feedback

It usually is fairly easy to recognize others' aggressiveness. A short, nasty comment, a glare, a menacing gesture—these responses are clear enough. But recognizing your own aggression sometimes is a very different matter. You are often unaware of the extent of your aggressive behavior because others may not give direct feedback. Therefore, it is ideal to identify a person whose judgment you trust and who is likely to see you in situations where you become aggressive. Enlist this person's help to give regular feedback on (1) how you handle specific stress-producing situations, (2) the specific aspects of your behavior (body language, comments, etc.) that are aggressive, and (3) positive suggestions on how you can handle situations differently.

Locating "Triggers"

One way to keep track of when you are aggressive is to keep a log. The log can help you find out what triggers your aggressive behavior. When you have this information, you will become more aware of sensitive spots and be able to stop the internal process that leads to aggressive behavior.[8] In your daily log, you should note the following:

1. Your aggressive comment or action.
2. A precise description of what the other person did or said just before you became aggressive.
3. The feelings you were experiencing (in addition to anger).
4. The thoughts that crossed your mind just before you reacted aggressively.
5. Your body language reactions just before your aggressive reaction.

Figure 20 (page 254) is a sample log. Collect this information for two or three weeks. Then read the log, looking for the common elements in people's behavior that trigger your aggression. For example, Sandy found her sensitive spots had to do with three things: (1) any sign of failure, especially academic failure, on her son's part, (2) any indifference her son showed about his failure, and (3) disagreement by her husband and children, especially in questioning her judgment.

Look for any *patterns* in the thoughts, feelings, and body reactions that come before your aggressive behavior. For ex-

Figure 20 Sample Excerpts from Sandy's Log

Aggressive Comment or Action	The Trigger	Feelings
I told David (son) that he was just like his Uncle Jerry who landed up in jail.	David was watching TV instead of studying.	Worried and mad
I told Mary, my sister, that only goody-two-shoes kids make the dean's list.	May told me that her daughter made the dean's honor roll.	Jealous
I lost my temper with David and grounded him for a month.	David's report card came—all D's and some C's—and he laughed when he gave it to me.	Mad—worried, too
I just looked at David disgustedly and shook my head.	David was assembling the lawn furniture and gave up halfway through the job.	Disgusted
I sarcastically told my husband that he was a model father.	My husband disagreed with my punishing David.	Scared and irritated
I told the encyclopedia saleslady that she should peddle her stuff elsewhere.	She said that all children's grades improve when encyclopedias are in the home.	Helpless and irritated

ample, just before Sandy became aggressive, she internally cursed and had thoughts about not being respected. Besides feeling angry, she usually felt worried. Her body reaction before aggression had this pattern: Tension began with her thigh muscles and quickly moved up her body until it reached her jaws. When her jaws tightened for more than a few seconds, she usually became aggressive.

Figure 20   Sample Excerpts from Sandy's Log (Continued)

Thoughts	Body Reactions Before Answering Aggressively
He's going to be a bum the rest of his life if I don't take a strong hand to him. If he really respected me, he'd study.	I could feel my jaws really tightening. I tried to keep my mouth shut, but I couldn't.
Why can't David be more like his cousin? She's got her nerve telling me that when she knows how badly David's doing in school . . . . Damn!	The jaws again—really tight. I wonder if that's why my mouth hurts sometimes?
Damn—all I remember is just cursing inside. The kid's got no respect.	I remember that as I read the report card I could feel my body becoming more and more tense, especially my face and hands.
Look at that—he's quitting already.	Nothing in particular that I haven't written already.
He's got his nerve telling me that; that's the reason why David's got no respect for me.	I could feel myself glaring at him—like I was going to bore a hole right through him.
Other people's kids do well in school. How come David doesn't? It must be all my fault. I guess I'm no good as a parent.	The jaws again. Also my hand got all tight into a fist.

Handling Your Triggers

When you have identified triggers, analyze them and change the thinking around your sensitive spots. For example, Sandy analyzed and changed her thinking about her son's failure (see Figure 21, page 256).

Watch for the types of situations that trigger your aggression. When the situation that normally triggers your aggression

Figure 21 Sandy's Analysis of Her Sensitive Spots

Incorrect Thinking	More Accurate Thinking
My son's academic failure means I've failed as a parent.	I've done the best I can as a parent. I don't know why he's not doing better in school. I need to find out.
I must get tough with him, or else he'll continue goofing off.	Getting tough hasn't worked. All it's done is get my son mad and up-set me. I don't know how to get him to stop goofing off. If I could just ask him directly, it might help him work harder in school.
It's all my responsibility to get him "shaped up."	He has some responsibility for himself too.
I can't show him I'm worried because that's weak.	Covering up my worry hasn't gotten me anywhere. It's only human to worry sometimes.
If he really respected me, he'd do what I asked.	Respect has nothing to do with this. I don't think he's so happy with his grades either. Something is definitely wrong. Maybe we all need to see a counselor. I do need to find out what's wrong.

---

occurs, internally label it.[9] For example, you might tell yourself, "Now that is an example of a disinterest-with-school-achievement trigger that usually leads me to attacking . . . . I had better pause for a moment and think of something else to say." When you label your trigger, you usually will gain a little more perspective on the situation.

Once you have realized and labeled what is happening, you can use coping statements to redirect your thinking away from thoughts that normally trigger aggressive action. For example, Sandy was particularly alert for her internal cursing since this was so closely associated with aggression. When she found herself internally cursing, she told herself to stop the cursing and, instead, to focus on what she wanted to say. She also gave herself the more accurate thoughts shown in Figure 21.

Coping statements often work well with exercises that relax specific muscles associated with your pattern of aggression. (See Appendix A.) You can also use coping self-statements to change those body positions that are typically associated with aggression. For example, Sandy deliberately relaxed her jaw muscles by dropping them so that they were no longer clenched. She also kept her hands open and not balled up in a fist. Lastly, since she often began staring before she became aggressive, she instructed herself to break eye contact and to casually glance around the room.

When you express yourself about a sensitive issue or concern, you should allow yourself to speak up while also telling yourself to edit what you say. Instead of expressing thoughts as they automatically cross your mind, internally check what you're going to say and edit or eliminate the aggressive components.[10] Guidelines for editing are:

Aggressive Components	Change To
You *should* do _____ .	I would like you to do _____ .
Global generalizations about another's character	Descriptions of specific behaviors you find annoying
Sarcasm	Directly saying what you want or object to
Questions which put down the other person (e.g., "Why don't you think of someone else besides yourself for a change?")	Edit out the questions completely or change to: "When you do _____ I feel _____ ."
Cursing	Edit it out completely or change to: "When you do _____ I feel very angry."

The following list is an example. Exercise 17 (page 258) will give you additional practice.

Sometimes your behavior is aggressive not so much because of the comments you make, but rather because of how you make those comments, i.e., your *style* of delivery. For instance, you may badger someone with a stream of questions without even realizing it. In these cases, it is helpful to get yourself to engage in behavior that is incompatible with the aggressive behavior you want to change.

If You Tend To	Try This Instead
Badger others.	Reflect the person's answer before you ask another question.
Talk too long and get into tirades.	Send verbal "telegrams." For example, consolidate your message into three short sentences, each beginning with "I think," "I feel," or "I want" instead of "You are."
Speak more harshly than is appropriate in the situation.	Lower your voice and speak more calmly or softly.

Exercise 17   Editing Your Comments

For each of the following situations, write down how you could edit your thoughts to make assertive instead of aggressive statements.

1. A neighborhood child has just cut through your property after you have told her not to do this. You think: "She must have been born in a barn! She's got her nerve cutting through the lawn."

2. Someone of your committee has just made what you think is a ridiculous suggestion. You think: "What a stupid idea. She should know better than that!"

3. Your boss asks you to run a personal errand during your lunch hour. You think: "I'm not a lacky. I don't get paid to do that work. She shouldn't ask me to do that!"

4. You and a car dealer have just agreed on a price on a new car and your trade in. He returns from checking the deal with his manager and says that the manager wouldn't approve the contract. The new price he offers is $300 higher than the one originally agreed upon. You think: "He's a crook. I saw this act on TV. If he thinks I'll stand for this, he's crazy!"

SUMMARY

There are several techniques you can use to handle others' putdowns, attempts at guilt-induction, and avoidance of your legitimate points. The intervention technique you choose largely depends on your goal in that situation.

Handling your own aggressive tendencies involves becoming aware of when you're aggressive and identifying what triggers your behavior. You can diffuse those things that trigger your aggression by labeling them and by using coping self-statements to instruct yourself to redirect your thinking and to relax. Instead of just giving yourself free hand to say whatever pops into your head, it is often better to instruct yourself to edit what you plan to say when you are dealing with your own aggressive tendencies.

Once you have a handle on your own aggression and know how to handle the aggression of others, you can act assertively and effectively. If, in the face of opposition, you persist by remaining goal directed, your assertive actions may increase the chances of getting positive results.

NOTES

1.   Jakubowski-Spector, P. *An introduction to assertive training procedures for women.* Washington, DC: American Personnel and Guidance Association, 1973.

2.   Strayhorn, J. M. Jr. *Talking it out.* Champaign, IL: Research Press Co., 1977.

3.   Strayhorn, J. M. Jr., 1977.

4.   Bower, S. A., & Bower, G. H. *Asserting yourself.* Reading, MA: Addison-Wesley Publishing Company, 1976.

5.   Whitely, R. Personal communication, October, 1977.

6.   Rimm, D. C., & Masters, J. C. *Behavior therapy: Techniques and empirical findings.* New York: Academic Press, 1974.

7.   Rimm, D. C., & Masters, J. C., 1974.

8.   Schmidt, J. A. *Help yourself.* Champaign, IL: Research Press Co., 1976.

9.   Schmidt, J. A., 1976.

10.   Gottman, J., Notarius, C., Gonso, J., & Markman, H. *A couple's guide to communication.* Champaign, IL: Research Press Co., 1976.

10
Conversational Skills

PRESENTING THE
REAL YOU

What do you do when you meet people? Many people panic when they are confronted by the ordeal of having to initiate and sustain a conversation, especially with a stranger. Their fears make it impossible to use whatever social and conversational skills they possess.

Even if you usually don't turn into putty in these kinds of situations, you probably feel at least a little nervous or uncertain when meeting some people. There are many possible reasons for feeling this way, but they usually are based on two fears: the fear of performance and the fear of rejection. Will I do it right? Will I be liked? These two questions consciously or unconsciously influence the fearful person's thinking, and when these fears become sufficiently strong, some people then convince themselves that it is easier to avoid the situation while others get depressed and berate themselves for their inadequacies. Still others decide to simply make themselves "visible" and hope that others will find them so appealing (without doing a thing) that they will initiate the contact. It seems much safer to be shy or coquettish or the "strong, silent type," and one can always rationalize any lack of initiative by the other person. (I didn't really get rejected; she just didn't catch my message.)

At the other end of the continuum are those who also worry a great deal about rejection and/or performance but overcompensate by talking endlessly, coming on too strong, or dominating the conversation for fear of losing control of the situation and failing.

You can make a great deal of effective change by focusing on changing specific behaviors. It is likely that as you are successful in using new behaviors, your attitudes and beliefs also will change. And the reverse is equally true: New, reasonable thoughts and attitudes can influence behaviors. That is, if you think assertively and rationally, you are more likely to behave assertively. Rational thinking can free you to enjoy the contacts you make with others more fully. Exercise 18 will help you pinpoint your irrational worries and rationalizations that may cause you to avoid social contacts.

Exercise 18   Avoiding Made Easy

1. List five irrational worries or thoughts that would lead you to avoid approaching and talking with someone you find interesting or attractive.
   a.
   b.
   c.
   d.
   e.
2. List three rationalizations that would help you justify avoiding that person at that time.
   a.
   b.
   c.

By trying, people can overcome their fear of social contact, just as John Emerson did. John Emerson is a highly successful engineer; yet about five years ago he was deathly afraid of people in small social settings when out of his professional element. As John progressed through college and had less family contact, he became increasingly aware of his conversational "inadequacies" (as he called them). Faced with increasing opportunities for social contact, John's fears of failure and rejection became greater and greater. He became withdrawn, was often depressed (not severely), and began to abuse a wide variety of drugs (hallucinogens, amphetamines, cocaine, and marijuana) which reduced his fears but also punished him. Fortunately, John became worried about his condition.

John's background is not as unusual as it might first appear. In fact, he had what most people would call a "normal childhood." He was not beaten or rejected or isolated or severely overprotected, although both of his parents were rather reserved and his father was a perfectionist. Though he had had little contact with schoolmates throughout elementary and high school, preferring to work on interesting projects and to read, he was a very pleasant and likable person. However, he could have had different experiences that would have facilitated his making contact with others more comfortably.

John wanted to meet more people. On the rare occasions that he did so, he enjoyed himself, even though he felt awkward. John used the steps described in previous chapters: He analyzed his behavior, made the appropriate changes, and practiced his new behavior.

First he identified his internal dialogues in several specific situations (one at a time). When he wanted to talk with someone after class, John would think, "What if he just ignores me? I don't have anything to say anyway. I can't just walk up to him. This place is so hard to meet people. Why doesn't somebody do something about that? Look, just go up and talk to him about the class. But, that's so stupid—nobody cares about this class. Oh damn, he's getting away! I blew it." He then identified the underlying irrational ideas. He discovered four that supported his thinking:

1. I must be liked by every significant person.
2. I must be competent.
3. It's easier to avoid difficult situations.
4. People (myself) who are bad deserve to be punished.

These are paraphrases of the irrational ideas listed as numbers 1, 2, 8, and 4 respectively (see pages 124-129).

Second, John challenged the irrational aspects of his internal dialogue and the irrational assumptions upon which it was based. He disputed their truth and accuracy by arguing

263

against them logically (of course, he won), and he decided that he didn't *have* to be liked and respected by everyone and didn't *have* to be perfect. Those were actually preferences, not "musts," and if he was rejected or if he was less than perfect, it was *not* the end of the world. He could live with imperfection and work toward changing his behaviors as he chose to do so. And he decided that it was *not* easier to avoid people, especially in the long run. Last, he decided that if he did get rejected or if he did not interact as effectively as he would like, he did *not* need to berate himself or get depressed by thinking how inadequate and unlikable he was.

The last step followed smoothly as he developed a series of brief thoughts he could think to himself before, during, and after approaching someone. These thoughts were more accurate statements about himself and his preferences. Here are a few examples:

- I'd like _____ to like me and respond with interest. If he does, great; if he doesn't I can live with it.
- I'd like to approach _____ in an effective, comfortable way. If I do, that's fine, but I don't *have* to. I can work on it if I choose to.
- I can handle my fear and go ahead and talk with _____ . I'm safe, and I can do this.
- If it doesn't turn out the way I'd like, I do *not* have to berate myself or punish myself. I will regret it, but that's all.

After John practiced thinking these thoughts several times, he set up a behavioral plan to gradually increase his conversations with others. (Although John's plan was somewhat different, he followed the guidelines that Ken used in Chapter 11.) He practiced a number of conversational skills that will be presented in the next section.

John made very significant progress. He stopped abusing drugs and actually began a richer and fuller lifestyle that included activities involving people.

Exercise 19 will give you practice in challenging your own irrational ideas and substituting more rational thoughts.

Exercise 19 How to Rid Yourself of Misery

Take each of the statements you listed in Exercise 18 and, first, identify which of the 10 irrational ideas supports such a thought (see pages 124-129). Then challenge each statement. Argue against it logically. Next, substitute more rational thoughts that would lead you to be more likely to approach the other person. Write those alternative thoughts below.

1. a.
    b.
    c.
    d.
    e.
2. a.
    b.
    c.

List all the personal rights you believe you have in this situation.

1.
2.
3.
4.
5.
6.

Another outcome of dysfunctional thinking warrants attention. When people convince themselves that they *must* impress someone (must be liked or respected), they decide that they must present a certain kind of image. Sometimes these images are limiting sex role stereotypes: for women, being "cute," sexy, not too bright, demure, shy, flirtatious, or mysterious; for men, being strong, tough, sexy, rich, intelligent, funny, clever, or eloquent. Regardless of whether the images are limited to one sex or the other (an important issue in itself), the images themselves are often restrictive and limiting. Trying to carry on a meaningful conversation, attempting to get to know someone and to share your thoughts and feelings—while at the same time you have to put everything through a strainer to make sure it fits your image is, at best, more work than it is worth. First of all it's hard work; second, it's distracting and keeps you from making more genuine contact with the other person; and, third, the belief that you will only be liked if you fit the image isn't true. Although it's true that *some* people only want to see the image, you don't *have* to be liked by everyone. It would be nice—but not necessary at all costs! If you choose to present yourself in a particular manner, especially for its intrinsic pleasure, that is certainly your choice. Many people label behaviors or styles as fake stereotypes when, in fact, they are genuine. However, it probably is a good idea to consider the degree to which you have accepted the notion that there is a way you *should* be when it's not the way you *wish* to be. If you like the ways you present yourself to others, then you can continue to act as you have in the past. If you want to change some of them, that is fine, too. But most of us want contact with others, and many of the ways we have learned to present ourselves are designed primarily to have a particular impact on others to make them think highly of us. Conversations and relationships based on such "image consciousness" become a means to an end—impressing someone—and the intrinsic enjoyment of communicating with others is then often lost or given a back seat. Of course, everyone likes to make a good impression and there is nothing wrong with wanting to do so *until* it becomes one's primary purpose and goal.

Many times this push to impress others comes from a belief that "I must be respected or liked and I must gain it by showing how bright (rich, witty, sexy, powerful, cute, suave, adventurous, or provocative) I am." This simply isn't necessary and is also untrue, for you may actually have some or all of these qualities. You do not have to impress people with them. If you have them, you will reveal them without great effort. If you don't, faking it will not last forever, and keeping up the front can be a self-imposed form of torture.

Most importantly, you don't have to adopt images in order to be likable or happy. You might choose to work toward

266

possessing certain qualities, but you should do so because it will be pleasurable to *you,* not because it will impress others. You are who and what you are, and you don't *have* to be anything else to be happy. You can seek improvement without demanding it or worrying yourself. When you try to change this way, the pressure is off and you are freer to enjoy others.

Although it is easy to fall into the "image trap," you may not have this problem and you may not be too concerned about it. However, it is a barrier to using the skills that are described later in this chapter. So, even if this is not a serious problem for you, Exercise 20 (page 268) will be a good way to analyze how well you present the "real you" to others.

DEVELOPING
CONVERSATIONAL SKILLS

You probably at least once have had the uncomfortable experience of being in a social conversation full of "pregnant pauses," during which people groped and strained to think of something to say just to keep things moving. In such situations you may begin thinking irrationally, which only increases your anxiety and reduces your ability to use the conversational skills you do possess. However, even if you removed all of your fears, you still have to say something.

The question is, What? You can use the "clever phrase" approach: "Hi, my name is Art, how do you like me so far?" Sometimes this will work, but if your purpose is to have an intelligent, meaningful, or at least honest encounter, you will be starting off on the wrong foot by relying on this kind of superficiality. Instead, practice conversations and think about what you might say before you approach someone. There are several simple yet very effective modes of response you can apply to any context. These responses are not pat phrases; they are general classes or types of responses like making requests, asking for information, or expressing feelings. Instead of being conversational formulas ("Would you like to see my pet rock?" or "What's a nice person like you doing in a place like this?") that are used mindlessly, these modes are principles that you can apply as you feel is appropriate.

Exercise 20 Developing Your Style

Although you can't be anything you want to be or have any quality you choose, you can control how you relate to others. Within the limits of your present thoughts, feelings, and behavior, you have a great variety of ways you can relate to a particular individual.

1. Observe other people in conversation and notice how they present themselves. Which nonverbal behaviors communicate their style of relating to the other person? Try to avoid stereotyping (a lover, a flirt, a brain, a dummy, a braggart); just identify the behaviors. Avoid becoming a "junior psychiatrist," and avoid interpreting your subject's behaviors and motives. The purpose of observing people is to get a sense of the variety of styles others use and to become more aware of the ways they get communicated.

2. Select two or three people to approach at different times. Decide in advance how you would like to relate to them:

   1. What is your goal?
   2. How do you want to present yourself generally?
   3. What will you do nonverbally to present yourself?
   4. What underlying needs to impress might get in the way?

   You don't have to have a predetermined script, but you should give some thought to each of the four questions. After you have asked your questions, assess your behavior in terms of your answers to the four questions above. Did you do what you said? What did you like? What would you change next time?

Asking Open-Ended Questions

The first mode of response is asking questions. Often when a conversation feels awkward or strained, one person is either asking too many or too few questions. While you certainly don't want to "grill" someone, the timely use of questions can help the other person "open up." However, an important distinction between open-ended versus closed questions should be made.

The purpose of asking questions in social conversations is usually to discover areas of mutual interest. The question you ask might be designed to maximize receiving what is sometimes called "free information," that is, information the other person is willing to share. Therefore, the more open-ended the questions, the more likely you will be to get more free information.

Contrast the open-ended and closed questions that follow.

Closed questions:
Q. Do you work at the university, too?
A. Yes.
Q. Do you like it?
A. It's OK.
Q. You been there long?
A. Three years.
Q. Do you live around here?
A. Yes, in Newport.
Q. Do you go to discos very often?
A. Sometimes.
Q. Do you like dancing?
A. Yeah.
Q. Isn't it hot in here?
A. Yeah.
Q. Don't you think places like this are depressing (or great)?
A. Yeah, really.
Q. Do you like Led Zeppelin (or Frank Sinatra)?
A. They're OK, I guess.
Q. Are you as bored as I am?
A. Yes!

Open-ended questions:
Q. Where do you work? (a somewhat closed starter).

A. At the university.
Q. Oh. What do you do there?
A. I work in the animal lab.
Q. Really, what do you actually do there?
A. I help raise and feed the animals they use in scientific experiments.
Q. You sound like you enjoy your work. What do you like about it? (If the person sounded negative, you might ask what he did not like about it. If he is indifferent, you might move on to something else or ask open-endedly what he thinks about his work.)
A. Well, I really enjoy working with animals and I especially like taking care of them. Sometimes I get attached to them, and when they get put into some of the experiments, I like to feel I'm part of a scientific enterprise.
Q. Yeah, I never thought of it that way. How did you get into that line of work?
A. Well, it was a lucky accident. I was having beer with a friend and we were talking about animal psychology. The guy next to us overheard the conversation and then he joined in. Turned out that he worked in the lab and knew about the job.

You may notice that a great deal more information resulted from questions that began very simply, with "What" and "How" as opposed to "Do you," "Is it," or "Are you." Not everyone wants to talk about his job, nor are all jobs interesting. The point being demonstrated is that open-ended questions give others a greater *opportunity* to share what is interesting to them.

If the job topic seems uninteresting to you or the other person, you might change to another area, but you should still use open-ended questions. ("What do you do in your free time for fun?" "How did you come to be at this party?") Admittedly, people sometimes volunteer a good deal of information even when asked a closed question, and open-ended questions will elicit only very brief responses (if the other person does not want to talk). Open-ended questions are simply an invitation for a fuller response. You might have noticed that *how* and *what* (and sometimes *why*) questions are inquiries for more than just

270

facts. They also seek descriptions, opinions, attitudes, explanations, feelings, and judgments. The process of getting to know someone goes well beyond the facts about that person, and open-ended questions can help you learn more about how a person thinks, what she believes, and what she values.

Often you will not receive answers to your questions. The other person may be intentionally avoiding the question or ignoring you, or you may unconsciously communicate that you don't really expect an answer (nonassertive body language). Or, the person you are asking may be insensitive or preoccupied. You may simply choose to restate your question. Some people tend to go along with wherever others take the conversation, simply not thinking in terms of what *they* want to discuss. Consequently, they find themselves in other people's conversations even when they initiated the contact. It's OK to restate your question when you don't get an answer to it as in the following:

John: What would you like to do for dinner?
Mary: (Pause) Say, did you see this ad for the Bogart film festival? I'd love to see Key Largo again.
John: Me too. Let's do it but right now I'm wondering what you want to do for dinner?

Exercise 21 (page 272) will help you practice asking questions persistently without being insulting.

Disclosing Information About Yourself
Open-ended questions like the ones listed earlier will enable you to stay focused on one area of conversation for a longer period of time without having to ask a million questions or make clever observations or tell witty anecdotes. Some people work much too hard at carrying on a conversation.

There are two other responses you may want to try. Even if you asked "perfect" open-ended questions, the conversation would be rather one-sided, for you would not be sharing much of yourself. Rather than just ask questions, you might share something about yourself that is related to the topic of discussion. You should use this tactic carefully, however. As we men-

Exercise 21   Asking the Right Question

1. Practice, preferably with another person rather than by yourself, asking only closed questions. (Do you . . . . ? Are you . . . ? Is it . . . ?) Do this for about two minutes and stop. Then start asking open-ended questions for two minutes. Don't do anything else but ask questions at this point. Have the person with whom you are practicing give genuine responses, but don't let them get so long that you don't get to practice. Do this exercise twice a day for about three or four days. Then you can practice as you like.

2. Initiate two conversations a day for three or four days. Be sure to ask three open-ended questions each time. The conversations may be very brief, and you can use other types of responses, but be sure to ask three open-ended questions each time. Afterwards, note what you liked about your questions and what you might do to change them. Also note what kind of responses you got (although they may be explained by many factors).

---

tioned previously, if your primary goal is to be very impressive, your disclosure will probably be less related to the subject and more designed to overpower the listener. Such underlying purposes can become serious barriers to a mutually pleasurable conversation. If you freely give information about yourself without launching on an ego trip, this essentially amounts to sharing your thoughts, opinions, feelings, beliefs, and preferences, which is almost synonymous with assertive behavior.

Self-disclosure is not difficult if you keep several ideas in mind. First, if you think more about what your ideas, opinions, likes and dislikes are and worry less about how other people are reacting to you, you are much more likely to *have* something to say. Second, if you practice and think about appropriate responses, you can continually expand your repertoire of responses. Third, you don't have to converse "spontaneously." You think about what you say and the way you say it (nonverbal behaviors). Thinking ahead about how you will conduct

272

yourself is not hypocritical if the kinds of behaviors you choose reflect your true self. Using cognitive restructuring steps (see Chapter 5) can help with the issue of worrying. The following examples of self-disclosure show how telling the other person about yourself can stimulate a conversation. Remember, you don't have to be eloquent or brilliant, and it's generally more effective to be brief and to the point. The following conversation occurred at an evening class offered to the public.

Clara: What prompted you to take this class?
Harvey: Oh, I've always been interested in history. I thought it would be fun to learn more about the history of our local area.
Clara: Me too. I wasn't sure what the class would be about, but I've really liked the presentations on what it was like here during prehistoric times.

The following is part of a conversation between strangers at a party.

Karen: What do you like about living in Southern California?
LaVerne: Oh, I love it. I live at the beach. I like to swim, and I like to fish, too.
Karen: Sounds great. I've thought about living at the beach, but I decided on an apartment complex instead. It's a little noisier, but I enjoy the pool, Jacuzzi, and tennis.

The following is a conversation on a coffee break.

Jack: What's your new job like?
Lou: Oh, it's all right. I thought I'd be given more responsibility, but I haven't so far.
Jack: It may be just a matter of time, but you may have to eventually go in and ask for it. I did, and it worked out fine.

These very brief examples simply demonstrate the combined use of open-ended questions and self-disclosure. Exercise

22 shows that the same combination holds true for more intimate or more intellectually stimulating conversations.

Exercise 22   Combining Open-Ended Questions and Self-Disclosure

1. Practice combining open-ended questions and making self-disclosures. Ask an open-ended question, get a response from the other person, and give some kind of statement of your own opinion, feeling, preference, or facts. Then stop, and start again with another open-ended question. This is still not a typical conversation. You are only practicing small segments. Practice this for about three days.
2. In your conversations ask an open-ended question and, after you get a response, tell the other person something about you. This may be what happened in number 2 of Exercise 21, but make it intentional this time. As you do these exercises, enjoy yourself, and don't get caught up in trying to do it perfectly.

Restating and Highlighting

Sometimes you just don't have an open-ended question in mind and don't have anything to say about yourself. At other times you simply are interested in what the other person has said and would like him to continue. One way to encourage the other person to continue talking is simply to highlight something he has said. In this instance you may want to give a response that is something between a question and an absolute statement, such as the following.

Other's statement:	I'm a teacher in an elementary school. I teach first graders. They're so much fun to work with. They're so open and curious.
Your highlight:	You really like working with these kids.
Other's response:	Yeah, they want to know about everything. I have to keep on my toes just to stay up with them.

274

Your highlight:	They can be a real challenge even at that age.
Other's response:	You said it!

Sometimes you can reflect the other's *content* in your own words, as in the above conversation, or reflect and highlight the other person's *feelings*, especially when he expresses them non-verbally. The following are reflections which highlight feelings.

Other's statement:	And she didn't even think to ask me if I wanted to go.
Your highlight:	You were pretty annoyed.
Other's statement:	I sure was, especially since she knew I was looking forward to going soon.
Your highlight:	So you were hurt that she didn't think of you.
Other's statement:	(with enthusiasm) I've got a great new job, and I've started meeting lots of new people.
Your highlight:	You're really feeling great.
Other's statement:	Yes. I'm happier than I've been in a long time, and it's super.

As you can see, when you highlight, you must listen attentively to what the other person says *and* how the person feels because you reflect her communication. Besides encouraging the person to go further, such responses let her know you are listening and empathetic. Exercise 23 (page 276) will give you practice in listening to both the content and the feelings that others express. Remember: When you highlight, you are not agreeing or disagreeing. You listen and possibly restate the important parts of what the other person has said.

We have suggested three response modes you might try: open-ended questions, disclosing information about yourself, and restating or highlighting the other person's response. After practicing each response mode separately, practice combining them into a comfortable style of conversation that flows smoothly for you. This integration of modes is important in

Exercise 23   Did You Hear What She Just Said?

1. Have someone talk with you for a few minutes and prac-
    tice restating or highlighting the main thought *or* feeling or
    both that the other person has expressed. Do only that for
    about two minutes even if it seems awkward. Afterwards,
    ask if you were accurate in identifying the main point or
    feeling each time.
2. Twice during five different social conversations, restate
    what the other person's feeling or thought was as you saw
    it. Don't preface it with too many introductory phrases
    like, "What I hear you saying is . . ." or "I'm hearing you
    saying that . . . ." Just restate the message.

---

getting over the initial awkward, almost mechanical manner that
comes with trying anything new. The modes will become less
awkward and more a part of your "normal" conversational
skills as they become integrated into your natural style. It just
takes practice, time, and perseverance.

The following is an example of an extended conversation
at a social gathering. Bruce uses all three response modes.

Bruce: Hi, how did you come to be at this party?
Shirley: Oh, I know Jane. We went to school together. We still
         see each other pretty often because we both work
         downtown.
Bruce: You've known Jane for some time then. I only met
         her a few months ago on a hiking trip.
Shirley: Oh yeah, Jane and I are always doing some kind of
         outdoor thing. We both love the mountains.
Bruce: What do you like to do most?
Shirley: Well, I guess it's skiing, but sometimes I really enjoy
         just walking in the woods. It's so peaceful and beau-
         tiful.
Bruce: I know what you mean. I grew up in the city and
         never really got to any mountains or country until I
         was about twenty-one. By the way, my name's Bruce.
         What's yours?

Shirley:	Hi, Bruce. I'm Shirley.
Bruce:	What do you do downtown where you work?
Shirley:	Oh, I work in a law firm as a researcher.
Bruce:	(with interested tone) A legal researcher?
Shirley:	Yes, I spend a lot of my time reviewing cases related to the ones the lawyer I work with is currently handling. About half the time I'm doing field investigations though, interviewing witnesses, following up leads. The lawyer I work for handles mostly criminal cases. She uses a private investigator for most of the field work, but I get to do a lot of it, too.
Bruce:	It sounds exciting; it sounds like you really enjoy your work.
Shirley:	Yeah, I really do. It's not always exciting, but I usually find it very interesting. What kind of work do you do?
Bruce:	Oh, I play drums in a small rock band.

If you reread this example, you might notice that Bruce could have used any of the three kinds of responses and different content at several points with equal effectiveness. For example, after Shirley's first response, Bruce might have asked where she went to school and what she studied and how it influenced her. Later, he might have picked up on her statement about skiing if that was one of his interests. This part of the conversation lasted less than a minute, yet both people learned more than just the facts about each other.

Although your responses may have been different, none of Bruce's responses were overdone or unnatural. Of course, if Shirley had not wanted to talk with Bruce, he would have had a much harder time of it. These modes of response simply increase the opportunity for having a fuller conversation; they do not make it happen. However, if you practice combining these response modes (see Exercise 24, page 278), you probably will notice how most people will "open up" when you talk to them.

REDIRECTING
THE CONVERSATION

What can you do when you find yourself in an uninterest-

Exercise 24   Combining Response Modes

With a friend, practice a five- or six-minute conversation, using all three skills: open-ended questioning, self-disclosure, and restating or highlighting the person's response. If at all possible, tape record the conversation. Feel free to respond in other ways as well, but try to integrate these three response modes into your conversation as much as possible. Listen to the tape and assess what you liked about your responses and how you might change them. This conversation, although it is practice, can be just like any conversation you might have. The distinction between role playing and the "real thing" is very thin here. Practice having conversations as often as you like. We hope you won't stop with just one practice.

Use all three skills in your day-to-day conversations. Get the feel of when and how to use them and let them become part of your typical conversational style.

---

ing conversation in a situation that you can't or don't want to avoid (in a car, on a plane, at work, at a bus stop, or in a jail cell)? You can always simply state that you'd prefer not to talk further, but in some instances you may be willing to talk but not about the current topic of discussion. Many people tend to follow a conversation wherever others direct it, even trying to stay interested (sometimes a difficult task) or "politely" nodding in agreement now and then.

This kind of charade isn't necessary. All parties to a conversation have a right to participate in determining the direction of the conversation. If you are not thinking of where you would like it to go, you probably are not involved in the conversation. (Some people have convinced themselves that they don't have much to say about *anything* when in fact they simply don't follow others' conversations and don't *think* of what they are interested in.)

You have a right to participate in the direction of your conversations when you choose to do so. It's OK to change the subject to something *you* are interested in. It doesn't have to be brilliant or better than the previous topic; it's simply what you would like to talk about.

When you are talking with someone you want to be with but are not interested in the immediate conversation, there are several ways to change the subject. Being direct, honest, and appropriate are the best ways. If the other person doesn't want to change the subject or doesn't want to discuss your topic, you may have to come up with a third alternative or end the conversation, but it doesn't have to degenerate into a power struggle over who is in control. The process can be mutually cooperative, and it often is.

For example, Bill and Betty work in the same office. They often find out about office "politics" and discuss the latest gossip. On one occasion, however, when Bill was talking about several "juicy" stories, Betty realized that she'd rather discuss something else at that point so she asserted her preference:

Bill: And I almost forgot to mention that Vice-President Higby was seen . . . .

Betty: Bill, I know we both usually enjoy talking about what's happening in the office, but right now I'd prefer not to. What did you think of the concert Saturday night?

Betty made an empathic statement recognizing their typical mutual interest but without apologizing or putting herself down. ("I'm sorry, Bill, but I'm not keeping up with you. I must be tired or overworked. Could we talk about something else?")

Bob and Harry were at a bus stop when Harry began talking about the last Dodger baseball game. After a few minutes of listening, Bob said:

Bob: You know, Harry, I don't follow the teams that carefully in baseball. I stay pretty close to football and hockey. What other sports do you like?

If you want to change the topic or direction of a conversation, you don't have to break into the middle of it. Most people will pause when they talk, and eventually there is an end to a story or the completion of a point. This is probably the best time to express your preferences because it is most considerate to both you and the speaker. It is most considerate to you because the longer you wait, the more frustrating it becomes and thus the more difficult it is to change the conversation without expressing a subtle yet critical exasperation or boredom. And this tactic is most considerate to the speaker's feelings because you are following the natural rhythm of the conversation. You are being honest without "rubbing it in." Also, avoid the rather commonly used "white lie": "Not to change the subject but . . ." (and then change the subject).

It's a bit more difficult to practice changing the subject (don't try it with someone just for the sake of practicing), so when a situation arises where you would like to change the subject, give it a try. See how it feels to express your preferences regardless of others' reactions. You might also observe others in conversation and note how and when they change topics or directions.

NONVERBAL ASSERTIVENESS IN CONVERSATIONS

The content of conversations is obviously important, but an equally important aspect of communication is the body language level. Just as you are more likely to know *what* to say when you are thinking and feeling assertively, you are more likely to know how you want to say it and to behave assertively when you have substituted rational thoughts for worrying, overreacting, or rationalizing. Practicing nonverbal behavior can be extremely valuable, and while there is no specific amount of eye contact or a certain "correct" tone, the following list can help you identify behaviors you might wish to change.

- Body posture
- Body position in relation to others
- Physical distance
- Body movements (legs, shoulders, feet, torso)
- Head nods and movements
- Eye contact—amount and direction (glancing; straight ahead; with head lowered)
- Facial expressions—smiles, eyes, brows

- Voice—tone, accentuation, loudness, rapidity, fluidity, and clarity

There are other nonverbal aspects of behavior, but these will give you an effective means toward assessing the way you come across. As you work on changes, use the assessment steps outlined in Chapter 2. Work on only one or two nonverbal changes at a time since they are often subtle and warrant full attention.

Nonverbal behavior is important because an essentially assertive statement can be completely distorted by a tonal quality or facial expression. Asking a good open-ended question in a meek, hesitant voice with a scared facial expression communicates more than just the question. It sends the listener underlying messages like: I'm afraid of you; I'm defensive; I've got to be in control; I'm helpless, please save me; Don't get too close; I'm evaluating you; I like you; I'm attracted to you; I'm less _____ than you; I'm more _____ than you; I'm feeling . . . ; You can't make me; How can I please you? You might want to explore some of the underlying impressions you give others and assess which of your nonverbal behaviors help to communicate that message. Many nonverbal expressions are subtle and habitual and can't be changed easily because some of them serve fairly important functions. Practice, like the kind provided in Exercise 25 (page 282), will help you change your nonverbal behaviors (body language).

EXPRESSING AN INTEREST IN SOMEONE

Sometimes in a more casual conversation, you may want to move to a more intimate or risky subject, like asking to get together again, expressing positive feelings for the other person, or asking someone with whom you would like to be friends to do something with you. Chapter 8, which explains making and refusing requests, can be very helpful here, yet the transition from the more casual (safer) discussion often can be difficult. As with all the stages of a conversation, if you are thinking irrational or rationalized thoughts, you are likely to have a

Exercise 25   Changing Your Nonverbal Behavior

Observe others in conversations and focus directly on their nonverbal behaviors. Using the list on page 36 as a guideline, identify what you liked and what you would think the person should change. Focus on specific behaviors. The purpose of observing is to get better at discriminating between nonassertive, assertive, and aggressive behaviors.

Next, pick one or two (no more) of your own specific nonverbal behaviors (speaking louder and clearer, putting more tone in your voice, being more expressive facially, making more eye contact, or speaking slower) you would like to change. Choose in advance a person to talk with and try making those changes during the conversation. Don't worry about anything else going wrong. As you continue to practice your new nonverbal behaviors, they will fit into your day-to-day style and you will hardly be aware of them unless you intentionally focus on them.

---

tougher time making the transition, so check your thinking out and change any worrying or other nonrational thoughts. When actually making the transition to a more intimate statement, there are only a few simple steps to keep in mind: Be direct, be honest, and be appropriate (remember the definition of assertiveness). So many times people know exactly what they want to say, but instead they beat around the bush, hoping the other person will get the point and rescue them by answering the question before it is asked. Statements such as, "I guess you have a lot of dates all the time, huh?" or "I only go first class when I go out—nothing but the best," or "You're not bad for a girl (ha, ha, ha)," or "You've probably already got lots of things to do with your free time but . . . ," are often designed to protect the speaker from rejection. If you want to ask something of someone, ask, and if you want to express your feelings to someone, do so. Remember that being appropriate means respecting your personal rights *and* the rights of the other person.

For example, Bruce (see page 276) may have wanted to ask

Shirley to get together again. He might have said something like this after having talked with her for some time:

Bruce: Shirley, I've really enjoyed talking with you, and I'd like to see you again. Would you like to have a drink after work some day this week?
Shirley: Sure. How about Wednesday night.

There is no single answer to the question of *when* to make such a request. You simply wait for an end or a break in a particular topic, but don't wait until you've exhausted all other topics. Your timing is likely to improve with the frequency of your requests.

The same criteria (directness, honesty, and appropriateness) hold true for the way you should respond to the compliments of others. It's all right to say things like:

- I really like you.
- I think you're very attractive.
- I like the way you think.
- You're a very nice person.
- I like your energy.
- You're very honest. I like that.
- I'm really attracted to you.
- I enjoy being with you.

Obviously, when you are attracted to someone, you don't have to verbalize every thought or feeling. Much of your attraction is communicated nonverbally (by distance, touching, facial expression, voice, etc.), so if your actions are direct, honest, and appropriate expressions of your feelings, the other person will probably realize how you feel. This doesn't mean that people should always be abrupt and get right down to the main issue of attraction (either friendship, sex, or both). The subtle and gradual development of a relationship is an exciting and pleasurable process, but you should avoid communicating your feelings so "safely" that the other person fails to understand them. Some people often "play it safe" to the point of watering down their feelings, expressing them inconsistently or contradictorily, or expressing them so indirectly as to distort what they really were originally. You don't have to play it so safe. It's OK to express your feelings verbally and nonverbally no matter how the other person receives them.

BEGINNING AND ENDING CONVERSATIONS

Starting or ending a conversation often can be more difficult than carrying on the middle part, the discussion itself. The context of the conversation and your relationship with the other person will probably influence your approach, but when initiating a conversation, you might try stating an opinion and/or asking an open-ended question. Your purpose is to invite the other person to talk with you, and making a factual statement doesn't accomplish this: It puts the other person in the position of having to initiate. Compare these two opening statements made during a class break:

Marsha: Hi. I sure do like this class. The professor is so interesting. I could listen to her all day. I've read quite a bit about social engineering, but this is really great.

Barry: Yeah . . . I like it too.

Marsha: All those questions she raises! Sometimes it's overwhelming to think of all the ways our lives are shaped by others. I'm not sure I like that.

Barry: Yeah. It's pretty scary.

Marsha: Hi. I really enjoy this class and Dr. Jacobs. What do you think of the class?

Barry: It's pretty interesting. I've never studied anything about social engineering before.

Marsha: Yeah, it's a fairly new field of study. What do you find interesting so far?

Barry: Well, I like thinking about the questions Dr. Jacobs raises for discussion, like who should get to make the decisions about things that influence the quality of our lives.

284

Marsha's comments were quite assertive in both examples; however, in the second case (1) she invites Barry to share more—and he does; (2) she expresses her opinions but more briefly and asks Barry (twice) for his; (3) she is not working as hard to carry the conversation. Of course, if Barry had wanted to initiate something in the first case, he certainly could have, or if he hadn't wanted to talk in the second instance, he might have said very little. But if a person is somewhat willing to talk, open-ended questions will help that to happen. Giving someone an honest compliment is often a pleasant way to make contact. "I liked your comments in class today, you raised some important issues" or even "I've seen you in class several times now, and I really wanted to meet you. My name's Marsha, what's yours?" are good opening statements that can be followed by an open-ended question.

Ending conversations is a separate and sometimes difficult step in itself. Sometimes you may want to stop talking with a particular person because you are uninterested in the person or the conversation, or you may sense that the conversation is becoming forced and you want to end it at a comfortable point. It is important to end your conversations before you get stuck or run out of things to say, and knowing that you can always stop when you want to can sometimes help you to relax and provides a greater sense of self-control. Telling yourself, "I can end this conversation when I want to," can reduce the fear of feeling trapped in an unpleasant or unsuccessful situation.

Although you should be direct, honest, and appropriate, you don't have to say that you are bored in order to be honest. If you are having a sort of low-key conversation, you might express your legitimate preference: "I'm going to get a drink and get around to see some other people" or "I see Bob over there and I've been looking for him for some time. Excuse me." If the person is someone you like and will seek out in the future, saying, "I'll see you again later," is certainly honest and appropriate. It probably is not a good idea to rely on many of the polite social phrases like "I've really enjoyed talking with you, but I must go," or "I've got to see Joan, but I'll be back later, OK?" or "Excuse me, I need to freshen up" *when they are untrue.* Besides being dishonest, these statements can be misleading or at least confusing, and you can state your intention more forthrightly without putting the other person down or being cold and abrupt. A great deal of the message is communicated nonverbally. A flat, disinterested tone, a bored facial expression, a look of annoyance, or an overly solicitous look of "I don't want to hurt your feelings but . . ." can do much to minimize your preference and maximize the negative impact of your statement. These nonverbal looks and tones are difficult to describe in words, but you can express your preferences in a pleasant, clear, and informational (as opposed to judgmental) manner that does not put the other person down or make you responsible for his feelings.

Occasionally someone will press hard to continue a conversation even after you've expressed your preference to do something else. The following example demonstrates the use of empathic and simple assertive statements in dealing with a persistent conversationalist:

Percy: So *she* said, "I don't know, but I'll find out in the morning!" Ha, ha, ha! (brief pause) Did you know . . . .
Jan: Percy, right now I want to see some other people at the party.
Percy: But, Jan, just let me tell you about . . . .
Jan: I know you want to tell me about this story, but I'd really prefer to get over and see some of the people here.

Jan might have decided to stay and hear one more story. Certainly you might choose to stay and listen to some people a little longer than you might want to for practical reasons (it might be your boss who would be offended and retaliate) or for personal reasons (it might be a respected relative whom you do not find interesting but regard very highly). If you choose to stay, then make the best of it and consider it a slight inconvenience.

It can be very difficult to be direct and honest about leaving a conversation unless the other person is very understanding. It simply is not an easy situation to handle. Try out various responses and judge which ones feel good and also seem asser-

286

tive. Exercise 26 will provide some helpful practice. Although sometimes it may seem easier to take the indirect route and tell a "white lie," don't do it. They can backfire and, besides, these little "deceptions" usually feel dishonest.

Exercise 26 Beginning and Ending Conversations

1. With a friend, practice *initiating* conversations as if the friend were a stranger or brief acquaintance. Try out varied approaches, using a combination of your statements and open-ended questions. Identify specific contexts and even specific people if you have some in mind.
2. Assume that you have been talking for a while and would like to end the conversation. Practice ending the conversation without demeaning the other person or lying. ("I must go" versus "I am going.") Try out several possible statements, and be sure to identify your personal rights at the moment.
3. At least twice during the week initiate a conversation. Also, twice, end a conversation (not necessarily the same ones you initiated). Assess what you like in all four cases and what you might do differently.

SUMMARY

The three response modes discussed in this chapter should help you improve your conversational skills so that you are able to project your true personality, not a false image, when you talk with people. Although the ideas in this chapter are easy to understand, putting them into practice is another matter. Using these skills is not really more difficult than understanding them, but you do need considerable practice and self-assessment. Try them out and stick with it: The payoffs for you can be great.

11
Developing Your Assertion Plan

You may be in an assertion training group right now. Many people reading this book probably are in a group. If you are in a group, you probably will make plans for improving your assertive behavior in situations outside of the group. Your plan of action is very important, and it is even more important if you aren't in a group, for you won't have the help of a leader or group members. This chapter lists important guidelines that you can use for developing a plan for becoming more assertive. These guidelines can serve as a helpful check list. But whether or not you are in an assertion group now or in the future, a well thought out plan will enable you to systematically make significant changes in your thinking, feelings, and behaviors.

When setting out to change your own behavior, it is a good idea to follow these steps:

1. Specify the situation clearly.
2. Determine your goals and subgoals not only in terms of *what* you want to see happen but also *how you* want to behave.
3. Identify the personal rights at issue for yourself and the others involved.
4. Explore your inner dialogue as you imagine yourself in the situation and look for and challenge any irrational (self-defeating, absolutist, exaggerated, or inaccurate) thinking, and any underlying irrational assumptions.
5. Establish a plan and try out the behavior. See how it feels, what the consequences were, and determine how close you came to the desired behaviors you chose in Step Two.

6. Decide how you could improve your plan so that you might be even closer to your desired behaviors next time.

Some of the changes you want to make in your own behavior can be well planned in advance, particularly if you have some control over the situation. We will focus here on one example where the person planned his assertive behaviors and did have a good deal of control over when he could try them out. In such a situation you don't need to plan every single word you are going to say or to plan for every possible response you might get from others. First, it is impossible to do, and second, if you try to plan your statements word for word and anticipate exactly how others will respond, you will force yourself into a rigid position that will not allow you the flexibility of responding to a particular situation. Instead, you can have a "game plan" and then use what's going on in the situation to carry out that plan. Being overly prepared can be as constricting as being underprepared when it comes to handling a specific situation.

STEP ONE: SPECIFYING
THE SITUATION CLEARLY

Ken is a graduate student who lived on the beach in California. He stated his assertion problem as follows: "I would like to be able to approach and talk with women I find attractive but do not know and to do so in an assertive manner." Ken had previously avoided initiating such contacts, and his social relationships developed mostly through friends or work relations. Those were effective means to meet people, but Ken wished to be more active and comfortable when seeking friends and romantic relationships on his own.

With this kind of general problem Ken's *first* task was really to set up a more specific situation. Since he lived on a popular beach, he chose to focus his plans on being able to talk on the beach with women he found attractive. Even that context can be defined more specifically (as he does later in developing his plan). As we continue with Ken's plan, you can follow step by step with your own plan by doing each of the exercises. Choose a specific situation for your assertion issue in Exercise 27.

Exercise 27 Being More Specific

There are at least two ways you can use to identify specific situations to work on. One method is to use the space below to simply describe your general assertion problem and a specific situation it occurs in. If you find it difficult to identify specific situations that currently pose a problem in your life, read Appendix B and conduct a self-assessment. The assertion inventory in Appendix B will likely stimulate you to think of specific situations where you have difficulty being assertive.

1. General assertion problem:

2. Specific situation:

**STEP TWO: SETTING GOALS
AND SUBGOALS**

Sometimes the 'most critical factors in changing your own behavior are *how* you select your goals and *which* goals you select. When you select goals, first think in terms of what you *want* and what you think would be better for you because *you* want it. Even with the person who, for example, wishes to change his behavior because others consistently see it as aggressive, the likelihood that he will be successful increases as he makes a commitment to change, not only because others will be more satisfied and pleased, but also because he will feel better about the assertive way he relates to others and will enjoy those relationships more. People who select a behavior change that they themselves do not particularly support often become rebellious and resistant. *You,* then, are in control of what you want to change, and you can decide what you are willing to work toward changing. This guideline is crucial when you select your own assertive goals.

Ken's next task (Step Two) was to start identifying his goals and subgoals. That is, he asked himself the following questions:

1. What do I hope to see happen?
2. What do I want to do to see it happen?

Many people mistakenly set their goals in terms of outcomes over which they have little control or in terms of situations in which the success of one's behavior is determined by how others behave (to get the raise or promotion, to have people like them, to live happily ever after, to be treated with respect). These are all legitimate wants, but they may not be attainable assertion goals.

For example, Ken would like to have the women he approaches respond positively to him, but if he defines the success of his assertive behavior in terms of their responses, he may be using an inaccurate measure. Ken might be very calm, effective, and assertive while talking with someone, and she still may not respond positively for a variety of reasons that have nothing to do with his assertiveness.

There are alternative approaches to this problem. First, list your goals in terms of your own behavior. Second, be highly descriptive when listing your goals so that you can clearly tell whether you accomplished them or not. Third, with a complex goal like Ken's, it makes good sense to break the larger goal down into a number of smaller ones. Below are some of the subgoals Ken set for himself:

1. Walking toward a woman he finds attractive.
2. Smiling at a woman he finds attractive.
3. Continuing to hold eye contact longer than just a brief moment (10 seconds at least).
4. Saying hello or some other greeting.
5. Making a brief comment or asking a good open-ended question that is general and sociable.

6. Listening clearly and attentively to her response.
7. Positioning himself (possibly kneeling or sitting) in such a way as to communicate his intention to stay a while.
8. Responding to the woman's response either with a reaction to hers or with a different comment.
9. Looking for indications of her interest in talking with him further.
10. Stating his *opinion* about something—the crowds, the sailboat race offshore, surfing, etc.

Ken's situation is not unique. Marsha had a roommate who continually agreed to and then did not do her share of the housekeeping. Marsha might have had any or all of the following goals:

1. Stating her concern clearly and specifically.
2. Expressing her opinions about sharing work.
3. Expressing her feelings of frustration and annoyance.
4. Expressing her opinion about her roommate's agreeing, then not fulfilling her agreement.
5. Expressing her hope that they resolve this problem.
6. Expressing her serious concern with this problem.
7. Asking her roommate to change her behavior.
8. Stating the consequences if her roommate does or does not meet this agreement.
9. Asking her to explain why she agrees to clean the room but does not follow through.
10. Asking for her opinion about her own behavior.
11. Asking for her to suggest a plan to solve the problem.

Depending on how her roommate reacted, Marsha might have wished to focus on how her roommate responds in this discussion as well. Marsha would not be able to accomplish all these goals at once because she would have to think clearly about what she wanted to say at various times during the conversation. In any case, making contact with the other person would have provided the opportunity to act assertively, to clarify the problem, and to specify subgoals.

Exercise 28 (page 294) allows you to list your own subgoals.

Exercise 28   Developing Subgoals

Figure 22 lists possible subgoals that you could have in a specific situation. Read these and then list all the behaviors you can think of as subgoals for your own situation, beginning with a few moments before you assert yourself until the interaction is completed. Write subgoals only about your own behavior. Be as specific as possible. Don't worry about how difficult the behavior might be for you. List everything you can think of for now, including improvements in body language (eye contact, voice level, etc.). For possible subgoals to strengthen your body language, review Figure 4 in Chapter 2.

My subgoals:

1.
2.
3.

Figure 22   Possible Subgoals

Self-expressions:

  Express positive feelings
  Express negative feelings
  State your personal rights
  Express your preferences
  State your point without defensively justifying or explaining yourself
  Express disagreement
  State your decisions
  Clarify your own idea or opinion
  Give information
  Express your opinions, beliefs, or ideas concisely and precisely
  Express concern
  Offer suggestions or solutions to problems
  Speak positively of yourself
  Clarify your intent or motives for doing something
  Give instructions or assign work
  State your interpretation of another's actions

Figure 22 Possible Subgoals (continued)

Start and carry on a conversation
End a conversation and leave
State a complaint
Admit mistakes

Confrontations:

Protest the behavior of others—unfairnesses, emotional overreactions, overt putdowns, passive or active aggression, rigid silences, "poor me" helplessness
Confront someone with his immediate behavior
Point out another's mistake
Describe someone else's behavior and state how that behavior has negative consequences for you
State negative consequences or results if someone persists in a particular behavior and positive consequences if the behavior changes

Requests:

Request services
Request a specific change in another's behavior
Ask for information
Ask for clarification
Request help or assistance
Ask why
Ask for:
    opinions
    feelings
    ideas
    preferences of others

Refusing Requests for Your:

Time
Property
Money
Body
Thoughts
Feelings

Figure 22   Possible Subgoals (continued)

Handling Negative Reactions:

Persist and restate your assertion
Disagree with the person's response and return to the original topic
Restate the seriousness of your feelings
Ignore the other's reaction
Agree, if honestly, with the other person and get back to the original assertion
Redefine and clarify another's labels of your behavior
Sort out and clarify any incorrect meanings others attribute to your behaviors
State negative and positive consequences of continued digression or attention

---

STEPS THREE AND FOUR: IDENTIFYING PERSONAL RIGHTS AND CHANGING IRRATIONAL THINKING

Step Three, identifying personal rights, and Step Four, exploring your inner dialogue and changing any irrational thinking and any underlying irrational ideas, have been covered in Chapter 5. The questions in Exercise 29 are designed to help you develop your own assertion plan.

Exercise 29   Identifying Personal Rights and Changing Irrational Thinking

1. What do you believe are Ken's personal rights? What rights do the women he approaches have?
2. What personal rights do *you* have in your situation? What rights do others have in your assertion situation?
3. What might be some of Ken's irrational (self-defeating or absolutist) thoughts as he considers carrying out his assertion goals?

   a. about himself
   b. about others
   c. about the situation

**Exercise 29   Identifying Personal Rights
and Changing Irrational Thinking (continued)**

What might be three underlying irrational ideas that might keep Ken from trying his assertive behaviors? (See page 124.)

a.

b.

c.

What would be four rational alternatives Ken could tell himself to help stay calm and comfortable instead of excessively anxious, angry, or depressed?

a.

b.

c.

d.

4. What are some of the irrational thoughts you have in your internal dialogue when you think about asserting yourself in your situation?

a.   about yourself
b.   about others
c.   about the situation

What underlying irrational ideas support your irrational dialogue? (See page 124.)

a.

b.

c.

Exercise 29 Identifying Personal Rights
and Changing Irrational Thinking (continued)

List four *rational* thoughts that directly counter your irrational thoughts and underlying ideas.

a.

b.

c.

d.

Below are some of the personal rights and cognitive changes Ken was able to make. Compare them to the ones you listed in Exercise 29. Ken decided he had a right:

1. To speak to others.
2. To be treated with respect.
3. To express his opinions and to make requests of others.

He also decided that others have a right:

1. To be treated with respect.
2. To decide that they do or do not wish to talk with him.

In analyzing his irrational thinking, Ken realized that he was quite anxious about being rejected and that his inner dialogue contained many catastrophic thoughts. ("What if she just stares at me with disgust?") He also recognized his excessive fear of being unable to start conversations with women he found attractive. ("What if I get all nervous and say something stupid? Or worse yet, say nothing at all! How embarrassing!") After going through the cognitive restructuring steps, Ken decided that he would think two new things to himself instead of the old dialogue:

1. I'd like this person to like me, and I will try to help that to happen. If she does, that's great. If she doesn't, I'll be disappointed, but I *can* live with it. It is not awful.

2. I would like to be calm and assertive while I'm talking with her, but if I do draw a blank or if there are awkward pauses, I can handle it. I don't have to be perfect. I can figure out what I'd like to do better and work on it. If she rejects me for something that I'm willing to change, I can figure it out and work on it. Anything else is out of my control, and it's unfortunate that we will not get to know each other.

Since these thoughts are fairly long, Ken also added a quick phrase that he would use any time: "I'm in control of myself. I can handle it."

STEP FIVE: PLANNING, CARRYING OUT, AND ASSESSING YOUR ASSERTIONS

When Ken has identified and classified his personal rights and corrected his irrational thoughts, his next step is to plan, carry out, and evaluate the behaviors that would lead to successful accomplishment of his subgoals. Ken's subgoals were stated as behaviors, but in many cases, more extensive plans can be developed to enable you to carry out the goals listed in Step Two.

Ken used three behavioral techniques to accomplish his goals. The first, called successive approximations, helps people gradually improve toward a new behavior. Ken was quite anxious about becoming more assertive, so he used the following plan to handle his anxiety.

Ken used the Subjective Units of Discomfort Scale (SUDS), which is a simple way to quickly rate just how anxious you are.[1] The scale ranges from 0 to 100 where at 0 you are so calm and relaxed that you are almost falling asleep and 100 means that you are extremely jittery. By determining your subjective discomfort, you can rank behaviors or situations according to their difficulty. You can also check your SUDS level to decide whether or not to use any techniques to calm yourself. The ratings do not have to be precise, and they do not compare to anyone else's ratings of you or themselves. They are just a

299

good guide for checking your own anxiety.

Ken decided that his SUDS level would be about 98 when he approached a woman on the beach. Consequently, he decided to plan a series of steps that gradually built up to his goal (this is called successive approximations). He developed the following list and added his expected SUDS levels so that he was fairly sure that each task would be a little more difficult:

1. Walk along the bicycle path by the beach and say hello to little children (SUDS = 15).
2. Walk along same path and say hello to older people working in their gardens, etc. (SUDS = 30).
3. Walk along same path, say hello, and talk very briefly to people working in garden or sitting in front of house (SUDS = 45).
4. Walk along path and say hello to women, particularly those he found attractive (SUDS = 65).
5. Walk along beach and stop and ask for directions from women he found attractive (SUDS = 85).
6. Walk up to a woman and strike up a conversation (SUDS = 98).

Ken used his list to gradually improve in small, managable steps rather than attempting a large behavioral change immediately. Exercise 30 asks you to develop your own list of successive approximations and to rate your SUDS.

The second technique Ken used to reduce his anxiety was to practice relaxing himself. Then, just before he actually set out to do one of the tasks, he could relax and reduce his anxiety considerably. There are many relaxation procedures available today that you can do by yourself. One procedure includes:

1. Tightening and relaxing various muscle combinations.
2. Breathing exercises.
3. Picturing relaxing scenes.

Appendix A presents this kind of procedure. A good way to practice is to ask a friend who has a calm, mellow voice to

Exercise 30 Checking SUDS and Setting Up
Successive Approximations

Decide what your SUDS level would probably be in your assertion issue: SUDS _____ . Now list about five or six behaviors, starting with one that would have a low SUDS and ending with behaviors that are closer to your SUDS level. Each behavior should be a little bit more similar to the actual situation you are trying to handle assertively.

1.
2.
3.
4.
5.
6.

---

read the procedure slowly into a tape recorder (noting the indicated pauses). You can then play back the tape whenever you want to relax yourself. Go through the entire tape once or twice a day for four or five days. After that, you will have learned the steps, and you will be able to do it any time and most any place. The entire procedure lasts about 20 to 30 minutes. However, when you do not have that much time, you can make up a shorter version that focuses on particularly tense parts of your body. Be sure to include all three aspects of the relaxation procedure: tightening-relaxing, breathing, and picturing relaxing scenes.

The third technique in Ken's plan was to reinforce himself for doing certain things during each of his approximations. He set up a series of subgoals or desired behaviors for each of the approximations he carried out. He decided to pay attention to *how* he wanted to behave, so he focused on nonverbal behaviors, such as making good eye contact, expressing his feelings by the tone of his voice, smiling, and using facial expressions. In addition, he practiced how to ask open-ended questions, how to respond to others' self-disclosures, and how to actively listen and reflect others' statements. (These are skills which can be improved in an assertion training group.) Ken reinforced himself when he did any of the behaviors he chose to focus on that time. He set up a flexible time schedule for going through each step of his approximations hierarchy and went on to the next step only after he successfully completed the previous step.

We use reinforcers for one simple yet powerful reason. When we are confronted with choosing between (1) talking with a woman (high anxiety and possible rejection), and (2) avoiding the situation entirely (disappointment but safety), most of us would opt for (2). You can work to reduce the anxiety and fear of rejection in option (1), and also make (1) more attractive and desirable by connecting other rewards to its occurrence. It's simple: Fight fire with fire. If watching TV or shooting pool is more immediately pleasurable than studying, you can *make* studying more attractive by connecting it with other pleasures you give yourself *when you finish studying.* These rewards, however, are contingent on studying.

In Ken's case the rewards he chose were contingent on (1) simply attempting a task (from saying hello to children at Step One to initiating a conversation with a woman he found attractive) and (2) successfully accomplishing the behaviors he chose (making eye contact, expressing feelings through his tone of voice, and asking two open-ended questions). His success was rewarding in itself, but Ken chose to use other reinforcers as well.

When setting up rewards, it is a good idea to use the following principles:

1. The reward is clearly defined.
2. The reward is immediately available.
3. You have control over giving yourself the reward.
4. You definitely connect the reward with behavior you plan *before* you attempt the behavior.
5. The reward is strong enough to influence your behavior.
6. The reward is connected to a small, brief behavior (smiling, asking two open-ended questions).
7. The reward is always given when you are successful. There should not be exceptions for successes or failures.

8. The desired behavior is clear enough so that you know when you should give yourself the reward.

Ken listed several reinforcers he could use: fishing, swimming, surfing, buying a new record album, taking a bike ride, playing his flute, reading a good mystery novel, calling a friend long distance, some special treat (not necessarily fattening), going to a favorite movie or concert. Use Exercise 31 (page 304) to pinpoint your own reinforcers.

Each day, before Ken carried out a part of his plan, he would write out the step in the approximations he was working on (see page 299), the behaviors he would focus on, and the rewards he would give himself if he succeeded in improving those behaviors. Ken did not have to be "perfect"; he rewarded improvement and went on when he judged he was ready. Develop your own plan in Exercise 32 (page 305) by using the outline form daily.

Monitoring your progress is very important. Keep a chart that shows each day of your plan and record what you set out to do, whether or not you accomplished it, and what reinforcer you used. The chart can be a record of your success and thus be reinforcing in its own right, but it can best be used as a systematic guide to adjusting your plan. Many people have intentionally set out to change their behavior and after a short time have failed and given up the whole idea of trying, often because of two factors that can be systematically controlled: (1) The subtasks were unmanageable and (2) The reinforcer was not strong enough for that person. For example, Ken might have had greater difficulty if he had set out to carry on a lengthy conversation with a woman on the first day he met her, or if he rewarded himself with watching TV, a reward he could take or leave. Many people who attempt to change their behavior do not pay enough attention to these two factors and, instead, decide that they do not have the "will power" or that "something inside them" (magical) keeps them from being successful. Actually "will power" has little to do with behavior change. It is more a matter of being systematic, thinking "small," and rewarding appropriately.

Exercise 31   Identifying Your Reinforcers

Reinforcers are unique to each person, and you can come up with your own. The most important criteria are: (1) Is the reward easily accessible to you? and (2) Is it strong enough to influence your behavior as you wish? The following series of questions will help you identify what things might be reinforcers for you.* Fill in the spaces after each question with reinforcers that also meet the criteria above. (Large reinforcers like a Rolls Royce or a trip to Hawaii are great if you are fortunate enough that they meet the first criterion.)

1. What kinds of things do you like to have? _____
2. What are your major interests? _____
3. What are your hobbies? _____
4. What people do you like to be with? _____
5. What do you like to do with those people? _____
6. What do you do for fun? _____
7. What do you do to relax? _____
8. What do you do to get away from it all? _____
9. What makes you feel good? _____
10. What would be a nice present to receive? _____
11. What kinds of things are important to you? _____
12. What would you buy if you had an extra ten dollars? Fifty dollars? One-hundred dollars? _____
13. On what do you spend your money each week? _____
14. What behaviors do you perform every day? (Don't overlook the obvious, the commonplace.) _____
15. Are there any behaviors that you usually perform instead of the target behavior? _____
16. What would you hate to lose? _____
17. Of the things you do every day, what would you hate to give up? _____

*From *Self-Directed Behavior: Self-Modification for Personal Adjustment*, Second Edition, by D. L. Watson and R. G. Tharp. Copyright © 1972, 1977 by Wadsworth Publishing Company, Inc. Reprinted by permission of the publisher, Brooks/Cole Publishing Company, Monterey, California 93940.

Exercise 32   Developing Your Plan

If you choose to carry out the plan you are developing here, write out your plan for that day using an outline like the following:

1. The step in the approximations:

    a.   The behaviors I will focus on this time (list no more than three):

    b.   The reward I'll use this time when I succeed in improving those behaviors:

2. Evaluation of my assertion:

    a.   What I liked that I did:
         verbal/content:

         nonverbal:

    b.   What I would like to do differently next time:
         verbal/content:

         nonverbal:

Ken then set out to accomplish each of his tasks, to work on improving specific behaviors during each task, and to reinforce himself for accomplishing tasks and improving any behaviors he chose. Plans many times do not work smoothly and thus require modification and adjustments. By carefully monitoring each step of the plan, additional tasks, new behaviors, and better reinforcers might be included. The process should be as flexible as possible. For example, Ken found that he was eventually able to ask a woman he found attractive for directions, but he had trouble moving to the next task: carrying on a conversation with her. Consequently, he added another task to his list: He would strike up a casual conversation, end it after only a few interactions, and move on. (Ken also decided to carry a bunch of grapes with him and offer some to the women as they talked. It may sound unusual, but Ken found it to be a comfortable way to make contact with someone, especially on a hot beach, and it provided a brief source of conversation. At this point Ken was only seeking brief, casual conversations.) These additions worked very well for him since his greatest fears now were about what to say next (earlier he even feared approaching women). As his fears decreased, Ken found that he could talk about many things. All along he also practiced carrying on conversations with his friends. Ken also decided to add some stronger reinforcers as he got closer to his final goal. He chose scuba diving, backpacking, and playing bridge, all of which were highly rewarding to him.

Within three weeks Ken was able to approach women he found attractive, to carry on extended conversations, and even to ask several of them to get together with him again. His anxiety was manageable, and he planned to join an assertion group to further improve his conversational skills. Once he got started, the fact that some of the women responded positively was itself a very strong reward, but if Ken had received a series of rejections, he wouldn't have had to feel like a total failure. He might have had to do some cognitive restructuring to keep from getting excessively down instead of just disappointed. This would have helped him analyze his situation to determine what he was doing that was not effective and make the necessary changes.

Ken's behavior change plan illustrates several principles and procedures that can be applied in most situations.

1. Set specific behavioral goals for yourself; you may have a global goal in mind also, but keep your subgoals small, manageable, and attainable.
2. Use SUDS to check how anxious you would be in each situation.
3. Set up a series of behaviors that progressively lead to the ultimate goal; each behavior is likely to be increasingly anxiety producing.
4. Learn a relaxation procedure that you can employ regularly and just before specific situations.
5. Identify the personal rights at issue for yourself and the others involved in each situation.
6. Analyze your internal dialogue and underlying assumptions for any irrational (alarmist, absolutist, or inaccurate) thinking.
7. Identify several reinforcers that are strong enough to help you accomplish your tasks.
8. Identify any specific behaviors you would like to improve upon as you attempt each task (e.g., making better eye contact, speaking briefly, putting more tone in your voice, or asking open-ended questions).
9. Set up a plan, possibly including a time schedule, where you make giving yourself the reward contingent on accomplishing a particular task *or* on making improvements toward specific behaviors you've selected to change.
10. Carry out the plan!
11. Monitor each effort to accomplish a task; adjustments are likely to be warranted. Each new task should be a relatively small step up from the earlier task. If the steps are too big, add another task before attempting the more difficult one. You may want to add more reinforcers as you think of them or as you need stronger ones. Be as flexible as you can as long as you seem to be progressing toward the desired behavior change. Do some trial and error experimenting.

Now that you are prepared, try out your plan. Stick with it and modify it as seems appropriate. It's *your* plan. We have provided some suggestions that might be helpful to you. Use those you believe will contribute to *your* goals.

SOME FINAL THOUGHTS
ABOUT PLANNING PERSONAL CHANGES

People seem to make their decisions to change their thinking, feelings, or behaviors when they (1) give themselves permission to do so; (2) feel safe and protected from serious mental, emotional, or physical threat; and (3) feel potent and somewhat hopeful of success. Giving yourself permission to change includes being willing to deal with any of the consequences of your new behaviors—that people might not like you all the time; that people might start liking you more and seek greater intimacy with you; that you might fail; that you might succeed; that people will want things from you; that people will not want things from you; that you will want things from people and not get them. Feeling protected while making changes includes having sources of support (yourself *and* others) who can help you deal with undesirable consequences in a reasonable manner rather than developing irrational or magical thinking about yourself or your future. Unconditional support from others can be valuable at any time, for it is truly comforting to know that such caring is not dependent upon your performance but rather that the people being supportive do so because they know that you believe the changes are likely to be good for you. Though specific situations may demand different treatment, the general principles we have given should work for you regardless of your situation. And making significant changes does *not* have to be a painful process. It can be rewarding and fun, too.

PRACTICING ASSERTIVE
BEHAVIORS

Many people who would like to be more assertive will never be in an assertion training group, and many of those who are in a group will often want to make better use of their time between sessions. As has been noted earlier, a variety of factors influence whether or not one acts assertively. One of those factors is that the person might have a behavioral "deficit"; that is, he is not really sure how to act in the situation or does not know how to act assertively, possibly because he has not behaved assertively in such a situation before. Therefore, before carrying out behavioral plans, it can be very valuable to practice the behaviors you think you will need for the actual situation.

> Albert was a high school teacher who was assigned to supervise the three most undesirable functions in the school: the early lunch period, the study hall during the last period of the day, and the after-school detention room for punished students. These assignments took up all his preparation time during the day. He wanted to assertively ask the assistant principal, who made such assignments, to change his schedule. He had been very shy and usually highly adaptive, but this time he decided to do something. However, he had never done anything like this before, so he decided to practice what he wanted to say and how he wanted to say it before he actually went in. He also assessed his personal rights, distinguished between passive, assertive, and aggressive responses, used cognitive restructuring, and set up a behavioral plan.

There are several ways to practice acting assertively. You might have a friend who would be willing to play the role of the other person, and while this is not the same as the real situation, you are still you, and if your friend is a good actor, you will be surprised by how realistic it can be. Another alternative is to use an audio tape recorder (videotape is even better) and act out your part of the conversation while imagining how the other person is likely to respond. You can also use the tape recorder if you do a role play with a friend. You might also practice making your assertive statements in front of a mirror. The mirror and recorder will provide valuable information not only on what you said but how you said it. All the nonverbal factors like tone, loudness, fluidity, clarity, rapidity of your voice, eye contact, facial expressions, body posture, hand gestures, and head movements can be observed and altered if desired.

When you try practicing, you should follow these steps:

1. Briefly plan what your goals are. For Albert it might be: "I want to tell her that I think it's unreasonable to assign all three supervisions to me, that I have no preparation time as others do, and that I would like her to change the schedule

309

of assignments."

2. Imagine yourself assertively handling the situation.

3. Practice (no more than two or three interactions between yourself and the other person). Check your SUDS before and after each practice. If it is up *very* high and stays there, you may want to do some more cognitive restructuring or work on a similar but less upsetting situation. If your SUDS level goes down, continue practicing.

4. Stop practicing.

5. Ask yourself (and your friend) to state what you liked about what you said and the way you said it. Describe your behavior in specific terms. ("I made good eye contact; I was brief and to the point; my voice was firm yet not aggressive," rather than "I really like that; I did pretty good. I liked the way I came across." The latter is complimentary but not very informative; the former helps you recognize and continue to do the specific things you liked.) It is also very important to focus first on what you liked about how you behaved. Most people tend to be critical and look for the "not OK" behaviors when assessing their own behavior or that of others. Unfortunately, such a focus often ignores their effective, assertive behaviors. No matter how many undesired behaviors there are, you can always find good things.

6. State two or three specific changes to make your own behavior more assertive the next time you practice. Do not pick more than two or three (even if there are scores) because most people can't keep more than three in mind while they are practicing. They get distracted trying to remember what behaviors they are working on and lose contact with the other person. Also, they usually are not able to improve on more than three and then believe they're not making as much progress. So, work gradually and select a few improvements at a time. For example, Albert decided he wanted to look a little more serious and not smile too broadly when he spoke to the assistant principal. Albert also decided he would ask her to change the assignment schedule rather than wait for her to offer. Also, he wanted to speak a bit slower and calmer. If you are

practicing with someone, you may also ask for their suggestions for improvements. You get to agree or disagree with the suggestions. Some people tend to "suggest" by firmly saying, "Well, I think you should . . ." and not leaving room for your reaction. Feel free to choose not to try any suggestion—you don't have to defend your decision.

7. Practice the situation again.
8. Then do Steps Four and Five again without going over all the same things you identified in Step Four, but especially focusing on improvements with the three specific behaviors you chose to change. Repeat this process until you have decided you are behaving as you like.

The focus of Steps Four and Five is on effective, assertive behaviors and specific suggestions for improvements. You are emphasizing positive aspects, not negative ones. There is no place in this process for a lot of useless attention to all the ineffective, nonassertive behaviors you might have been doing while practicing.

For example, in Step Five Albert might have cited "problems" like, "I looked foolish with that silly smile while here I am trying to be serious and assertive," or "I talked so fast it didn't matter how firm I sounded, you could tell I was jumpy as could be." Both statements might be true, but even if they are, such critical, negative thinking is a dead end. Albert instead chose to focus on how he could improve and what specific changes he could make: look a bit more serious and speak slower. Consequently, Albert was working toward changing without putting himself down in the process. Try it and see if there is less of a critical putdown quality when you cite specific improvements you wish to make. You might also check if your SUDS level is going down as you practice and if it feels good to be acting more assertively. It might feel new, even awkward, but you also will feel direct, honest, potent, genuine, and respectful of yourself and others.

While you first practice your assertions, have the role player be relatively cooperative (or imagine the other person being cooperative if you are practicing alone). After you are satisfied with your own behavior, you may then want to practice asserting yourself when the other person is responding either non-assertively or aggressively. Very often we give up our own assertiveness when faced with hostile, defensive, pushy, hurt, helpless, guilt inducing, passive, or depressive behaviors from others. We often respond to someone else rather than initiate the interaction. The issue often becomes, What do I say after I say something assertive and the other person does not cooperate or respond assertively? If this happens to you, it probably is because some form of irrational thinking is getting in the way of your responding assertively. When you "escalate" your practice sessions to handling difficult situations, you should first look for any irrational thinking you may have. After substituting more rational thoughts, practice responding to nonassertive or aggressive responses. Focus on your own assertiveness—not the other person's behavior—as a measure of your own success. Some people will be nonassertive or aggressive no matter what you do. Even more importantly, your own behavior is the only measure of your assertiveness.

IN VIVO
SELF-ASSERTION TRAINING

The previous sections focused on planning change and practicing specific responses. In some situations, it is impossible to plan your responses—planning simply is not an option unless you take a "time out," and of course these kinds of situations don't allow you to do so. The following techniques will prove helpful in these difficult situations.

Sometimes you would like to be assertive, but you feel excessively anxious, intensely angry, or depressed. You can use those feelings as a cue to begin asking yourself a series of simple but important questions. These questions are designed to help you to get control of how you are thinking, feeling, and behaving and to interrupt those disruptive thoughts, feelings, and behaviors. Ask the questions in the following order:

- What is my SUDS level?
- What am I doing?
- How am I feeling?

312

- What am I thinking?
- What do I want to be thinking, feeling, and doing?
- What thoughts, opinions, preferences, needs, or feelings do I want to express in this situation?
- What do I want the other person to know?
- What *thoughts* are keeping me from doing what I want?
- What do I think is appropriate to express?
- How can I go ahead and express what I want?

It may seem that it would take forever to answer these questions, especially when you are right in the situation. While it would be better to be able to take a brief "time out" from the situation to think these questions through, you probably will be able to answer them in just a few seconds without being very distracted from the situation. And you can be selective: You don't have to ask and answer all the questions in every situation. Use those that apply specifically to the situation you are in. They can be valuable guides to help you get control and redirect yourself toward more assertive responses.

You must, of course, use these questions judiciously, for they can be answered in a variety of ways, some of which are less helpful than others. For example, George answered the self-assessment questions as follows:

Questions	Answers
What is my SUDS level?	102 and rising!
What am I doing?	Punching my boss in the nose for berating me unfairly in front of my friends.
How am I feeling?	Extremely angry and vengeful and exhilarated.
What am I thinking?	I'll show the creeps of the world they can't get away with berating me! But now I'll have to change since I'm trying to be more assertive.

What do I want to be thinking, feeling, and doing?	I want to be on a yacht in the Caribbean, feeling rich and powerful and thinking about the last million dollar deal I just made.
What thoughts, opinions, preferences, feelings do I want to express in this situation?	I'd like to tell my boss that I'm really a nice guy at heart and that I hope he recognizes that.
What do I want the other person to know?	After this, I won't hold it against him that he berated me.
What thoughts are keeping me from doing what I want?	Thinking about how I will get fired and get a bad reference and the possible trouble I will get into for felonious assault.
What do I think is appropriate to express?	Well, maybe I could apologize.
How can I go ahead and express what I want?	I did! I did!

Besides being unrealistic, George's responses did little to help him get greater control. Since he was already assaulting his boss, it was probably too late to use any questions. But instead assume that Archie is also berated unfairly by his boss in front of his friends. Below are some guidelines for using the self-assessment questions in a more productive manner as well as a discussion of how Archie responded to them.

It's probably a good idea to check your SUDS level regularly in any uncomfortable situation. Then, rather than waiting until you are ready to explode, you can catch yourself at a lower level of anxiety and start asking yourself the sequence of questions. Assume that Archie rated his SUDS at 75 when his boss started berating him.

When checking what you are *doing* you might look for verbal or nonverbal clues that indicate that you are losing self-control. General descriptive statements, like "I'm standing here waiting for my boss to stop berating me," are usually less valuable. Keep the focus primarily on yourself. Archie realized that his stomach was tightening up, that he was gritting his teeth, that he kept glancing between his boss and his friends, and that he snapped back with "Hey, just one minute here, buster!"

When checking how you are feeling, look for one of these basic feelings first: mad, sad, glad, or afraid. Then see if there are any feelings in addition to the one you are most readily aware of. For example, Archie was most aware of feeling angry, but he was also embarrassed (afraid of what his friends might be thinking of him) and even hurt (sad that his boss would be so nasty when he really works very hard). Very often one feeling will seem to "cover up" another either because: (1) the person has decided that it is not OK to show the underlying feeling (show anger instead of hurt or sadness) or (2) there are actually several feelings going on, and one is stronger and more prominent than the others (showing fear and anxiety when you are also angry). Consequently, you should look a bit beyond the feelings that are most prominent. On the other hand, don't become a Sherlock Holmes in search of your "elusive" feelings; don't "overpsychologize" or "overanalyze" yourself. Some people get so caught up in the search for their "real" thoughts and feelings that they tie themselves in knots.

When checking what you are thinking, use the techniques presented in Chapter 5 for identifying your internal dialogue. What are you saying to yourself about yourself, the other persons, and the situation? Archie realized that he was thinking: (1) that his boss was a louse and had no right to treat him this way; (2) that he was worried about what his friends were thinking of him; (3) that he felt demeaned and that his boss deserved to be rebutted in kind; and (4) that if he didn't respond aggressively, he and his boss and his friends would think he was a coward and that would be awful. He was also aware of being quite anxious that maybe he *had* made a mistake and that would be terrible, too, since he prided himself on his accuracy.

You can base your decision about what you want to be thinking, feeling, and doing on the changes you would make in your thinking. For example, Archie decided that he did not

315

want to be treated the way his boss was treating him, but that he was not going to worry about being a coward. Therefore, he wanted to think: "I will be firm and assertive; I don't have to be aggressive to prove I am not a coward. I can live with whatever my boss or my friends think, and it's unlikely any of them will think I am a coward because I acted assertively instead of aggressively. If I did make a mistake, I can live with that and do all I can to correct it. But I don't deserve to be berated for it." He decided that he wanted to feel serious and alert but not overly anxious or overly angry. And he decided he wanted to try to disarm his boss's anger and discuss the problem more calmly.

The next four questions on the list are designed to help you plan what you will actually do. Archie decided that he wanted his boss to know: (1) that he did recognize that he (the boss) was very angry, (2) that he (Archie) wanted to discuss the matter but not in such an angry manner, and (3) that he (Archie) was willing to sit down and talk about the problem further. He also decided that he would confront his boss later in the day with a request that he not berate him like that again, especially in front of his friends. He decided to put the confrontation off because he believed his boss would be less defensive then and more able to hear Archie's request. Most importantly, Archie decided that he would express all these points without adding any aggressive comments or saying them in a sarcastic, condescending, hostile, or nasty tone. Rather, he would be firm, serious, and direct. By deciding how he wanted to think, feel, and behave, he was more easily able then to decide what it was he wanted his boss to know and when it would be most appropriate to express it.

Self-assessment questions are guides to help you gain self-control in a situation that might be difficult for you. As with other techniques, the more you practice, the better you will get. (See Exercise 33.) They can also help you to set a more assertive direction in the way you respond in that situation.

Exercise 33 Using Self-Assessment Questions

1. Imagine yourself in the following situation. Your neighbor or a friend often criticizes you for things like the way you handle situations or particular decisions you make. You like her generally and you would like to stay friends but her continued criticisms annoy you. You decide to say something about it to her and she is at your home for a visit. You are not sure how she's likely to respond and there is a good chance she could feel hurt, resentful, or angrily defensive. Assume that you have made yourself excessively anxious in this situation and answer the assessment questions with that assumption in mind.

    What is my SUDS level? _____

    What am I doing (specific behaviors)? _____

    How am I feeling? _____

    What am I thinking? _____

    What do I want to be thinking, feeling, and doing? _____

    What thoughts, opinions, preferences, or feelings do I want to express in this situation? _____

    What do I want the other person to know? _____

    What *thoughts* are keeping me from doing what I want?

    _____

    What do I think is appropriate to express (remember personal rights)? _____

    How can I go ahead and express what I want? _____

2. Think of a real situation in which you found yourself feeling excessively upset, anxious, or angry while the situation was occurring. Imagine to yourself exactly what was going on and try to make yourself feel some of those feelings again. Then think through each of the questions above and see if you are able to gain a sense of control over your thoughts, feelings, and the resulting behaviors.

SUMMARY

Any time you try to make a significant personal change, a good deal is at stake. As you work toward increasing your assertiveness, approach your changes with an attitude of serious concern and enjoyment. Making significant changes does not have to be painful, and you don't have to struggle or suffer through them. Admittedly, not all changes come easily, but you can do a great deal to keep yourself systematically directed toward those desired changes and at the same time maximize your enjoyment and fulfillment as you approach those goals. Your attempts to increase your assertiveness do not have to be perfect. Use your own resources and share your successes with others who will appreciate and support your efforts.

NOTES

1.   Wolpe, J., & Lazarus, A. A. *Behavior therapy techniques.* London: Pergamon Press, 1966.

Appendix A
Relaxing Yourself

Some people become so anxious in certain situations that they find it very difficult to employ the cognitive and behavioral techniques that have been presented in this book. You can learn to relax enough to begin thinking clearly and maintaining greater self-control. When most people find themselves extremely anxious, they try to *make* themselves stop by self-ridicule ("Stop being such a baby!") or by trying to talk themselves out of it (see Chapter 5 on coping statements). The former often does not work and the latter is often done haphazardly.

You can learn to use the following method for relaxing. The first step is to either have someone read the procedures below while you do them, or better yet, have someone slowly read the statement below onto a tape recorder. Go through the whole relaxation procedure at least three or four times with the tape until you are able to go through the process from memory. You can then use these techniques at any time. When you find yourself extremely anxious, you can go through just a portion of the process if you do not have the time or you are not in a convenient place. These techniques have been used by many people to reduce anxiety.

The following directions are a suggested format for a brief relaxation procedure including deep muscle tension and relaxation, breathing, and picturing relaxing scenes. (If you wear contact lenses, remove them before beginning.)

Make yourself as comfortable as possible, loosen any tight clothing that you can, and get relaxed in your chair. Just focus on your body and feel the tension flow out as you relax more and more. Now, stretch out your legs, lift them slightly off the floor, point your feet back toward your face as much as you can. Tighten your toes, your ankles, your calves, and your thighs—tighten and tighten, as tense as you can (tighten about 10 seconds). Now, relax . . . feel the warmth of relaxation in your legs and feet as you relax. Feel how pleasant it is to feel that warmth as it flows through your legs even to your toes (relaxation should be 15 to 20 seconds).

Now tighten your buttocks and stomach as hard as you can. Tighten and tighten. Hold it a bit more (again about 10 seconds total). Now, relax . . . buttocks and stomach. Notice the pleasant contrast between the relaxed feeling you experience now and the tightness you experienced a moment ago. Take a deep breath now. As you slowly let it out, also let out the remaining tension in your feet, legs, buttocks, and stomach. Continue to take deep breaths and let them out slowly as we go on (again 15 to 20 seconds of relaxation).

Now tighten your back muscles, your chest, and the muscles just under your armpits. Harder. Hold it a little bit longer (10 seconds). Now relax. Let yourself feel the tranquil flow of relaxation as it moves up your body into your back and chest. Imagine the word *calm* or the word *relax* and think that word to yourself slowly about ten times. Take a deep breath and let it out slowly as the tension drains away (45 seconds of relaxation).

Extend your arms and make two fists. Tighten your triceps, your forearms, and your fists. Hard. Really hard. When I say relax, let your arms fall to your lap with the pull of gravity (10 seconds). Relax. Notice the tingling sensation of relaxation in your fingers and hands. Feel the warmth in your arms. Enjoy this beautiful relaxation. Imagine a peaceful, tranquil scene that is really relaxing. Picture that scene and how warm and comfortable that image is for you (45 seconds of relaxation).

Now, hunch up your shoulders as though you are trying to touch them to your ears. Tighten your neck, too. Tighter and tighter. Hold it just a bit more so that your neck actually shakes (10 seconds). Now, relax. Feel the heaviness in your shoulders and the warm feeling of relaxation. Take a deep breath and slowly let it out. Imagine saying to yourself, "I am calm and relaxed." Enjoy the comforting feeling of being tension free (45 seconds).

Now, open your mouth as wide as you can. Wider. Hold it a bit more (10 seconds). Now, relax. Feel the warm, tingling sense in your face. Let your mouth hang open as it relaxes. Breathe deeply (15-20 seconds). Now, furrow your brow and tighten your cheek and face muscles into a tight grimace. Tighter. Hold it (10 seconds).

Now, relax. Feel the flow of warm relaxation enter your face and eyes. Enjoy the wonderful feeling of relaxation through your entire body.

Now take a deep breath and hold it (hold it for 10 seconds). As you let it out fully, let any tension drain from your whole body. Imagine that your body is being immersed in a warm fluid which absorbs any remaining tension. Feel your body little by little sink into this pleasant fluid and the tension seep from your body. First your feet and legs, then your torso, your arms, your neck, and your head. Breathe deeply and enjoy this relaxed feeling. (Pause a few seconds.) I will count to three. On three you will open your eyes and be refreshed and relaxed - one, two, three.

Appendix B
Self-Assessment, Goal-Setting, and Decision Making

SELF-ASSESSMENT AND GOAL SETTING

Assessing your current assertive behavior and setting specific goals for changing yourself are important steps in developing greater assertive skills. By completing the Gambrill-Richey Assertion Inventory you can identify your strengths and weaknesses.[1] This inventory can also help you set goals for your own assertiveness program.

Gambrill-Richey Assertion Inventory*

On a scale of 1 to 5 rate your degree of emotional agitation in the space *before* each situation listed below. Degree of emotional agitation refers to the amount of interfering emotion you experience in the situation, for example, anger, anxiety, guilt, fear.

1 = none
2 = a little
3 = a fair amount
4 = much
5 = very much

(Inventory begins on page 326.)

*From "An Assertion Inventory for Use in Assessment and Research," by Gambrill and Richey. *Behavior Therapy*, 1975, *6*, 550-551. Used with permission.

Degree of Agitation		Situation	Likelihood
_____	1.	Turn down a request to borrow your car	_____
_____	2.	Compliment a friend	_____
_____	3.	Ask a favor of someone	_____
_____	4.	Resist sales pressure	_____
_____	5.	Apologize when you are at fault	_____
_____	6.	Turn down a request for a meeting or date	_____
_____	7.	Admit fear and request consideration	_____
_____	8.	Tell a person you are intimately involved with when he or she says or does something that bothers you	_____
_____	9.	Ask for a raise	_____
_____	10.	Admit ignorance in some area	_____
_____	11.	Turn down a request to borrow money	_____
_____	12.	Ask personal questions	_____
_____	13.	Turn off a talkative friend	_____
_____	14.	Ask for constructive criticism	_____
_____	15.	Initiate a conversation with a stranger	_____
_____	16.	Compliment a person you are romantically involved with or interested in	_____
_____	17.	Request a meeting or a date with a person	_____
_____	18.	Your initial request for a meeting is turned down and you ask the person again at a later time	_____
_____	19.	Admit confusion about a point under discussion and ask whether they can give clarification	_____

Degree of Agitation	Situation	Likelihood
_____	20. Apply for a job	_____
_____	21. Ask whether you have offended someone	_____
_____	22. Tell someone that you like them	_____
_____	23. Request expected service when such is not forthcoming, e.g., in a restaurant	_____
_____	24. Discuss openly with the person his or her criticism of your behavior	_____
_____	25. Return defective items, e.g., store or restaurant	_____
_____	26. Express an opinion that differs from that of the person you are talking to	_____
_____	27. Resist sexual overtures when you are not interested	_____
_____	28. Tell the person when you feel he or she has done something that is unfair to you	_____
_____	29. Accept a date	_____
_____	30. Tell someone good news about yourself	_____
_____	31. Resist pressure to drink	_____
_____	32. Resist a significant person's unfair demand	_____
_____	33. Quit a job	_____
_____	34. Resist pressure to "turn on"	_____
_____	35. Discuss openly with the person his or her criticism of your work	_____
_____	36. Request the return of borrowed items	_____
_____	37. Receive compliments	_____
_____	38. Continue to converse with someone who disagrees with you	_____

Degree of Agitation	Situation	Likelihood
_____	39. Tell a friend or someone with whom you work when he or she says or does something that bothers you	_____
_____	40. Ask a person who is annoying you in a public situation to stop	_____

Go over the list a second time, and in the space *after* each situation rate the likelihood of acting the way described if you were actually presented with that situation. For example, if you rarely apologize when you are at fault, you would mark a "1" after that item:

1 = never do it
2 = rarely do it
3 = do it about half the time
4 = usually do it
5 = always do it

It is important to place a piece of paper over your emotional agitation ratings while rating the situations a second time. Otherwise, one rating may influence the other, thus making it unlikely that you will get an honest assessment of your behavior.

Four Basic Patterns

As you look over your ratings on the Gambrill-Richey Assertion Inventory, you may find that your behavior falls into one of these four patterns.[2]

The Nonassertive Pattern. If you rated yourself as having high degrees of agitation and low likelihood of acting as described in the inventory item, your conduct follows the nonassertive pattern. This pattern suggests that you will need to develop skills in assertive behavior as well as specific skills for coping with your emotions (Chapter 5).

Don't Care Pattern. If you indicated a low probability of acting and low degrees of emotional agitation in many situations, your behavior probably follows this pattern. This pattern suggests that you may not really care about being assertive in those situations and may not be interested in changing your behavior. If you have this pattern, Chapters 3 and 4 may be of particular help to you.

Agitated Pattern. If for many situations you indicated a high likelihood of acting as described in the inventory item and high degrees of emotional agitation, your behavior may fit the agitated pattern. This may indicate that though you act assertively, you are anxious when doing so. For this pattern the methods described in Chapter 5 for dealing with emotions will be of particular importance for you. If your emotional agitation is mainly one of anger, this pattern may indicate aggressive behavior.

Nonfearful, Assertive Pattern. If you indicated high degrees of acting as described in the inventory item and low degrees of agitation in many situations, your behavior fits the nonfearful, assertive pattern. This is a pattern of a comfortably assertive individual.

Deciding on Your Training Goals
Look over the list of situations on the Gambrill-Richey Assertion Inventory and select approximately five situations in which you rated a low likelihood of acting assertively and a fair amount of emotional agitation. The five situations should be ones that you feel need to be changed and offer you a reasonable chance of successfully asserting yourself after some training.[3] It is important that you do not immediately start asserting yourself in highly threatening situations where you have a low likelihood of success because you probably will get overwhelmed by the situation and feel defeated and discouraged about changing your behavior. Rank the five situations according to the degree of discomfort they hold for you.

329

Least Discomfort

1.
2.
3.
4.
5.

Most Discomfort

Now set your goals by making each of the five general situations more specific: Describe who the person is that you have difficulty with, what that person does that poses a problem for you, what the situation is, what your problem behavior is, and what you want to do.[4] For example, Rita listed "admitting ignorance in some area" as one of her five situations. Her more specific description of the situation was as follows:

> When the topic of discussion at parties shifts to something I don't know much about, like politics or sports (*situation*), I feign more knowledge than I actually have (*problem behavior*). I want to be able to admit my ignorance in a self-affirming way and to ask for information (*want*). This situation poses a problem for me with both friends and strangers who seem to be very knowledgeable and sure of themselves (*who*) and they assume that I understand what they're saying (*what they do*).

It is possible that for each of the five general situations you have listed, you may want to describe more than one specific situation that you want to work on. For example, Rita continued to identify two other specific situations in which she had difficulty admitting ignorance.

> When I get lost driving the car (*situation*) I don't ask for directions until I'm hopelessly lost (*problem behavior*). I want to ask for clearer directions the first time they're given to me (*want*). This is particularly a problem when the other person is someone I don't know very well (*who*) and is in a rush (*what they do*).

In my job as a fabric clerk, customers often ask me how to put
together clothing patterns, make estimates on how much upholstery
material they need, etc. (*situation*). I act like I know what I'm
doing (*problem behavior*). I'd like to tell them that I don't know
(*want*) or say that I'm willing to help them figure it out but that
I'm not 100 percent positive (*want*). This is particularly a problem when the customer looks like she's critical (*who*) and she just
assumes that "of course" I know the answer (*what they do*).

General Situation 1 _____
   Specific Situations

      a. _____

      b. _____

      c. _____

General Situation 2 _____
   Specific Situations

      a. _____

      b. _____

      c. _____

General Situation 3 _____
   Specific Situations

      a. _____

      b. _____

      c. _____

General Situation 4 _____
   Specific Situations

      a. _____

      b. _____

      c. _____

General Situation 5 _____

   Specific Situations

    a. _____

    b. _____

    c. _____

       Now that you have your list of goals, you can start your assertiveness program. You can revise this list as you reach your goals and gradually deal with situations that are more difficult for you.

DECISION MAKING

       The following questions are useful when you are truly undecided about whether you want to take the risk of being assertive in a problem situation.

1. Describe the problem situation and how you are considering being assertive.

2. List the positive gains that could occur if you were assertive.

	Importance	Likelihood
a.	_____	_____
b.	_____	_____
c.	_____	_____
d.	_____	_____

Rate the importance of each positive gain to your self-worth and happiness on a 10-point scale (1 = not at all; 10 = extremely important).[5] Rate each positive gain on how likely it is to occur (1 = not at all; 10 = extremely likely).

3. List the negative costs that could take place if you are assertive.

	Upsetting	Likelihood
a.	_____	_____
b.	_____	_____
c.	_____	_____
d.	_____	_____

Rate each negative outcome according to how upsetting it is to you (1 = not at all; 10 = extremely upsetting). Rate each on how likely it is that the negative outcome will occur. Be careful that you do not exaggerate the negative effects (1 = not at all; 10 = extremely likely).

4. Are there any other ways of handling the situation that will achieve your objective and maintain your sense of personal integrity? Is compromise a viable alternative?

NOTES

1. Gambrill, E., & Richey, C. An assertion inventory for use in assessment and research. *Behavior Therapy*, 1975, *6*, 550-561.

2. These four basic patterns are modified from Eileen Gambrill and Cheryl Richey's work.

3. Bower, S. A., & Bower, G. H. *Asserting Yourself*. Reading, MA: Addison-Wesley, 1976.

4. Bower, S. A., & Bower, G. H., 1976.

5. Bower, S. A., & Bower, G. H., 1976.

About the Authors

Patricia Jakubowski is best known for originating the empathic assertion, as the first person to focus on assertiveness training procedures for women, and for conceptualizing the four-phase assertiveness training model. She is codirector and co-author of the film *Assertive Training for Women,* published by the American Personnel and Guidance Association, which also published her monograph *An Introduction to Assertive Training Procedures for Women.* She has published extensively in professional journals, contributed chapters for edited volumes, and has presented papers at many professional meetings. In addition to being a keynote speaker at several conferences, she has given approximately 150 all-day workshops on assertiveness training to such diverse groups as banking personnel, nurses, police officers, librarians, media technicians, mental health workers, nuns, homemakers, secretaries, college deans, employment services workers, teachers, trucking workers, and business managers and supervisors.

Dr. Jakubowski is currently President of the North Central Association for Counselor Education and Supervision and former Associate Editor of *Counselor Education and Supervision* as well as former Senator of the American Personnel and Guidance Association. She has received service awards from the College Student Personnel Association and the Association for Counselor Education and Supervision. In addition, she has been a consultant for the American Personnel and Guidance Association National Sex Equality Project.

Dr. Jakubowski is licensed as a psychologist in Missouri and she is presently Associate Professor of Education at the University of Missouri— St. Louis where she teaches group counseling, counseling practicum, assertion training, and behavior modification. She received her doctorate in counseling from the University of Illinois and conducted her own behavioral counseling firm in Chicago for two years. She was formerly a counseling psychologist at Washington University in the Student Counseling Service where she was a therapist and also supervised the work of other counselors. She is listed in *Leaders in Education, Who's Who of American Women,* and *The World's Who's Who of Women.*

She is co-author of *Responsible Assertive Behavior: Cognitive-Behavioral Procedures for Trainers* and a contributor to the film *Responsible Assertion.*

335

Arthur Lange received his Ed.D. degree from American University and has done post-doctoral work at Southern Illinois University.  He is currently Director of the Counseling Center, University of California, Irvine, a lecturer in Social Science and Social Ecology, and a faculty member of the Rational Emotive Institute in Los Angeles. Dr. Lange has conducted over 250 workshops and training programs for universities, hospitals, government agencies, private practitioners, and secondary schools. He has also conducted over a hundred assertion training groups and workshops for lay persons, including workshops at national conventions for the American Psychological Association, American Personnel and Guidance Association, and the National Council on Family Relations—American Association of Child and Family Counselors. He has lectured both nationally and internationally and is the co-author of *Responsible Assertive Behavior: Cognitive/Behavioral Procedures for Trainers,* as well as a contributor to the film *Responsible Assertion.*